Almendro
Under the Almond Tree

By Pato

authorHOUSE®

AuthorHouse™
1663 Liberty Drive
Bloomington, IN 47403
www.authorhouse.com
Phone: 1-800-839-8640

First published by AuthorHouse 9/15/2010

ISBN: 978-1-4520-7877-9 (hc)
ISBN: 978-1-4520-7878-6 (sc)
ISBN: 978-1-4520-7879-3 (e)

Library of Congress Control Number: 2010913311

Printed in the United States of America

This book is printed on acid-free paper.

Second Edition

From the Author

Almendro is Spanish for Almond Tree

This is a true story

Names have been changed to protect the privacy of those who were instrumental in helping me survive a near five year ordeal.

I dedicate this book to them and to the beautiful people of the Caribbean, in particular Dominica, who taught me how to survive, to live and love again and be whole.

To you with love

Pato

Contents

Prologue
May 2009

Dam you Jim, Dam you to hell! Now we're both dead and all because of your dam stupidity.

I pulled as hard as I could at the cord around my neck but it wouldn't budge. The look on her face as she slammed my head back again – stretching my neck over the arm of the sofa for the third time, was as frightening as what lay ahead for me. If I could only get free for a few seconds, I would kill her and she knew it.

Sam where are you? I heard his whimpering turn to howls and a thumping sound. He was trying to break through the screen. Do it Sam, do it – save mommy; I won't scold you if you break down the house and take a chunk out of this bitch. Dam dog!

She was going to get away with it again. If I couldn't bring her down, nobody could and I wasn't going to be on this earth much longer. I prayed to God to help me as flashes of those I loved so much ran through my mind. I was never going to see them again. Seron, oh how I love you so and it took all these years to find you. Why did you have to pick today to go to town? Dam men!

The buzzing in my head came with a bright glare followed by shadows of people who once lived. I saw my mother and father and Jim. I hope he's on the other side when I get there so I can beat the crap out of him. I felt the darkness coming and could fight it no more. The last of my air left my lungs as a kaleidoscope of colors danced in my head. I felt myself floating into the unknown.

You won't get away with this girl. I will come back and make your life hell.

Almendro

Introduction

May 2, 2008, Flight 806 made its final approach into Chicago O'Hare International.

Not being a particularly chatty person, especially on an airplane, I am now berating myself for not engaging in conversation with the young lady sitting beside me until the last hour of our six-hour flight from San Juan.

Ms. Gonsalves, an attractive lawyer seemed more than anxious with the delays we'd been experiencing. Unable to use her cell phone in flight, she wasn't able to let the seven senior partners know she was hovering thousands of feet above them and would be late for the meeting. After several interviews, today is the day she would learn their decision; was she the successful candidate who would head their new subsidiary legal firm in San Juan?

Learning of her profession with specialization in family law, I couldn't chat with her enough. Was this a coincidence or the hand of God once again leading the way to my destiny?

When I told her I was entrenched in a messy and bizarre family law matter and on my way to see my Canadian lawyer, her interest piqued as I rattled off my tales of woe in the short time we had left before landing.

For the first time in my life I wished I lived in Chicago instead of Niagara Falls. I had to remain for at least another hour on the plane before I could have a cigarette. My daughter Samantha was picking me up at Buffalo International Airport and by now she would be cursing. Unfortunately, I didn't have a cell phone to let her know. Fortunately, I didn't have any luggage to wait for.

For the past five years I have made my home and new life in the

Caribbean. Not knowing how long I will need to be in Canada, and being short of money, my ticket was one way.

Ms. Gonsalves was spellbound over the condensed version of my life. I was grateful when she gave me websites to visit and specific issues that should be discussed with my own legal counsel.

Before parting company, she wished me good luck while handing me her business card.

Her last words to me were: "I want to know how this turns out. Please let me know. Regardless of the outcome, sell your story. Get in touch with publishers in New York, get an agent, and call Oprah. You must write a book. With a story like yours, you cannot lose."

The last leg of my journey was filled with thoughts of our conversation. I made a promise to myself to let her know the outcome.

This is my story.

Chapter One
Laura & Jim

Seventeen years earlier

*I*n December of 1990 I met Jim Cassidy at a cocktail party hosted by good friends Bunny and Blair Lloyd. This annual event was well worth attending but this year after Bunny informed me of the eligible bachelors invited in my honor; I faked the flu and stayed home.

With my bowl of popcorn, remote and two new releases in hand I settled on my sofa just as the phone rang. Bunny ranted on knowing I was no sicker that she was. After listening to her crying attendance was poor, many expected guests were calling to cancel because of icy road conditions, I gave in. My condo was less than a mile from her home and there was no way she was letting me off the hook.

Not bothering to shower or shampoo I jumped into my black leather mini skirt, black cashmere sweater, high boots and fur coat. Finding a parking spot on her busy residential street took longer than the drive to get there. So much for low attendance as many cars were parked near or close to her home and on her snow covered front yard.

As I entered the room the first person I noticed was Jim. Aside from his good looks he stood out. The man was well over six feet tall with a full head of silver white hair. His ski sweater and pants meant he had either come from the slopes, was heading for them after the party, or had no taste. It was as plain as day he was one of the bachelors as he strutted to the entrance hall to greet me, nearly knocking a few guests over in his haste to beat the competition also heading my way.

For the remainder of the evening Jim was my shadow, catering to my every wish. Quickly I learned not to make any sudden moves for fear I would collide with him which I did several times. There was no escaping this eager bachelor. Blair as usual, became his own best guest letting his charming wife do all the work. Normally, I would have lent my friend a hand but that meant Jim would be in the kitchen which wasn't large enough as it was.

Bunny looked smashing as always. Her jet black hair was bobbed short with bangs that set off her brown black eyes. Her full voluptuous mouth was painted the reddest of red which only she can carry off. That color on me made me look like a hooker. Bunny looked as though she had stepped off the cover of Vogue in a full length, skin-tight black wool dress.

Later in the evening, after most of the guests had departed, Bunny finally flopped into a chair saying she would kill for a cigarette. We were both trying to kick the nasty habit - I had been several weeks without but the thought of one now had great appeal. No sooner were the words out of my mouth when Jim was out the door to fetch a pack.

As the last of the hangers on were about to leave, Jim asked if he could escort me home which brought bursts of laughter from our host and hostess. Jim had walked to the party, living less than a block away and I was a mere half mile and had driven my car.

Jim went home and I drove to my place where I hurriedly showered and shampooed before he arrived. We made tea and sat for hours chatting, each of us on one of my matching love seats.

He was extremely intelligent, which along with his enthusiasm about every subject we covered, I found refreshing. Jim's wife of 28 years and the mother of his three grown children had passed away with ovarian cancer only six months earlier. His youngest daughter, in her last year of university, was living at home with him, while his eldest - a son was in the process of moving into his own newly purchased house. His middle daughter and son-in- law lived 200 miles away in a world of their own. They seldom visited if ever which was the first sign of disproval I witnessed in Jim. While his wife was in the final stretch of her life, his middle child was too busy to come to her mother's bed side.

Bunny managed to tell me a few things at the party when Jim was out of earshot. He had left his wife for another woman five years before she died. He moved back into the home he once shared with his family only days before her passing.

Jim was eager to tell me everything, much of which I was not ready to hear. I didn't let on that I knew anything about his past. When the time was right, he would no doubt get around to filling in the blanks. He was intense and sincere, becoming emotional as he revealed the recent events in his family.

I couldn't help but like this man who was at least 20 years my senior. While that was a concern of sorts, he was in terrific shape and took care of himself. He drank very little, had never smoked, and was active in sports. I already was looking forward to our mutual interest in each other. For more than 20 years, he worked for the largest school board in the Metro Toronto area, holding a key administrative position. Prior to that, he had been a practicing minister and remained ordained. But he had left his congregation for a better paying position with the board, since he had a family to raise.

I became a very young grandmother for the first time two months earlier. My plans for the Christmas holidays were carved in stone. For the first time in several years my family would spend Christmas together. Leslie, my youngest, was flying home and I would not be soaking up the sun on a tropical island as had been my custom for the previous few years.

Samantha and Guido were having Joseph christened as part of the holiday celebration. Guido was a fabulous cook, having helped his mother and aunt with their catering business since he was old enough to carry a tray. He could cook as well as, if not better than the elderly ladies who retired from the business long ago. We were guaranteed to come away after the holidays at least ten pounds heavier.

Jim also had his plans made for a week of skiing with friends over the holidays. When he asked if he could call me, I gave him Samantha's phone number which I later regretted. His numerous calls became a nuisance as did the teasing I received from my family.

I wouldn't have traded the week with my family for a free month on an island in the Caribbean. We all cried when we said our farewells and as much as I hated to admit it, I loved being a granny.

The two hour drive back to Toronto in heavy traffic on New Year's Eve restored me to the familiar road rage and stress of my hectic life. The last thing I wanted was to go out again for dinner with Jim, who had returned to the city himself the previous day and called to ask me out.

My phone was ringing when I opened my apartment door. It was Jim – all apologies for not being able to secure a reservation anywhere. I told him to come over anyway; I would happily throw something together.

He arrived two hours later and two hours too early carrying a bouquet of long stemmed red roses. He looked smashing in a dark pin stripe suit, white shirt, and sharp red and black striped tie. I looked pretty good myself in my old jeans, sloppy football sweater (my Christmas gift from Guido) and bare feet.

He took in my attire while struggling to find something nice to say, then began laughing. I made no attempt to change my clothes and suggested he get rid of the jacket and tie, roll up his sleeves and help me cook dinner.

The man was totally useless in the kitchen but willing to accept any orders I dished out. A moron can peel potatoes but Jim cut his finger on the peeler. My prime rib was already in the oven while he had the pleasure of setting my dining room table after I relieved him from potato duty.

Jim loved my tastefully decorated condo and was full of questions. I barely got one answer out when he bombarded me with another. He wanted to know everything about my job, friends, what sports I enjoyed, and what type of music I liked and how I spent vacations. He was fun to be with in spite of being a klutz.

I hadn't been involved in a relationship for a long time—a topic that seemed to interest him most. There was nothing to hide. I had been severely hurt when my fiancé called off our wedding a week before our wedding. That was four years ago and I was totally recovered.

With the topic now open this was his chance to fess up about the relationship he concealed when we first met. Although he downplayed the affair, he did reveal he left his wife because of the other woman but the relationship didn't work out. Again, there was some untruth to this as Bunny and Blair had dined with the couple weeks before his wife died.

We got off the subject and moved to the sofas with coffee and brandy. We chatted about anything and everything, exchanging a few kisses in between. Passion was not one of Jim's strong suits, or maybe he was more nervous than he appeared.

Once again, as he had done the first night, he became quite serious and emotional. He had tears in his eyes when he said he had something to tell me. Not sure I wanted to hear this I gave him the green light, sat back and waited to hear about his fatal brain tumor.

If he launched into his broken heart story concerning the "girlfriend," I would bring the evening to a speedy end and send him on his way. My little shoulders had it hard enough holding my bra straps in place without having some big fat head leaning on them. Not long ago, I was the crying post for a very good male friend who wore me out with his tales of woe. Men don't want advice as much as they want a mother to make their pain go away until some other unsuspecting female takes her place.

Without any preamble he told me he was sexually dysfunctional. This was a topic I was unfamiliar with but I had the feeling I would have preferred the brain tumor. This was far too personal for a first, and likely the last date.

"Why are you telling me this Jim?"

"I'm falling in love with you Laura and hope we can make a life together."

Dear God – beam me up please. I should have saved the prime rib and made hot dogs.

"Jim you are a lovely man and I like you. I think the timing of such revelations is premature and I am not comfortable talking about sex issues with you."

He fumbled through an apology, regained his composure and carried on with the same subject. Shit, thought mois, as I sat back to endure what was becoming a bummer of an evening. Hopefully there was a punch line coming – this had to be a joke.

He told me all about the girlfriend and the wife. Everything was their fault of course. His wife wanted nothing to do with him after their children were born. She shunned his advances which left him impotent. Then the girlfriend wanted only what she could get out of him and also shunned his sexual advances and eventually ended their relationship. I should have seen the red flag but instead I felt sorry for him.

Our evening ended soon after bringing in the New Year, but not before I threw my good crystal champagne glass over the balcony to welcome 1991. Jim stood motionless at the spectacle and soon followed suit with his own glass. This was far too much fun! We tossed the remaining six glasses and then the empty bottle. I had major clean up to face first thing in the morning.

We made a date to have dinner the following week.

My annual check-up was scheduled for the morning of our dinner. Dr. Boyle frowned when I brought up the subject of erectile dysfunction.

"Why would a healthy young woman like you be asking the question?"

"I met a very nice man who seemed it appropriate to tell me he suffered from the problem on our first date."

"How old is this man?"

"I think late fifties but he's in very good shape – very athletic, doesn't smoke, drinks a fair bit and eats like a pig."

"Well Laura the problem has to be major for him to declare it like he did."

"Is it something that can be cured?"

"I've been your doctor for too many years to let you walk into a relationship with potential for disaster. I don't know the man's medical history and can only speak in general terms but it sounds as though it is a major problem for him already. I wouldn't like to see you involved with something that will only bring your heart ache."

I was a long way from promiscuity but sexual pleasure was important to me. I was in my prime and wanted more than anything to be in a meaningful relationship. Not knowing Jim's medical background, Dr. Boyle said there was no point in guessing at a prognosis and advised me to be very sure before I leaped into a relationship.

Jim took me to a quaint French restaurant in north Toronto named Pour quoi Pas. It was a small old two story house built in the early thirties and nothing on the interior had been altered since. The original kitchen served only four tables; two in the living room and two in the dining room. Lighting was dim to give an ambiance reminiscent of those early years and the food was wonderful. I was impressed with Jim's choice and having a wonderful evening until he proposed.

"Laura I want you to be my wife."

"Are you out of your mind Jim?"

I pulled my hand out of his and stared at him in disbelief.

"I know it's sudden but I know how I feel and I'm so sorry because I have upset you."

"No Jim – you got it wrong. I'm not upset; I pissed off big time. Do you have a fatal brain tumor after all and want a wife at your side when you hit see the big white?"

"I'm very sorry. I promise I won't bring the subject up again."

That night we slept together at my condo for the first time. Although not entirely in the mood I figured we might as well get this part out of the way. We could have won an award if we had it on film. Jim was clumsy and I was grateful you didn't need a potato peeler to have sex. He was nervous - sweating profusely and I didn't appreciate being dripped on.

There was nothing wrong with him that I could tell but then again I didn't see stars, hear music or want to accept his proposal when we were done fifty five seconds later. First times are usually bummers and I did like him very much. I wasn't about to toss him aside.

We saw each other every weekend or mid week if our busy schedules allowed. We shopped to bring Jim's wardrobe into the current century and then moved on to a new vehicle for him. I swear the man had the first dollar he ever earned. Clearly he had money to spend but that didn't stop him from moaning and groaning at every price tag. His new look drew attention and compliments from work colleagues and friends. He started shopping on his own and with help from many over eager middle age sales women; he managed to make some nice purchases.

Never before had I experienced this much fun with a man. I took skiing lessons and when spring came, out came his Gold Wing Bike and off came the shutters at the summer cottage. He met and liked my friends and what few he had were as much fun. There was never a dull moment with so much going on.

His agenda was marriage and the sooner the better. When we dined at that sweet little French restaurant one month to the date after our first dinner there, he proposed again. Jim needed a wife. From what information I had, he had never been without a woman for very long and aggressively looked for one when he was in between. Some men are just not complete without a partner. Other women began to show an interest in him and why wouldn't they? He dressed well, was very handsome, spent money without abandon and now drove a new Lincoln sport coup.

Jim's three children, James, Sarah and Kathy were great to be with although I sensed reluctance on their part to get too close to me. I attributed this to the short time since their mother's death and my arrival into their lives. They made an effort to accept me and tried to embrace their father, who wasn't the least bit interested in what his kids thought or how they felt. It was much later that I learned they believed I was the woman he left their mother for.

*O*ver the summer months we spent every weekend at the family cottage located two hundred miles north of Toronto in the Haliburton Highlands close to Minden. The old cottage had a long history – Jim's parents being among the early cottagers to summer here since the 1930's. It was a time when accessibility was by boat alone and a two day trip by car.

Progress changed many things since the cottage was built. Highways from Toronto to Bracebridge, where the cut off to reach the family hideaway was, shortened the trip from two days to two hours and an additional half hour to reach the lake. Close by now were amenities that included a hospital and a fire department.

We entertained every weekend with our city friends and Jim's children and their significant others. We had cooking contests where the guests were responsible for one meal which also kept our costs minimal. Water sports and camp fires were the main events.

On the few occasions we didn't have guests, we often had dinner at a quaint lodge on Eagle Lake – Sir Sam's Inn. We fell in love with the place after our first visit and chose no other after that. We were familiar to the staff who gave us preferential treatment as a regular customer.

*I*n September Jim went to great lengths to make a reservation. One was not required at this time of the year but he was adamant he wanted the corner table by the biggest window with the best view of the lake. I had a hunch what he had up his sleeve and was ready.

He took the liberty of telling the staff he was going to propose to me. Complimentary drinks were served to us in the lounge prior to dinner and when I caught the kitchen staff peeking through the port hole windows from the kitchen, I knew what was coming and was enjoying the fanfare.

Jim liked an audience but he also liked approval for his actions and by telling the staff of his plan, he gained their support and encouragement.

He waited until our meal was finished while I enjoyed watching the staff become impatient. Our waitress, Connie, who always served us, made it a point to remind Jim the kitchen staff wanted to go home. In other words hurry up.

She brought our desert out with a china cover over mine. I had never had a cover over a slice of carrot cake before. Rather than return to the kitchen, she stood off the side while three little faces peered though the port holes and the manager stood in the hall – all were watching.

Beneath the china cover was no carrot cake but rather a black velvet box containing the most exquisite diamond ring I had ever set eyes on with the exception of the one Richard gave to Liz Taylor. A magnificent diamond weighing at least a pound was the centre stone of three set in a unique modern setting my friends later referred to as the condo. The ring seemed too big for my finger but when I put it on I knew I had a ringer (pardon the pun).

"Don't ask me to marry you again Jim. The answer is yes."

He was about to get up to come kiss me when the kitchen doors burst open to let the staff thru and the manager arrived with a bottle of champagne – compliments of the house.

We had a lot to discuss and many decisions to be made. First order of business was the wedding date and the second was where we would live. When Jim's son James became engaged two weeks following our engagement, we had to re-think our wedding plans which I wanted for the next summer but now collided with his son. We decided on March 13th 1992 and that didn't give us much time to do what we wanted to do.

Jim's house was beautiful albeit extremely out of date. It was two storeys with a center hall entrance through now modern double frosted glass doors. The hall was gloomy and dark with the previous wooden doors with small upper peek windows. The new doors added light and with the hall walls leading to the kitchen now completely mirrored, the space appeared three times larger.

We knocked out almost every window and walls to put in large sliding glass doors off the dining room and kitchen eating area. The kitchen wall that blocked the den was opened up to allow for an eating bar that looked through to the den and the fireplace. The den window was replaced with an oversize bay window that now captured the beauty of the newly landscaped back yard and patio.

The Kitchen itself was the biggest challenge. We hired a designer who blew our minds with his sketches. It was horribly expensive but we both wanted it. Our new kitchen was totally white, modern with Italian flair and re-arranged for efficiency, proper lighting and gourmet cooking. What once would only accommodate one cook now allowed for a group to work at one time without colliding with another person. We were ecstatic with the outcome and it soon became my favorite room.

The sale of my condo was coincident with our wedding. I moved into my new home one week before our small but elegant wedding held in an old estate home – The Heinsman House in North Toronto. Bunny was my Maid of Honor while Blair walked me down the aisle. Jim's son was his best man and master of ceremonies at our candle light dinner reception.

Kathy was the only one of Jim's children living with us. She was a busy girl finishing up her final year of university and kept busy with a different boyfriend every month. She became upset when I used towels in our bathroom that once belonged to her mother. Kathy also made it clear to me when we had dinner alone one evening when Jim was out that the house belonged to her. She then proceeded to tell me what various furnishings and properties, such as the cottage belonged to James and Sarah.

Mona and Kirk, who were long time friends of Jim and his first wife, visited often. They lived some four hundred miles south of the Canada/US border but came almost monthly to spend a weekend with us. I liked them both very much. The four of us had many good times together until Mona began to overdue the reminiscing of the good times they had with the first Mrs. Cassidy. Jim spoke to her about it and also reminded her I was the lady of the manor now and he did not appreciate it when she arrived with her menu and supplies for the weekend and took over the kitchen.

I had not complained to Jim but he did tell me of the conversation he had with her. However, nothing changed and she continued to invade my space and then it did bother me a great deal. I spoke to Kirk about it and he agreed Mona was overstepping her bounds. He said he would talk to her.

He never revealed to me if they had that promised conversation but not long after my chat with Kirk, while Mona and I were alone one evening, she asked me if Jim and I had a good sex life. I was appalled at this invasion of privacy and asked her why she would ask me something so personal.

"Oh Laura, I have known for years about Jim's problem. He even told me himself and I talked to my daughter's husband Joe who is a doctor."

"How dare you discuss Jim's business and especially something so personal with me or anyone else? Our sex life is none of your affair."

"..."

They came less often after my confrontation with Mona but the meddling continued with visits to James and Sarah. Because Kathy was living with us, the way she chose to get at her was paying her way and that of the current beau to visit them.

Jim was outraged when he learned of this. He made the mistake of showing Mona the ring he had made for Kathy's upcoming graduation, which Kathy had invited her to. She was only allowed three guests for the ceremony and chose her brother James, Mona and her father. I was not offended at being excluded and stayed home to prepare a lavish party for Kathy and her friends.

The ring was designed and made by the same gemologist who made my engagement ring. The center stone was an exquisite emerald once worn by his mother. Jim had the gemologist add a sizable diamond on each side of the gem and set in a gold band very similar to my ring. The outcome was sheer beauty.

Sarah's birthday was six weeks after Kathy's graduation. The gemologist was making a floating pendant for her using the center diamond from the Sarah's mother's engagement ring. We planned to take Sarah and her husband Beau to dinner in celebration of her birthday at which time he would present her with the lavish gift.

Mona knew about both gifts but on a visit to Sarah, prior to Kathy's graduation, she revealed to her the details of Kathy's ring and showed her a photo that she took of it without Jim's knowledge. Sarah was devastated and angry at her father. Mona did not tell her about her own special birthday gift.

Mona was a shit disturber – creating problems between Jim and his children that were unnecessary, and cruel. We believed she wanted to be the mother they lost and for reasons unknown undermine Jim, I put my foot down.

James, Sarah and Kathy still grieved for their lost mother. It was not Mona's place to appoint herself as surrogate parent or meddle in Cassidy family matters. I suggested to Jim that he become involved with family therapy to help his children heal but first he had to put a stop to Mona's trouble making and he should deal with it head on with both Kirk and Mona. He would not hear of it, saying the damage was done and what good would it do now? As for family counseling, he flatly said he wasn't interested. They were adults now and had to come to terms with their own grief.

Our sexual life became non-existent within a week of our marriage which is why I took such offence to Mona's question about our sex life. Had Jim told her of this as well? My life was full with many good things that kept me busy and happy. I missed the intimacy but we did have romance that made up for the absence of sex.

Since the first night Jim and I met I continued to smoke. Now that we were married he insisted I kick the habit. Although I resented being given the order; I knew he was right and with the help of acupuncture gave up smoking completely eighteen months after we were married.

In those first two years we continued to dine out at a variety of restaurants and entertain at home. Our work day ended with cocktails and lavish dinners I prepared that included a bottle of wine. Candles were lit in the rooms we were using while romantic music played softly in the background.

Jim went on a health kick and became a vegetarian and gave up drinking. The burden of preparing special meals for him wore me down. Not wanting to prepare two separate meals after a long day at work, I ate what I prepared for him. But when I continued to have wine with my dinner, Jim complained. Before long there were no candles or soft music playing.

With romance now gone from our marriage, the absence of intimacy began to haunt me. Discussing sex with Jim was like talking to the moon. It was a subject he avoided at all times. I grew angry with myself for continually broaching the subject when there was nothing to come of it. We began to argue about anything and everything with each argument beginning with our non-existing love life but ending up on just about any other subject as long as it kept the fight going. When he told me he simply wasn't interested in sex or romance, I gave up and resigned myself to a life of celibacy.

Jim went to his office on the second floor that was once his son's bedroom when ever I was in the house. He had to be called to the dinner table and after silent meals with me, he returned to his office.

He complained we were eating dinner too late – he wanted to be fed no later than seven o'clock. He argued if I had a glass of wine and insisted I give it up. The joy of cooking and spending time in my beautiful kitchen was soon lost. I stopped eating with him. I spent Sunday afternoons preparing food for the coming week and froze it in serving size containers. He could use the microwave and feed himself.

I became friends with the woman who was our next door neighbor. Cindy was once good friends with Jim's first wife which I did not know until we became acquainted. Her husband David was retired and seldom home. Her early evening hours were the time of day she enjoyed most because she enjoyed her husband's absence for much the same reasons I was enjoying my time without Jim.

Cindy was a cute little blonde lady of leisure who could have been a calendar girl for the high society martini drinkers club.

I began joining her when I returned home from work which infuriated Jim. Cindy did drink too much and if I didn't be careful I would be too. I could not afford to have a foggy head in the morning but I thoroughly enjoyed those few hours I spent with her several nights during the week and the more Jim complained, the more I went to visit Cindy.

Most of my friends no longer came to visit because of Jim. If I saw them at all it was over lunch or a drop in at their homes after work or on the weekend. Jim called them drunks and not the kind of people he wanted to be associated with. Nothing was further from the truth. They were beautiful people with interesting lives and he was simply intimidated by them. I was very lonely for friends.

Cindy sensed Jim and I were at odds when I arrived one evening for our now regular happy hour. Prior to arriving, I dropped my briefcase and laptop at home. As I was about to make my exit, Jim stood in front of the door blocking me. He said the door would be locked when I came back if I went to Cindy's house. I went upstairs to get my overnight case – empty of course and went to Cindy's.

She offered me the use of her guest room but I had no intention of staying anywhere other than my own home. Jim could not put me out and I wasn't going to take his crap much longer.

This event brought Cindy and me to a new level of friendship. We now confided in each other and from her I learned a great deal about my husband who Cindy hated with a passion.

Cindy talked about Jim's first wife – what a wonderful person she was and how her heart was broken and her life destroyed when Jim left her. I hardly felt she was being fair to Jim. Infidelity was not unheard of and didn't warrant the venom coming from Cindy.

Cindy agreed with me but clarified her feelings toward Jim were not based on his cheating but rather the manner in which he walked out on his family and for five years made no effort to contact his children. I had no idea he was totally estranged from his family for so many years and was now curious to know more about the man I seemed to know little about.

"I didn't want to meet you let alone get to know you Laura because I believed you were the woman responsible for breaking up Jim's home but I found out a few months ago that I was wrong."

"How do you learn that I wasn't the one Cindy?"

"David and I had dinner at the club a few months ago after the wrap up bonspiel. She was there with one of the members who has been seeing her for some time. Her name is Shelley."

"That still doesn't confirm anything."

"Sorry, there is more to it. David knew for some time but the rat didn't bother to tell me. These guys like to get information but they don't like to pass it on, especially to wives. Brian, the club member dating her, asked David if he ever met Shelley before. Of course he said how could he have ever met her? Brian then told him that she lived with Jim for several years and he once owned a home next door to ours."

"Cindy I think you have shed some light on something that has been bothering me. If you thought I was the other woman then it is possible the rest of the neighborhood thinks the same thing and that would explain why I am snubbed by them after more than a year living here."

"Oh yes, I believe that most do still believe it. They were outraged when Jim married you and moved back into the house."

I wanted to set the record straight with our neighbors and although Jim didn't give a dam, he agreed we would have a Christmas cocktail party. We turned our home into a wonderland for the holiday season and invited every neighbor. Cindy and Kathy helped me with everything including delivering personal invitations.

Every neighbor came to the party but it was soon evident they came out of curiosity. Some even had the audacity to eat our food, drink our wine and snub Jim. I wasn't treated much better which proved what Cindy and I talked about. But women being more curious when it came to other people's business put on a false face and engaged me in conversation. I was grateful for the laryngitis I developed during the day.

Cindy was at my side when one lady came right out with it. Her hostility was evident before she opened her mouth but Cindy played bridge with her and figured she was the designated one to start trouble.

"You have a lovely home Mrs. Cassidy. I'm sure it must have cost you and Jim a bundle. Carl and I have been wanting to renovate ourselves. Maybe you could give me the name of your interior designer."

"Thank you for the compliment. We are very proud of our home but I did the design myself with the exception of the kitchen. We hired the designer from Bins Kitchen in Oshawa to do that."

"Is that a hobby for you or do you teach and do interior decorating?"

There it was. Shelley was a teacher.

Cindy – forever quick and wonderful, answered for me.

"Gladys, where did you ever get the idea Laura was a teacher. She's a senior executive with North American Life Insurance."

Our hospitality was not reciprocated that Christmas or any other. We never received an invitation to any of the many parties in the neighborhood but I did get a wave from a passing car now and then.

Jim retired six months later at the end of the school year. To celebrate I threw a surprise party for him in our gorgeous back yard with over seventy friends, Jim's work colleagues and family. Other than Cindy and David, no other neighbors were invited.

During the summer months and well into the fall, we continued to spend every weekend at the cottage. It was our place to relax after a busy week in the city. We had two canoes and bought a small sailboat. I loved the quiet of the old place and didn't care if I never left my lounge chair the entire weekend. The call of the loons through the night is the most beautiful sound on earth. Jim often stayed beyond the weekend now that he was retired while I had to tear myself away and fight heavy traffic back to the city every Sunday.

We took lavish trips to Europe, the Caribbean, Mexico and Florida in the winter months. While I looked forward to vacations, I did not look forward to the anxiety that was even more marked when we were away from home. It bothered me immensely to see other vacationing couples holding hands and snuggling over a candle light dinner.

I could have found what was missing in another man and there was plenty of opportunity, but then what would become of that? I wanted my marriage, my home and the bright future that was possible if Jim would at least show some affection. Our children were getting married, more grandchildren would come soon and I looked forward to all of it. My home was my castle and I had my job.

Jim resented my time away from home, even my work and began to interfere with career and what little personal time I afforded myself. My lunch breaks were my only opportunity to work out at the gym, located in the basement of the Xerox Tower where I worked. He began showing up unannounced at my office shortly before noon to take me to lunch. At first I didn't mind and thought it was sweet of him, but when it escalated to several times a week, I wasn't happy. My squash partners and my personal trainer did not like being cancelled at the last minute.

If I had to stay late at work, which was happening more and more as rumors spread of a corporate take over, he accused me of stepping out. I had no time for myself and what time I had with Jim now left me anxious and resentful.

I liked to shop in the evenings during the week when I had the time and I didn't want Jim's company. I could not escape him even at my work now and certainly not at home. I was too busy to spend more than an evening a week with Cindy and sometimes even less. I missed our times together.

Jim accused me of seeing another man and often interrogated me. He followed me a few times and was not very good at playing detective. I found it amusing to the point of laughter – I had nothing to hide other than the amount I was spending on clothes, most of which I never wore. My daughter Samantha encouraged me to keep shopping – we were the same size.

My workouts graduated to lifting weights and like it or not Mr. Cassidy – my lunch hours were the only times my trainer could accommodate me.

He wasn't happy when he showed up at my offices, in spite of being told I had a session booked, and I refused to cancel for him.

Jim harassed me day and night. If it wasn't one thing, it was another. First was the change in my appearance. I was looking pretty good and was happy with the results of my efforts. He told me I was too old and a fool to think I could have the body of a younger woman. He didn't like my new clothes and the way men looked at me. Well the men always did and my new clothes only reflected the latest styles - I couldn't win. The better I felt about myself the more he pulled me down.

In our fourth year of marriage, what had been rumors became reality. My company was under siege and soon I would be out of work. The bright side was my status warranted an attractive package and I would be a fool to turn it down.

I agreed to stay on to assist with the corporate transition for another year under contract which placed some restrictions on me such as time off. They gave me three weeks vacation time that could be used immediately or I could take the extra pay when my contract was up. Other than statutory holidays, I was expected to be at work every day until the end of my term. We decided to take a vacation in the sun.

We drove to Florida – a familiar trip, and settled into a rented condo on the beach in Panama City. The weather was cool for February but ideal for tennis which we both loved and were equally skilled. The sun shined bright and from our balcony we could enjoy sunsets. It was too cool for Jim to work on his tan.

Jim was a sun worshiper and worked on his tan on many previous vacations and in the summer months at the cottage. He never wore sun screen and was a red head before he went grey. He took a tan well for his complexion and he knew it. Several times I drew his attention to the abrasions on his legs and arms. I bought creams for his rough skin but nothing seemed to work on the scabbing type scales on his body.

While playing tennis on the third day into our vacation, Jim wasn't himself for our game. I beat him the first three games and then noticed he was struggling and breathing heavy. He asked if we could call it quits for the day – he wanted to have a nap.

Later that day we went for a walk on the beach to watch the sunset. We hadn't walked far when Jim had to stop and rest. A second attempt to continue our walk and we had to turn back. He was gasping for breath but refused to let me take him to a hospital.

"Jim don't be such a dam fool. It may be nothing which will put our minds at ease and if it is something serious, then you need to address it before you get into serious trouble."

"I'm not seeing a dam doctor Laura. I'm catching a cold – that's all. I'll take two Tylenol and get a good night's rest. Next time we will fly. I'm getting too old for the long drive."

"I did most of the driving Jim while you slept."

"It was still a long trip."

"…"

There was no arguing with Jim. He was a stubborn man and had to learn things the hard way when it came to himself. Over the next two days his condition worsened. I packed our things, loaded the car and bullied Jim into getting in it. I drove the next twenty three hours to get us home.

Jim was diagnosed with Atrial Fibrillation, the most common cardiac arrhythmia involving the two upper chambers of the heart. He was placed on medication and scheduled for further testing. The medication didn't work resulting in his admission to hospital where a procedure was performed to stop his heart and re-boot it. For three months he seemed back to normal when he began having difficulty again. The procedure failed the second time. He was placed on a regimen of medications that would be with him for life. A month later he started treatments for skin cancer.

The corporate transition completed after fourteen months of hell. Jim was settled into a casual lifestyle with many changes he didn't like and in particular the number of extra hours I had to work. I brought work home on weekends to at least be in the house with him but that was not enough. He wanted my undivided attention. He nagged me – breaking my concentration when I worked at home and called me several times a day when I was at work. He wanted me to break my contract and retire. I couldn't get it through his head that to do so would mean I would lose my package which was close to a quarter million.

I was glad and ready when I finally walked out of the Xerox Tower for the last time in June, but I wasn't happy about now being a housewife and nurse and planned to find something else after some well needed rest. We closed up the house and went north to the cottage for the summer. No more fighting week end traffic.

This was the first time I had ever spent more than a week at one time at the cottage. I loved it and dreaded returning to the city as did Jim. Over the summer we discussed moving to the north permanently – the idea had great appeal.

We both loved our city home and had put a lot into it. For me it was a big decision but there were merits to selling and moving. Kathy was out on her own now over a year and doing very well. The house was huge for two people and expensive to keep up. We had very few friends in Toronto and seldom entertained or were entertained. The downside was we couldn't live in the cottage in the winter months.

We made the decision in late October after we were home for a few weeks. We put our house on the market and began looking for a house design suitable for the north. Jim returned to the cottage in early November with James and a few of his buddies to tear down the old cottage. We had a small cabin we decided to leave standing for our use while construction was underway. The first building to go up was a three car garage with attached work shop. We wanted that finished before winter for storage.

We found and paid for the blueprints for a large chalet but we didn't want a prefab house. Jim hired a construction crew who came from Labrador in April. They brought their own trailer and set up camp in our yard.

The serenity of life at the lake amidst the tall pines and wild life would be good for us both and was the change we both needed. I could hardly wait to make the move but I had to stay in Toronto until the sale of our house was complete and to keep the wheels turning while Jim was north overseeing construction. Gradually we moved many things into the new garage and weeded out what we didn't want.

We moved in two weeks before Christmas – fourteen months since making the decision to re-locate. Already we had a few feet of snow but it was totally unlike city snow and slush. Everything was pristine and with each new snowfall we sat by the fire watching the wonderland at our doorstep through any of the many large windows of the chalet.

Neighbors were few and far between and many only came on the weekend but they were very social and before long we had many new and wonderful friends. We joined the local church and became actively involved with church events. We took up the sport of curling which Jim was familiar with from his younger days but it was totally foreign to me. I found the arena very cold and kept falling until I got used to the technique of sliding down the ice with a slider on one foot. I came to love the sport and got pretty good at it. We looked forward to our twice a week games and the socials that followed with another group of new friends and acquaintances.

I longed to get involved in something that stimulated my brain. When cottages opened the following spring; I was asked to accept the position of president for the lake association. That same summer I became chairperson for the township waste management committee and joined the ladies golf league.

Every few weeks we drove to Toronto for Jim's routine medical check-ups. His skin cancer was under control as was his arrhythmia. The two hundred mile drive in one day was becoming too much for both of us but I refused to allow Jim to make the drive himself. He was wearing down and I did my best to slow him down. His driving skills in particular were becoming frightening.

Over the next few years Jim grew old before my eyes. He was crankier than ever but I accepted it and ignored it. He was meticulous about his medication and never missed. His hygiene went down the drain but again I accepted and ignored it until one day I walked into the bathroom as he was stepping out of the shower I bullied him into taking. As he raised his arms to towel dry his back, I noticed a black mark under his left breast that was about two inches long and an inch in width.

"Jim, how long has that been there?"

"What are you talking about?"

"Go to the mirror and look."

"I've never seen that before."

"Don't you ever look in the mirror? Remember the doctor told you to check your body regularly and to use a mirror to see those areas where your eyes can't reach."

"…"

The melanoma was removed from Jim's chest one week later.

Going into our fifth year at the chalet Jim underwent more tests. We were advised on October 3, 1999 he needed a quadruple heart bypass operation. Surgery was scheduled for January 16, 2000. Until then he had to have total calm and quiet.

We cancelled our trip to Morocco scheduled for New Year's Eve. Christmas dinner with our children was postponed until Easter. We gave up curling and asked friends from the church to take over our volunteer commitments. Other than attending church services, we stayed home to prepare for Jim's convalescence.

On the 20th of December, Jim's color changed to ashen. He assured me he felt fine when I repeatedly asked him how he felt. He was irritable, had no energy and wasn't eating. His condition worsened almost hourly but the stubborn old man would not let me take him to the local hospital. We argued constantly which didn't help him but my frustration got the better of me. I was no medical person but I was sure something was amiss. We were already socked in with snow and it was frigid cold.

Two men from our church came by on the evening of the 21st to assist with assembling a computer station I purchased to set up in the den for Jim. After his surgery he would not be able to sleep in our room upstairs. The guest room was on the main floor with a full bathroom. The den was close to the kitchen, had a fireplace and a set of ten foot sliding glass doors.

Charlie and Len found Jim looking not so good either. They had the unit assembled within an hour and needed only a different type screwdriver than the one they brought with them. Jim went to the lower level to fetch one and could barely make it back up the stairs.

The men wanted to take him to emergency – something I had been attempting for two days. He refused and became angry with all of us. Len and Charlie didn't want to leave and turned to me for direction.

"There's nothing you can say to Jim that will make him get medical attention. I have been trying and he just gets himself upset arguing with me. Why don't you fellows go home to your wives? I'll call you if I need anything."

We argued after the men left. I was near panic with worry but the more I argued the more agitated Jim became. He went upstairs to bed while I sat alone in front of the fire with a glass of wine. I slept in the guest room that night but didn't get much sleep. Through the huge bay window, I watched the steady snow fall and worried more.

At 4 a.m. I awoke to find we were buried in snow and prayed Jim wouldn't have to be driven anywhere. I called our groundskeeper Norm to bring in his plow.

"Laura, when I get myself out from under all this snow; I will come right over but it's going to be a while."

Feeling guilty over the previous night's argument, I went upstairs to check on him. The bed side lamp was on and Jim was sitting up in bed. His color was better and he seemed more at ease than he had been the previously. He assured me he was catching a cold, something we had been trying to avoid with his pending surgery.

"Jim, I'm sorry I have been such a nag; I was just worried.

"I know sweetie – no harm done."

"Can I get you a cup of tea?"

"Yes and please bring me two Tylenol."

"What do you want the Tylenol for?"

"Chest pain – I feel like an elephant is sitting on it."

I took the stairs two at a time to get to the phone in the den. Jim followed behind me, his old plaid flannel robe flapping all about. After tearing the phone from my hand he threw it against the wall smashing it to pieces.

"Laura, what the hell is wrong with you?"

"It's too late Jim. I made the call."

The fire department arrived within twenty minutes. They were less than a mile from us, knew our exact location and us very well. The ambulance had to come fifty miles from Lindsay in winter storm conditions. They didn't know us or our location and we were not easy to find.

Deputy Chief Tony Aymon thought I was the patient when he entered the house. I was hysterical and Jim was still acting like a lunatic. Somehow I managed to give Tony the information he needed. He was taking no bull from Jim - ordering him to lie on the stretcher. After some resistance, Tony threatened to knock him out if he had to. Jim got on the stretcher and was immediately given oxygen.

Tony was sure Jim suffered a heart attack as was I. But once I had thought I was pregnant when I had a bladder infection and another time I thought I had a bladder infection and I was pregnant. I wasn't taking any chances.

The fire department was not equipped to deal with this situation when they learned of Jim's pending surgery. We had to wait for the ambulance which should have reached us before now. They were lost and had long ago passed the cut off to our driveway. Tony was in radio contact with them but the weather had turned into a major blizzard which further handicapped the ambulance. Tony sent the rescue unit out to the highway to bring them in.

Following instructions, I gathered up Jim's medications and drove to the newly built hospital in Minden. Jim was appointed to the Board of Directors only a few months earlier when the hospital opened. Although the ambulance was coming from Lindsay – some fifty miles away, the new Minden hospital was only ten miles from our home. Tony told me they would take him there first to get stabilized. It was too risky to travel back to Lindsay in the storm with Jim.

It took me thirty minutes to find the hospital in the blinding storm. I had only been there once or twice and wasn't familiar with the area. Our little community was very proud of the new facility and they had every right to be. The hospital was a fine example of community effort. This small town in Ontario was everything a good life can be with a strong community spirit, respect for all and good time traditions and values.

Tony and the ambulance paramedics were standing off to one side in the emergency room with Jim when I arrived. Jim was sitting up in bed looking happy and laughing as he relished in the attention he was receiving from the doctor and nurses. After all he was a board member and their first real emergency.

The doctor approached me when I entered the room and asked if I was Jim's daughter, a question frequently asked. He confirmed Jim did have a heart attack - over 20 hours ago. The look he gave me was accusatory. Why didn't I get him there sooner?

Jim lunged at me when I approached his bedside.

"This is your entire fault Laura."

The doctor ran back into the room while the nurses rushed to Jim's bedside. They believed, as did Tony, that Jim was going to hit me. Tony came to stand beside me where I stood frozen. I rushed out into the corridor with Tony on my heels.

"Laura, you have every right to be upset. I know how hard you tried to get him help. This is not your fault. Try to stay calm for Jim. You can beat the crap out of him later. Hold that thought."

Tony was right. The last thing I needed to do was make matters worse. I cried while Tony stood by me.

"Tony, I hate that man. I want to belt him right now but I won't. I will do what I have to do for Jim but this is the last time – I swear it's the last time."

I don't know what they did to stabilize Jim. He looked pretty stable to me and I didn't care what his situation was. He was transferred to Lindsay two hours later. When I learned that was where they were taking him I went to see the doctor.

"Why are you taking him further north? Why not take him to Toronto where he's scheduled for surgery?"

"Toronto is closed. I've been trying since your husband got here to get him there but they won't receive him."

"What can Lindsay do for him? He's technically a triage patient of Toronto General. Can't he be sent to a hospital in the other direction?"

The doctor walked away from me.

I stood in the background as Jim was loaded into the waiting ambulance and went home. Even if it had been a sunny day in July, I still would have gone home.

My sister Mary and brother in law Hector were already en route to my house. I left a message on their answering machine before I left home earlier.

They had only returned from their annual trip to Mexico the previous day and I didn't expect them to come. I just needed to talk to my sister but they were on their way – was the message on my voice mail when I arrived home. Their home was in Niagara Falls. They had to drive through Toronto – a hell of a drive and then two hundred miles further north to reach me. It would take them at least four hours and I had no idea what the weather was on the other side of Toronto but they were in for a ride once they got north on the highway.

I spent the next several hours on the phone. I couldn't get past the switchboard at Toronto General and none of Jim's doctors answered. I left messages for those I could not reach and called anyone I knew who might be able to help. I had to get Jim to Toronto.

It made no sense to rush to Jim's bedside and I didn't want to see him. Much more could be accomplished from home where many long distance telephone calls had to be made.

Fresh coffee was brewing when Hector and Mary came through the door. Their trip had been rough and they were still jet lagged from the previous day. I was so grateful when they walked in the door. Hector was willing to go right back out in the cold to take me to see Jim but I said no. I called Lindsay Memorial every few hours to get a report. He was stable and resting. Good!

The following day, after a good night's sleep, we drove to see Jim. He was in good spirits and happy to see us. We stayed only two hours before returning to the chalet. Roads were not sanded yet and many of the side roads, which we made the mistake of travelling on in the interest of saving time, were not even plowed.

Christmas Eve morning I was on the phone while Mary and Hector slept. I wasn't making any headway and became frustrated to the point of desperation. I called friends who had connections - I called strangers who hung up on me. I called other hospitals who advised my only option was to make contact with Toronto General where Jim was technically their triage patient.

After a late breakfast we drove once again to visit Jim. The nursing supervisor was eager to get Jim transferred – putting the onus on me. They had made their call and were not following up with Toronto until after they re-opened. I found it somewhat ironic that such responsibility had fallen on my back but it was Christmas and if I didn't take the initiative it was clear no one else was anxious to do anything.

We returned to the chalet after spending the afternoon with Jim.

Hector braved the weather and barbequed steaks on the deck while Mary and I drank wine and made a terrific Caesar salad. It was Christmas Eve.

Later that evening I reached the surgical nurse, Ruth Gordon, who was sister in law to Mona and Kirk. I didn't realize her position in the surgical wing was the most senior and I never even thought of her as a contact. It was Cindy, who I spoke with frequently and earlier that day, who suggested I call Rut h at home.

Ruth agreed Jim had to be transferred immediately and set about to make it happen and explained why I wasn't getting through.

"The hospital never closes Laura, we simply cut back for the holidays but we are there for those emergencies that need us. Sometimes it is hard to get through to anyone on the telephone. Had you arrived in person we could have had Jim transferred right away."

"Had I known this Ruth I would have had him transferred to Toronto from Minden instead of letting them send him to Lindsay. The doctor here said he tried to reach someone in Toronto but wasn't successful."

"I find that hard to believe."

"What about the weather and road conditions?"

"Those ambulance drivers are the best and can drive through anything. They're equipped and they could have a police escort if needed or they could use air ambulance. Nothing's impossible Laura."

"So what happens now Ruth?

"Leave it with me for a few hours. I will get back to you. Sit tight and don't do anything else. I will take care of it."

Mary and Hector left after breakfast Christmas morning. They had their own family with plans made long ago. They had a long drive ahead of them but had enough time to play Santa and cook their turkey. We hugged in my round about driveway as they set out. The storm had passed; skies were cloudless and sea blue. The Canadian North country is so beautiful at this time of year, yet I felt so alone in the vast wilderness.

Ruth called less than an hour later. An emergency surgical team was on standby; an ambulance would be dispatched before evening. She told me where to go within the hospital to get myself a place to sleep and to stay calm.

I packed a suitcase and headed for toward Lindsay Memorial. Roads were still icy but with literally no other traffic, it wasn't as bad as I feared. I prayed for Jim while I drove listening to Christmas carols.

I waited with Jim until the ambulance from Toronto arrived several hours later. Against the advice of the drivers, I followed on their tail at high speed arriving in the emergency bay of Toronto General seconds behind them at 9 p.m. I had never driven that fast in my life and felt light headed once the commotion of getting Jim settled was over.

Jim was taken immediately for testing. I waited in the deserted lounge for hours before another nurse came to advise me he was going into surgery at 6 a.m. He suffered considerable damage to the heart and was high risk but without surgery he had no chance at all.

A security guard escorted me through the underground tunnel to the dwelling Ruth suggested. Once a residence for student nurses, the building was now used as a guest house. The following morning, Jim's daughter Kathy arrived to wait with me during the surgery. Her apartment was close to the hospital and a short walk. I spoke to all three of Jim's children before leaving home the previous day. Only Kathy was close by and available. James lived in Ottawa with his wife and the weather there was worse than anywhere. Sarah lived in the country and was socked in.

Jim came through the surgery but was in a coma when Kathy and I went to see him for the first time. I encouraged Kathy to go home and get some sleep – I would let her know if there was any change. I pulled the old leather chair in the I.C.U. up to Jim's bed side and spent the next seven days there.

Thoughts ran rampant through my head as I watched him and listened g to the life support machinery that was keeping him alive. At times I wished he would pass quietly into the next life - other times I prayed for his recovery. In truth I didn't really know what I wanted.

New Year's Eve 1999 - I left the hospital for the first time in six days. Dressed warmly, I inhaled clean cold fresh air as I walked toward the Eaton Center. It had been a long time since I wandered through the famous three storey mall in the heart of downtown Toronto. The boutiques were unchanged from the days when I roamed and shopped here with girl friends for the latest fashions. I had no need now for designer clothing and the shops were closed as it was. Looking in the windows was enough to satisfy my need for the moment. My memories of the good times I had here, whether shopping of eating in one of the many trendy restaurants was what I needed.

I was hungry and wanted something special. The streets were empty when I left the Center – only the odd vagabond looking for a handout crossed my path as I wandered the streets looking for the right place. It was still early evening – the rush had not started yet.

I walked for an hour before coming to a steak and lobster restaurant just opening their doors for business. I was their first customer. A cute little waitress, who was no more than nineteen, ushered me to a small corner table beside a window. This time was for me. I wanted a good meal and to be alone.

I seldom drank anymore much to Jim's delight but he wasn't with me now and I didn't care what he thought anymore. I ordered a martini. When my dinner came, I ordered a bottle of wine.

The meal was delicious as I took my time savoring every mouthful. I left nothing on my plate but a 50-dollar tip under it for my waitress who couldn't do enough for me.

Feeling warm and renewed, I walked back to the hospital at 9 o'clock. As I sat looking at my husband, I prayed the New Year held better things for both of us. Never before had I felt the sadness I was now feeling as one century ended and a new one began.

On the seventh day, Jim's intubation tube was removed and his medication lessened. Within four hours he was conscious and moved to a private room. He was confused, delirious and suffered hallucinations for the first few days.

Using a soft sponge and special soaps purchased at a local Body Shop, I bathed his foul smelling body. I treated his bed sores with ointments provided by the hospital before dusting him with baby talcum powder. Like dressing a child, I put on the new pajamas I purchased for him along with a new robe.

I clipped his finger nails and helped him brush his teeth. I sat with him through every meal to ensure he ate all. Often I brought in foods from local restaurants to better please his palate. We prayed together every night before I retreated to my own room.

Hospitals were so understaffed and what help was there were too busy to give patients the attention they needed. I didn't relish bathing my husband but it had to be done and if I didn't do it who would?

We returned to our home three weeks later. Jim's recovery was rapid, his strength and vigor returning. His appetite was ravenous.

Never forgetting the night he was first taken to the hospital, I asked him if he remembered. I was sure he would not and would deny if he did. My heart sank once again when he quickly answered that he did remember and still held me to blame.

When Jim was so incapacitated I had to take over our finances. To my horror I discovered we were heavily in debt. How could that be? We paid cash for our chalet and had plenty of money left over from the sale of our house and my severance package. We were paying high interest rates on our debts and if this continued we would lose everything. My anger was renewed that Jim allowed this to happen and kept it from me.

I loved the chalet and the community but there was no way to salvage if we didn't clear the debts and that meant sell the house. Half of my severance was invested in my own portfolio and I wasn't about to dip into that to save the day. I was a lot younger than Jim and had to face the possibility of being on my own one day. I had to take care of my own affairs hence forward.

When I confronted Jim with our financial situation, I didn't give him an option. We were selling and he agreed. As much as I loved Toronto, the city that brought so much into my life and the place I still called home; I didn't want to move back. We bought a new town house in the Niagara Peninsula on the shore of Lake Ontario.

Jim was totally recovered by the time we settled into our new home. If he followed doctor's orders, he would have many more years of life to enjoy. Without telling a soul, I made a decision to give our marriage one more year. I had to care about myself.

Chapter Two
Trial Time

Snowing again! Another dark dreary day as I sit by the fire looking out over a very angry Lake Ontario. With a glass of wine in hand, Celtic Dreams playing softly on my stereo, I become relaxed as I do daily with this ritual. This is my one hour a day to meditate; a time when Jim leaves me to myself. It is my time to remember where I came from and to cry softly as I almost always do at this time.

Memories of the mother I lost 15 years ago float through my mind. She speaks to me in my thoughts and says she is sorry we never had the relationship I wanted.

My father, now gone five years also speaks to me and tells me he too is sorry he didn't teach me what I needed to know about men--how to pick the right one, how to be happy.

I tell them they did the best they could and I am not angry with them. I tell them I love and miss them. I ask for their help to find my true happiness. They tell me it will come but I must be brave and strong as I have always been. They tell me to take better care of myself. Before fading away, they tell me they will always be watching over me.

The aromas from my kitchen arouse me from my hour of self indulgence. Six neighbors will be arriving in less than two hours for our weekly Sunday evening dinner party. Tonight is my turn to be hostess and I look forward to an evening of socializing.

I consider myself a gourmet cook. I love being in my kitchen creating new dishes or doctoring proven ones. My pantry is filled with cookbooks collected over the last 20 years; books of any kind being one of my hobbies.

Looking out the kitchen window with my apron on and utensil in hand, I note it is snowing much harder than before. The neighbors will be here on time. They live in the same luxury townhouse complex and can skip along the back-decks without getting snow-covered. Most will arrive without coats.

My concern is for my husband Jim who has not returned from the errand I sent him on hours ago. That little Echo of his doesn't handle very well in this weather. I swear I don't know where that man goes. A simple task is a major expedition for him. He will spend an entire afternoon going from place to place on the premise of looking for the best price, when in fact he just likes being out and about.

It's been ten years since he retired and he has yet to find a hobby of interest. He still putters in his office for several hours a day – doing what is mystery. I'm not complaining since we seem have found a harmony between us since moving to the peninsula. I no longer play sports or work out but I have a job – a recent happening and pray it works out for me.

Finally I see him turn onto our street swaying and skidding to a halt in our driveway. At least he made it home in one piece and before the arrival of our guests. I suppose I should feel grateful for many things but my love for him died a long time ago. We are room mates.

I stopped beating myself up years ago. I tried for many years to make a good marriage but it simply didn't happen. I wasn't happy and doubted I ever would be but at least I didn't cry about it anymore. Jim is simply not easy to be with. He can be nasty and manipulative and then become like a child when he is cornered for his ways.

The force of the wind nearly blasts him through our front door. Dripping snow and mud on the foyer tiles he calls out his familiar greeting:

"Hi Sweetie – I'm home."

My heart goes out to him as he hands me a beautiful bouquet of tropical flowers. I love getting flowers on a regular basis – something he did every Friday in the first few years of our marriage. Exotic flowers were not available in the Canadian north and artificial ones were often used on our dining room table. In summer months I grew my own in the garden and cried when the first frost came. Surrounded now by many nurseries in the peninsula, we had fresh flowers throughout the year.

"Thanks honey, these are beautiful but remember I warned you tropical flowers were reminders of the Caribbean and some day I want to live on a beautiful island in the sun."

"Nothing is holding us back sweetie. We can do whatever we set out to do."

My dreams of living in the Caribbean have become my personal escape. I spend hours at my computer searching out every piece of information on every island. Who in their right mind wouldn't want to live in such paradise? In my heart I know I will not spend the rest of my years with Jim and the Caribbean is where I want to be. Maybe it is just a dream but there is no harm in having a dream.

Table talk during dinner covered everything from religion, politics, economics and grandkids. None of us knew each other prior to moving into the complex. All came from a variety of professions and life experiences, making our times together interesting as well as fun. Some of us have taken weekend trips together in small groups. As most are retired or almost and moved to the area from far away places, we are eager to make lasting friendships. I am the only one who secretly knows I will not be around for life long friendships with them. I hate to see the evening come to an end but tomorrow is a work day for me.

The dishes are loaded in the dishwasher, the kitchen tidied up and back to normal. A quick mop of the floor where wet shoes left marks is my last task. After a quick check of the entertainment area to ensure candles have been extinguished, I'm off to the second floor for the night.

One last look at the beautiful tropical floral arrangement before turning out the lights leads me to my computer. The glory of these flowers never ceases to takes my breath away. Where would the world be without the beauty of nature?

It is still early, only 11 o'clock. Sleep will not come to me after such a wonderful evening for at least another two hours but before I reach the top floor I can hear Jim snoring. In a matter of seconds my computer comes to life – hello Caribbean, what have you got to offer me?

After two hours in front of the screen, tiredness overcomes me. Tomorrow is a big day for me at the office. With visions of surf, sand and palm trees, I head for my bed.

Chapter Three
Stephanie

The snow continued through the night making the drive to work an unpleasant challenge. The streets were blocked with stalled and abandoned vehicles. I had to climb snowdrifts to get into the 6-storey office building that houses the most successful personnel agency in the area.

The President and CEO is my long time good friend Stephanie Buchanan. We met and worked together at a local radio station CJRN Niagara, when we were both still wet behind the ears with not a lot of experience to offer. It was the first job since college for both of us and a time when jobs were plentiful.

Stephanie and I had much in common in those days twenty fives years ago with matching type-A personalities, an eagerness to learn and move forward and both of us single moms. With two small daughters each close in age, we became instant friends.

Stephanie was still a very attractive woman with enviable natural blonde hair. Standing nearly six feet in height with a healthy voluptuous body, she made a statement with her mere presence. Standing next to her I had to look up. We were nothing alike when it came to physical appearance. I barely made five feet – three inches, could be blown over in a strong wind and was a brunette.

We struggled to raise our kids, pay our bills and still have some time for ourselves. When we did manage to take some personal time out it was always Stephanie who was the self-appointed organizer. She had the most outgoing personality of anyone I have ever known. When she enters a room, she takes over, keeping her admirers captivated with a winning smile and quick wit.

We left the radio station within six months of each other. I was offered the career opportunity of a lifetime with a Toronto insurance company that was my dream come true. I packed my possessions, loaded my two little girls in my old VW and drove the 100 miles to my new life.

Stephanie fulfilled her dreams by opening her own company. She struggled in those early days but if anyone could do it – she could and she did.

We didn't keep in contact much over the years and I hadn't seen her for nearly fifteen years when I walked into her office not long after we moved into our townhouse. My career in Toronto was everything I could have possibly wished for but it kept absent from my home town and old friends. Raising my two daughters Samantha and Leslie took up what little spare time I had. Stephanie was living a life similar to my own. Someday we would catch up with each other. Good friends are for life and she was one of mine.

As I sat in the reception area waiting for my scheduled appointment with her, I took in the beautiful surroundings. Everything was authentic, warm, welcoming and comfortable. My friend had no idea who was waiting to see her. I made the appointment using my married name deliberately. I wanted to surprise her.

The receptionist approached me to say that Ms. Buchanan was ready to see me. She led me down a long hall and left me before a set of oversize double mahogany doors. I knocked lightly and heard a familiar voice telling me to come in.

She was on the phone facing away from the spot where I now stood. She took a quick glance at me and motioned to a chair for me to sit down. She was holding the phone in her right hand, turned slightly to her right in front of her computer screen. She kept her left hand, beautifully manicured and donning some impressive gems in a gesture to me which indicated be with you in a minute.

Age had been kind to my friend. She was even more beautiful than when I had last seen her. The stunning thick hair was bobbed just below the ears; the honey blonde of yester years now evenly toned ash blonde. Her make-up was perfect with shades of taupe and ivory on the eye lids to pick up the lilac leather suit and ivory silk blouse she wore. She had come a long way from the days of sharing lipstick with me. When her call ended she turned to face me and was about to speak when recognition hit her. She had only given me a quick glance upon entering the office but now she was staring at me.

"I don't believe it, - I don't believe it."

She was out of her chair and hugging me before I could lift my butt out of my own chair. We flung our arms around each other; my head just barely reaching her chest. We babbled at each other for several minutes - neither one of us making any sense. Finally, she grabbed her purse and said:

"Let's get out of here."

She whirled me around and through the offices introducing me to her staff as we flew by them. Bursting with pride she took me into two adjoining executive offices where her two little girls, now grown women, held senior executive positions with their mother's company. Of course they didn't remember me. It had been years since I last saw them and they were been barely out of diapers. Now, they stood almost as tall as their mother and were the spitting image of Stephanie with her poise and confidence.

We headed to the underground parking area where her white Mercedes was parked. Still laughing and holding my hand, she managed to maneuver her car out of the garage. We drove across the street - something only this crazy woman would do and pulled up in front of the restaurant known as The Mermaid. It had been 25 years since I had been in this restaurant. I couldn't believe it was still in business.

"They still have the same staff," she said laughing while voicing my thoughts.

"I wonder if they will remember you."

The answer to that came soon after our coats were checked. Philippe', the maitre de, rushed to greet us. There was no doubt in my mind Stephanie was a regular. The Mermaid was and still is the favored place for business professionals in the city of St. Catharines, Ontario.

After Stephanie managed to pry herself loose she turned Philippe's attention to me for introduction. None was needed; he remembered me and gave me the same hugs and squeezes just given to my friend.

Our four-hour lunch that started before noon was a trip down memory lane. As Stephanie had remained in the area all these years; she was in touch with many of our mutual friends and business associates. Sadly, some were no longer with us. Many had divorced and remarried. Some were retired while a few were now total alcoholics. We reminisced over the many lunches we literally shared for lack of funds and gossiped about those who weren't as successful as we were. I cried and laughed at the same time over the mischief we got ourselves into in those years of our youth gone by.

Memories are a wonderful thing that we carry with us until the end. If there was one line of work I would never want to go back to it was radio. The parties were endless, the people were nuts and if you didn't get out in time, you were doomed.

Before parting company, I invited Stephanie to have dinner with us the following week. She had never remarried while I had shortly after moving to Toronto and was divorced less than a year later. Jim was my third husband and hopefully the last.

Jim fell in love with Stephanie at first sight. He was an excellent communicator and listener and above all, a charmer. They hit it off immediately, chatting non stop, while I went about making drinks, preparing and serving dinner. It was well past two in the morning when Stephanie left. There was no mention of a future get together as we hugged each other good night. Stephanie was a very busy woman and I was grateful for our reunion but I was a housewife and the ball was in her court for further contact.

A week later she called to invite me to lunch at the Mermaid. I was glad to hear from her fearing it may be months before we got together again. When I arrived at the restaurant she was already seated enjoying a martini. We hugged and before I knew it there was a martini in front of me. We enjoyed a lunch of lobster salad – the house specialty and a bottle of wine. This could be dangerous! Stephanie was always a big drinker but she could handle it. I couldn't and didn't' want to go home drunk. We ordered cappuccino but I passed on the cognac to go with it.

"Laura I have a business proposition I would like to discuss with you."

"Wow, I wasn't expecting this. What's on your mind?"

"I want to open a new division for executive recruiting. For years I have been waiting for the right time and the right person to head it up for me. I believe now is the right time and you Laura are the ideal person to run it. With your past experience, you are perfect for the job."

Going back to work was the last thing on my agenda but I was excited at the prospect of working again and especially with Stephanie. Jim was so demanding of me that I wasn't sure what to think, but this was an opportunity I didn't want to turn my back on.

"Laura you have the talent, experience and skills to do this job. You are comfortable working with executives and I just know this is the right fit. Don't make a decision now. Think about it - talk it over with Jim if you want to but at least give it some consideration. I will be straight up with you. Once receivables are on the books, you will get 35%. Until then I will provide you with an assistant and any other office support you need, a full expense account including all travel and parking."

An opportunity like this doesn't come along often and I didn't need or feel it was necessary to discuss it with Jim. He wouldn't like me working again but I didn't care what he liked or didn't like. I wanted the position more than I had wanted anything in several years. I knew I could do the job albeit somewhat different from what I did before but of one thing I was sure; I wouldn't let Stephanie down.

"When do I start?"

After six weeks, numerous mail-outs, follow-up phone calls, announcements in local papers sporting my photo and credentials, dozens of lunches and dinners with high profile corporate executives, I had clients.

Stephanie spared no expense getting word out to the business community about her new Executive Recruitment Division. She introduced me to every member of the country club where she was a member and where I soon would become one. She was respected as well as admired. People were eager to give her referrals which of course she passed on to me.

Jim was happy for me which came as a surprise. He supported my every effort and offered his help whenever I needed it until my work took me into an area he hadn't counted on. Executives looking for employment could not be seen entering my offices nor could I go into their places of work. Meetings were held in restaurants, coffee shops or bars and always a safe distance away from their domain.

The men and women I was working with were interested only in boosting their career. They were not into small talk and seldom gave away personal information. When they did I made note of it. After initial contact, cell phones were used. I had no personal data on these potential clients other than their name and the company they were currently employed with. Confidentiality was a top priority and Jim was not happy when I discussed my day but never revealed the identity of the people I met.

My office and home computer kept what little data I had. I made quick notes of family member names if they were given or some special event or happening they may have mentioned. I consulted my notes before each meeting. If the client mentioned a sick child at a previous meeting or some special event worth remembering, I made a note of it and asked how the sick child was or how was the wedding when I saw the client again. They seemed to appreciate this and never failed to give me an up-date.

Jim did not like the idea of me being out for dinner or drinks – especially with men. His rational was I had an office job that should end at five o'clock each and every day. I tried to assure him I would make every effort to keep my evenings free for him but it wasn't always possible. If I wanted to succeed I had to meet the client's needs, not my own.

Although he claimed to understand, he didn't or he did and didn't like it. I wasn't sure which applied and I didn't care. His antagonism toward me mounted with each new meeting. I dreaded talking to him or telling him I would be home late. When dinners were unavoidable, I ate light. Once home I ate with him or we went out. I was never later than eight o'clock arriving home but that was three hours after my curfew of five o'clock.

On the nights when I arrived home after such a dinner meeting that was totally unavoidable, Jim was in a foul mood. Whether we ate in or went out he was miserable and condescending - referring to my meetings as dates. He never asked about my meetings. He was more interested in the age and appearance of the person I was with and whether or not they were married. I gave away as little information as I could manage but not because I had anything to hide other than the identity of my clients. The more Jim harped, the more I protected information relevant to my clients. I didn't trust him.

I don't know if I should have, could have or would have seen what was coming. Jim's behavior worried me based on past experiences, especially when we lived in the North. Regardless of what I was involved in, he had to be part of it. He made whatever went on in my life his reason to be. He had his own interests that kept him busy enough to squelch boredom but when I was involved in anything, including selling Mary Kay cosmetics for a year, he had to make it his business. I had nothing to hide and never felt intimidated by him – just annoyed.

If I could have taken Jim with me for my after hour meetings, he would have been quite happy. He would join in the sales pitch and make my job his. He would be first in line also to take any glory. It was one thing to take him to a Mary Kay house party with a dozen women but it was quite another matter to take him on an executive recruiting interview.

After an evening appointment with a client, I arrived home to find Jim dressed and ready to go out for dinner. Expecting to arrive home for another argument with him and likely going to bed without dinner, I had a full meal with the client. I tried to get away with an appetizer and a salad but this particular client insisted on ordering for me. His choices were heavenly and I enjoyed every morsel. The man was also a diabetic and had to eat at a certain time every day. I was home at eight o'clock.

I didn't let on to Jim I had eaten a full meal but rather told him it was a great idea for us to go out. He told me to hurry and change into something sexy - we had reservations.

Much to my horror our reservation was at the very restaurant I had just left only an hour earlier. From the coat check clerk to the maitre de to the head water, I received warm welcomes and strange looks. They must have thought I had a little business going on the side or an insatiable appetite. I was grateful for their discretion.

Once we were seated with drinks in front of us he asked me how my date went. I tried to make light of everything not wanting to draw attention to our table but I knew exactly where this was going. This restaurant was not one we had been to before but I did learn from the client it was one of his favorites. It was quite possible I might find myself here again. The last thing I needed was a scene with Jim and I was very curious as to Jim's choice of restaurants.

His innuendo continued throughout our meal. As much as I tried to change the subject he kept bringing it back to where he wanted it. It was hard to think when I was with Jim; it was similar to fencing with a skilled fencing opponent. I was always on the defensive and his constant battering brought me close to tears.

We said little in the car on the way home and I was so angry by the time we reached I was ready to take him on or anyone else who took a shot at me. Jim's choice of restaurant was no coincidence. I was now determined to meet him head on with every derogatory comment he made. We were no sooner in the door when he started again by asking if I had the same meal twice or did I try something different with him. For the first time in our marriage I slapped him across the face.

….I asked him to leave. Enough was enough and I was at the end of my rope. Jim packed a bag and left for three nights.

I bounced off the walls for those three days. What on earth was wrong with Jim? I hated confrontations and arguments but how much more of this could I endure? I was relieved when he came home and gave him a warm greeting but it was all so very superficial because I wasn't sincere with the warm welcome. I didn't want him back but he was so pathetic that I did. He was full of apologies and remorseful for his behavior – so he said. He was no more insincere than me and I had to wonder what held the two of us together.

Finally I had a client, Mr. Nixon, who was eager to come on board with us. I was so excited that I told Jim but didn't mention the client's name – only the nature of the situation. He wished me well and expressed excitement when I headed off to work on the Monday morning following our dinner night with the neighbors.

Heading for the staff lounge leaving a trail of wet snow behind, I bumped into Stephanie who had also just arrived. We thawed out together over a fresh brew and discussed the day ahead of us.

"Are you sure Laura? Do you really think Mr. Nixon will sign on with us?"

"Absolutely; when I met with him on Thursday he asked if I had the contracts with me. I told him our legal department would have them ready today."

I went over my plan for the two of us to meet him for dinner that night – something Mr. Nixon was expecting. After reviewing the contracts he could take them with him if he chose to have his own lawyer look at them or he could sign during dinner. The choice was his.

Stephanie had two companies searching for a CEO and Mr. Nixon was a suitable candidate for both. Each offered a starting salary with perks that far exceeded what he was currently earning. Stephanie was very good at connecting the dots and knew when to play her card. Once I earned the respect of the business community I would be able to do much of what she had to do until then.

Mr. Nixon was not aware of the two opportunities nor would he be until he signed. I didn't even know what they were. Stephanie would handle that part during dinner. I knew he would be pleased.

"We make a great team Laura. My calendar is open for the rest of the day – let me know where and when."

She hugged me – my feet were barely touching the ground.

I dropped Jim's medications at home before picking up a French Vanilla Cappuccino at the Tim Horton Drive Thru and found a quiet side street to enjoy my coffee and make the call.

"Good morning Mr. Nixon, this is Laura Cassidy. I hope your family enjoyed your surprise ski weekend at Collingwood. Stephanie has kept her calendar free to meet with us later today and has extended an invitation for dinner. If this meets with your approval and schedule, what time would you like to meet?"

There was a long silence before he spoke.

"Laura please do not call me again. Do not call my office either. I want nothing to do with you, your company or any person associated with it."…
Dial tone - he hung up.

Stunned, I sat there staring out the windshield. My heart was racing and I felt like vomiting. What the hell happened? Had I in some way offended him? Other than Stephanie no one in the office knew his name or anything about him. Could there have been a leak? Had confidentiality somehow been compromised? I had to find out.

I couldn't talk to Stephanie about this yet. She would not know any more than I did. There was no point upsetting her yet. I punched in his number again.

"Mr. Nixon please may I ask for just a few minutes of your time. I don't know what's happened. I respect your request there be no further contact and I will not call you again after this call. But this is a new job for me and you were to be my first client. I need to know what changed your mind. Please help me sir."

There was a deafening silence for what seemed forever. I thought maybe he hung up but my phone displayed we were still connected. Finally he spoke.

"My dear you are being followed. We didn't have our family ski weekend because my wife got an anonymous letter delivered to our mailbox at the end of our driveway on Friday. She didn't see who put it there. There was no postmark. The letter said I was having an affair with a brunette who drives a 2002 Toyota Camry, License Number 469 238. They met six times and the places where we had met were all mentioned in the letter."

"I have given you what you wanted to know and I have nothing further to say. All my thoughts and efforts now are to get my family back. My wife is pretty upset and I have my work cut out for me. I will give it everything I have. I don't want to lose my wife and children. I will take legal action against your company if I have to - if they are in any way responsible for this." He hung up without another word.

I drove around for hours fighting back the tears. Who would do such a thing? Was Mr. Nixon telling me the truth? Maybe he was seeing a woman who drove the same kind of car I did. But the meeting places and times and the license number! Only Stephanie and I had that information. I didn't even carry a day timer, I used my computer to track appointments and make comments.

I left a message at the office there would be no meeting that day and went home.

"Hi Sweetie." Jim called out as I arrived home.

"Laura honey, you don't look well – is something wrong?"

"Pour me a glass of wine please Jim and light the fire. I'm going to have a shower and change into something comfortable."

Two glasses were poured, the fire was lit and soft music was playing on the stereo when I came downstairs. I didn't know where to begin or even if I should. I felt like a total failure.

"How did your meeting go sweetie?"

"There was no meeting Jim. The client cancelled."

"Oh really, I thought you said he was willing to come on board with the firm."

Through tears, I told Jim what happened. He knew nothing other than my first client was about to sign and I was to have dinner with him and Stephanie that evening.

"I don't believe this. Who would do such a thing? You worked so hard for this sweetie – I feel bad for you sweetie. Is there anything I can do? I bet anything it was some jealous employee at the office who was overlooked for your job."

"No Jim, that's impossible. No one other than Stephanie was privy to any information regarding the recruitment division."

He insisted I call Stephanie to tell her and suggested she might know something or may have heard from the client. After the way Mr. Nixon spoke and his threat to take legal action, I doubted very much Stephanie knew anything.

"If she heard from him she would have called me and all I want right now is peace, quiet and the space to think it through."

I was missing something here but be dammed if I could put my finger on it. My antennas went up because my inner voice told me the answer wasn't far away.

Jim's body language was out of whack. His reaction, words and attitude were not in sync with his body. Could he have been responsible for this? I put the incident secondary in my mind and focused on my husband as we continued to talk. He also refilled my glass repeatedly and opened a second bottle. That was definitely a red flag.

It was difficult to conceive he would sabotage my career in this way and our marriage if I found out it was him. By the end of the evening I was sure he was responsible. Deciding to give him the benefit of the doubt, I chose not to address it until after I spoke to Stephanie, had a good night's sleep and got away from Jim for a few hours. If he was guilty the consequences would be astronomical for him – of that I had no doubt.

Little sleep came to me that night. I analyzed every word Mr. Nixon spoke. My license number and make of car - anyone at the office could easily gather that information. Our meeting places, dates and times were noted on my computers which were secured with passwords. If Jim was responsible, he would go to his death denying it. In my heart I hoped it wasn't him. The guilty party would have to be someone with no moral values, a truly evil person. Was Jim capable of this?

As I lay awake I recalled the many times Jim used my computer. His excuse being his was giving him trouble. Another time I caught him creeping up the stairs when I was on my computer. I went to the top of the stairs to look over and witnessed his progress before quietly going back into the room and calling his name. I returned to my viewing spot and watched him back down and stomp two or three times on the floor to mimic walking before calling - "did you call me sweetie?"

I was on a roll as many memories of incidents I paid little or no attention to at the time, now came flashing back and took on meaning. The many times Jim showed up where I was and claimed coincidence and happiness to bump into me. How many times I was almost certain he was behind me in the car but passed if off as just another silver Echo. How many times I searched the house for my cell phone and Jim magically finding it under the sofa cushion or in the powder room.

Stephanie called me later the next day and was all business. She asked no questions other than to ask me to have lunch the next day. I arrived a half hour before our scheduled time intentionally. I needed the relaxing atmosphere of the restaurant, a glass of wine and time to figure out how to break this news to her.

It would not be fair to Stephanie or her company for me to remain. This could and would happen again. She could replace me with one of her senior people to keep the momentum going until she found someone else. I did not want to deceive Stephanie. She worked too hard for what she had and Mr. Nixon wasn't kidding with his threat. My heart sank. This job was something I really wanted and now it was all gone. Was there any point in having a dream?

Stephanie arrived at the scheduled time. We did not exchange the usual warm greetings when she got right down to business.

"We lost the Nixon account, didn't we?"

"Yes, did you hear from him? Is that how you found out?"

"No I didn't hear from him but I remember how it was when I started out and lost those first accounts. This is not your fault Laura. I knew when you called the deal fell through and when you didn't come into the office yesterday I knew how you were feeling. It's not the end of the world Laura."

This was your first crack at it and I don't want you taking any shame or guilt about losing it on your own shoulders. We may be able to get him back. If not we move on to the next one. Tell me what went wrong."

She wasn't prepared for what I told her. I did not tell her about suspecting Jim; only the facts as they actually happened. She would come to her own conclusions and hopefully together we could find some answers.

...."I won't be returning to work Stephanie. I am grateful for the opportunity you have given me but it won't work and it is best for you to find someone to replace me."

She studied me a long time without speaking.

"It's Jim Laura. You are making this very easy for me honey. If word of this got out my company could be destroyed. I cannot take that chance Laura and I am grateful to you for thinking about me."

"How can you be so sure it was my husband?"

"Who else could it have been? I didn't like him when I met him although it was an enjoyable evening. He tries to control you Laura and he is jealous of you. He's cunning and a manipulator and when he called me the day after our dinner and asked me to give you a job, I was sure my first impressions of him were accurate."

"What do you mean he asked you to give me a job? I know nothing of this."

"I thought you knew Laura. He said he was worried about you – that you were bored and drinking too much. The funny thing was I already planned on making you a job offer and Jim's call gave me second thoughts.

"You have to get to the bottom of this. It had to be Jim, who else could it be?"

"I wish I had known about that call."

"That's history now honey. I'm glad you came on board and I'm not happy about losing you but I have no choice now. He will continue to meddle in your life and look what's happened. A family is probably destroyed and my company may get hit with the backlash of his action."

"Well Stephanie, I also suspect Jim and am convinced now that I hear your side of it. I didn't want to admit what my suspicions were until after you heard all the facts and offered your opinion. It was him and I know it but how to deal with it is another matter."

"I don't know how you can stay with him Laura. After what you confided

44

in me about his impotence and now this. He's old enough to be your father and he will never change."

Stephanie was so right. I didn't know whether to throw up, cry or just kill myself and get it over with. I had no idea he called her to ask such a huge favor. What other things in my life has he meddled with and manipulated that I don't know and will likely never know?

We ordered lunch, selected a wine, and sat back to enjoy it. We exhausted each other with speculation about other possibilities but always came back to the same conclusion. I didn't know what to do.

When we parted company at 4 p.m. Stephanie told me I was welcome to continue to use my office for personal use. I would have liked nothing better if for no other reason other than escaping Jim for a few hours a day but I never stepped for in her offices again.

I lunged at Jim when I arrived home. It wasn't in my plans but when he greeted me with the usual Hi Sweetie crap, I wanted to vomit.

"You dirty bastard. You are the one who destroyed an innocent family and came close to destroying the company my dear friend worked so hard for. I want the truth and you won't have a minute's peace from me until I get it."

He continued to maintain his innocence with empty promises to get to the bottom of it himself. His hands shook and his face was scarlet. He knew he was caught and was pathetic as he groped for anything and everything to blame. He was angry with Stephanie and about to call her when I told him I no longer worked there.

"She can't do that to you."

"Of course she can you dumb ass. It's her company - she can do as she pleases. Just because you begged her behind my back to employ me doesn't give you any right to further negotiate or beg with her, and just for the record mister she didn't fire me – I resigned. I'll give you a little advice too you might want to consider. If I was Stephanie I would sue you."

Jim confessed at 3 a.m.

Chapter Four
St. Horatio

Several weeks passed with little spoken between us. I was miserable and eager to put my focus on something productive which led me to on-line studies for interior design. As long as Jim was part of my life I couldn't work for anyone other than myself. I wanted out of my marriage but knew he would make my life miserable. What started as a dream to live in the Caribbean was now a passion. I was determined to do it – it was the only way I could see to be free.

Eleven months after Jim admitted he was responsible for the fiasco with Mr. Nixon, I found a business with appeal on the island of St. Horatio. I had four more months of studies before earning my certification for interior design – a field I was enjoying immensely.

For the past year I kept a keen eye on our finances and took over many things that Jim once did. We were in good shape financially but if he suspected I was about to pull the plug, I didn't put it past him to find a way to stop me and money was the key. It didn't matter that everything we owned or had was in both names. Too many times I saw sneaky horrible things done to the other partner when a marriage went down.

There was no choice now that I was about to turn the wheels of change. I had to break the now semi-silence with Jim.

"Jim, I'm taking a trip to the Caribbean to look at a potential investment."

"Wonderful idea Laura - tell me about it."

"I plan on moving the islands Jim. You know this is something I have wanted for a long time but I need to earn a living and now that I'm almost a certified interior designer, I think it would be a good start."

"When are you planning on taking this trip?"

"Next week. I found an art gallery on the island of St. Horatio and have spoken to the owners who are Canadian. They won't be there when I arrive but they gave me the name of someone who will show me the property. More than anything I want to check out the island."

"Have you booked your flight yet?"

"No. I was going to do that today."

"Book us both."

"I wasn't asking you to accompany me Jim. This is my dream and something I plan to do on my own."

"You forget Laura that when you retired you gave up your credit cards and now carry my cards which show your name but I am the keeper of the credit cards and will cancel you as spousal carrier in a minute if I have to."

We left ten days later.

St. Horatio was a beautifully exotic small island in the West Indies. It took no more than a couple hours to drive completely around the island. The east side - the Atlantic was quite different than the west side on the Caribbean Sea. A neighboring island, part of the same Federation is accessible by ferry or private boat only and is clearly visible from the west coast of St. Horatio.

We stayed at a small inn overlooking the Atlantic for ten days. I had always longed to live in such an exotic place and prayed this trip would be the turning point I so desperately sought. I was prepared to do what I had to do and wasn't worried about finances. A large portion of my severance was tied up until I reached age sixty. I had a ways to go but it was my security for the future.

We owned our town home jointly and had other joint investments. He could not take what was rightfully mine away from me and I would fight him if he tried. It was too soon for that now. First things first and as it was his credit cards paying for my search for freedom, that was fine with me. It was his choice to come along.

Ten days was not enough time to properly evaluate the gallery or the island but I had a good feeling about everything. It was now early October and off season. Many people told me the island would be quite different once the expatriates returned. We found a small cottage close to the sea; paid two months rent commencing mid December and went home.

Jim took over my dreams. He told friends over dinner we were buying a business and moving to the Caribbean. It took everything I had to keep the wind in my sails. He wasn't going to get away with it this time but I had to stay calm and keep my mouth shut. I would never forgive him.

The island was quite different when we returned on December 13, 2004 – it was a hub of activity. Yachts and sailboats dominated the waterways on the Caribbean side of the island. Reservations were required at restaurants and early arrival at Sunday services might guarantee a seat. It was all wonderful!

Through the church we attended we met a many lovely people who were as anxious as were we to make new acquaintances. Soon our social calendar was filled with invitations to lunches, days at the beach or dinner at local restaurants. Jim was thrilled with all of it. His health appeared to be better – he looked better and was full of energy.

Jim could be charming when it suited him and St. Horatio did just that. His animation was refreshing. For the first time in our marriage, he was the one who made friends, organized activities, which often excluded me, and found interests to keep him busy. He played bridge with the ladies in the afternoons and golfed with the men. When we went out to dinner with the group, I was ignored. I knew what he was up to – he was planting his own seeds to get his own support network in place. He knew I had an agenda and he wasn't going to make it easy for me.

Midway through our two month stay I made the decision not to proceed with any further interest in the gallery. It wasn't what I wanted and there were other options worth considering. The main decision was already a given – I was going to live the rest of my life on St. Horatio.

I met Selina Dorian shortly after arriving on the island. She was a successful realtor and a fascinating woman. She was my age, single, successful and beautiful. We spent many hours together touring the island. She was on the historical society board and knew all there was to know about island history, culture and politics. We graduated to having lunches and spent time walking the beach with her dogs.

Through Selina I met Beatrice Wade – a Canadian who did most of what I wanted to do. With literally nothing to call her own, she made a new life for herself in the Caribbean. Bea was again in my age category, small, blonde and full of bubbles. We became a threesome and I felt blessed to have two wonderful new friends.

Bea had stories to tell about her new beginnings as did Selina. They kept me entertained for hours over lunches and often dinners at Bea's home on the Atlantic coast. Selina lived in a small cottage – much like a little doll house, on a cliff overlooking the Caribbean Sea. From her five by five foot balcony, she had a view of everything.

Jim liked both my new friends but I did my best to keep him away from them although at times it was difficult. All too often Jim interfered with friends in Canada and I ended up with none. Stephanie was a prime example. I put nothing past Jim and if he thought I was enjoying myself or in some way going to benefit from knowing these women; he would find a way to spoil it for me.

Selina showed me many store front type dwellings that could be used for the start up of an interior design business. Rents were high and I would also need a place to live. The weeks were flying by and I was growing anxious. I didn't want to go back to Canada without something tangible to bring me back to the island.

Selina was very wise and knew more about my situation than I gave her credit for initially. She suggested that I do not look for a place to start a business and focus on a place to live first.

"There is no reason why you can't run a business out of your home Laura."

"I never thought of that Selina. That's a good idea."

After we had seen several properties that were far too expensive, Selina suggested we bring Jim with us in the future. We spent the next week looking at many properties. The more we saw, the more excited Jim became. This is what I feared – now he was a part of it all and the one thing I was trying to avoid.

Selina invited me to have dinner with her alone on a Friday night. It was the only evening she had free as most of her evenings were spent with clients. This was the same night Jim and I had dinner with the group each week. I didn't enjoy these dinners and didn't want to pass on an evening with Selina, but I had to be diplomatic with Jim. If he thought I was up to something he would seize the opportunity to make life miserable for me.

"Jim, do you mind if I don't join you for dinner on Friday? Selina wants to take me to that place on the other side of the island that I have been dying to try and it's the only night she has free for the next few weeks."

"I don't mind at all sweetie. You go ahead and I will make your apologies to the others."

The restaurant we went to was the place where British Royalty has often stayed, in particular Princess Diana. I still mourned her death and felt her presence as Selina and I dined on the veranda.

Jim's group ate early and he could quite possibly invade my time with Selina and I didn't put it past him. He had done this many times in the past with other friends of mine. Whatever it was Selina wanted to talk to me about had to be done with before he invaded us.

"Laura, I think I have a pretty good idea what your situation is and I hope you don't mind my addressing some things with you."

"No Selina, I don't mind at all. In fact I wanted to get a little more personal with you so you would better understand what it is I want.

"I know what you want Laura but you have to be careful how you go about it."

"I know you're not happy in your marriage. I've been there and went about it all wrong when I didn't have to. Men like Jim can be uglier than satan when you cross them. You may be entitled to half but that's in Canada and you want to be here. Am I right?"

"You are right on the mark Selina."

"If you begin the process of ending your marriage before you are established here, you will never get here. He will tie you up in court for years to fight you and that will have to be where your property is – Canada."

"Yes, you are right about that and he can be one nasty old man when he wants to be."

"I can see that already but he does care about you or at least he doesn't want to lose you. That's not my business so I won't go there but it's what you want and how to go about getting it that I want to help you with."

"What are suggesting Selina?"

"Jim wants to be here as much as you do so there's no trickery here. He knows your marriage is hanging by a thread but if this is what he really wants then you should work together with him to have it. He would probably fare much better here as a single man than he would in Canada anyway."

"You're right. I hadn't really given much thought to what would happen to him after we separated but here he already has social connections and seems to be happy."

"Yes and he wouldn't have to cope with bad weather. Everything here is within an arm's reach and his health would be better. If you both lived here and decided to end your marriage, you would have a better chance with the courts here than you would in Canada. It could take years in Canada to settle on who gets what and the cost of lawyers would eat you alive."

"O-k, you are making a lot of sense and here is where I want to be more than anything. I can put up with Jim a little longer and I wish I didn't feel this way but if you knew the things I have had to endure for so many years......"

"I understand Laura. We are not young women anymore and like it or not, we will soon be old women. You can make a go of it here with interior decorating. There is only one on the island that is any good and he charges a fortune. You will do alright so don't worry about that for now. Find a place to call home. Close down anything in Canada that can be taken away from you. Put your money off-shore. I can refer you to a man here who will help both you and Jim in this area."

Three days later Jim and I bought an acre of land and met with the developer, Jason Dupree. Jim was more excited than I was. The last thing I wanted to do was build again – such a head ache but we found nothing that we liked and would spend a lot less by building our own home.

There was no alternative but to sell our Canadian home to fund our new life in the Caribbean. This was a far cry from my original plan for Jim to stay in Canada but either way, our town house would have to be sold and as Selina so aptly pointed out, it could be years before I saw a penny.

Jason Dupree was a dream to work with. He was in his early thirties, very tall, handsome and charismatic. He worked 16 hours a day and was at our beck and call. With several floor plans to consider and in hand, we packed our bags to return home. Construction would begin on our new home as soon as a fat down payment was wired to Jason and that we planned to do as soon as we returned.

To celebrate the sealing of the deal, Selina, Jason, Jim and I had drinks and dinner on the beach. The evening air was balmy as the sun set in clear blue skies over the sea. This was truly paradise and I couldn't have been happier than I was at that moment. It was a perfect ending for our two months and for the first time in several years I wondered if Jim and I could make it as a couple.

Enthusiastically, I went over the plans Mr. Dupree had given us. With my design books close by, I made changes and enhancements to the one floor plan Jim and I agreed on. Although my original plans had been severely altered, it was good to see Jim so happy. Perhaps this was the right thing for both of us but I still didn't trust him.

Our townhouse sold within weeks for far more that we paid for it. Once again I proved my marketing skills to Jim. He would have been happy to get what we paid for it two years previously but money and investments were my area of expertise and he seldom argued with me on those issues.

Time flew by as we packed and prepared for this major move. Jason called daily with a progress report- insisting Jim come in June for the first inspection. While there he began the ground work for my company and purchased a vehicle.

Jim called me from the office of our St. Horatio financial advisor to announce that Beleza Dentro (Spanish for Beauty Within) was now official. I celebrated at home with friends while Jim celebrated with his group of friends on the island.

I returned to St. Horatio in September leaving Jim at home to finalize what had not yet been done. Beatrice hosted a welcome dinner for my arrival, serving delicious food on her large veranda where the crashing surf from the Atlantic provided the music. Selina left the next day for several weeks abroad, leaving me with the use of her cottage, jeep and the care of her dogs.

Mr. Dupree was the first person I called upon my arrival. We met at the construction site where he greeted me warmly with a kiss on the cheek. Proudly, he walked me through my new home – far from complete and pointed out the many changes I had made. It felt good to see my work now in concrete and I didn't do too badly at all with my ideas now a reality.

The first person he introduced me to as we roamed through my house was his foreman, Mr. Gavin Brown. He also was welcoming and charming.

Mr. Brown, Mrs. Cassidy will be visiting the site daily and I hold you personally responsible for her safety. Take good care of her always sir."

Everyone was very formal with one another – always address each other as Mr. or Sir. Gavin Brown was gorgeous, gracious and very protective of me when I arrived daily. He never left my side while I was on site and always escorted me to my car when I departed. The man was mesmerizing. It was all I could do not to hug him.

Time was passing quickly with not enough hours in a day to get all that needed to be dealt with accomplished. I had to select cabinetry, counter tops, knobs and other odds and ends. My evenings were filled with planning a grand opening for Beleza Dentro in early December. I could think of no better way to tell the entire island other than having an art show and cocktail party.

The party room at a local inn was available for the evening of December 11th. Two local artists were invited to present and sell their work and co-host with Jim and me. With help from my friends, invitations were personally addressed and sent out. I was nervous as hell!

Progress on the house was falling behind and Jim was due to arrive soon. We spoke daily, each giving the other a report on activity at both ends.

Jim was now staying with friends since ownership of our house had changed hands. He still had much to do to close down all that we had in Canada. He closed bank accounts, transferred funds to our financial advisor in St. Horatio and arranged for the shipping of all our worldly goods.

I was cozy at Selina's cottage but it wasn't large enough for two people and our house was not going to be ready in time for Jim's arrival. Selina's was due to return the end of October. Jim and I had to find a place to live. Jason, we were now on a first name basis, assured me he would have a house for us if ours wasn't ready and indeed he did provide us with a very large home not far from where we were building our own. He promised we would be in our new home by the first of December but the thought of organizing the Beleza Dentro opening and moving into a new home at the same time didn't do my blood pressure any good.

Not a day passed that I wasn't on the job site and always the charming Gavin Brown, now openly flirting with me, was at my side. He was a very small man, standing only an inch or two over my own height. He had a beautiful smile and the best teeth imaginable. There was no doubt I was smitten with the man. Believing I was a fat, middle aged frump, his attentions revived the woman in me. My self-esteem was long overdue for a complete overhaul and I was getting it from Mr. Brown. What was the harm? My interests were exclusively my business and my home. The last thing I needed or wanted was trouble.

Jim arrived a week before we were scheduled to move into our loaner home. He wasn't in the door five minutes when it hit home Selina's place was going to be a tight squeeze for the next week. Her bed fit me fine as we were both the same size but Jim hung over six inches at both ends.

Our first task was to pick up our new jeep. We were headed to the bank to pay the balance when it died in the middle of the road so back it went to the shop for inspection and repair. Selina's jeep was still at our disposal for a few more days which was a blessing as no rentals or loaners were available in high season.

Discouraged over the jeep and tired, Jim suggested we spend a few hours at the beach. We parked in an open area at the edge of the sand where we could keep an eye on the jeep. I had left the windows open the night before and it rained heavily through most of the night. We left all four doors open to dry out the upholstery while we enjoyed the sand and surf.

We floated in the blue water for over an hour, both looking like first day tourists with our sun screen and broad rimmed Tiley hats. The excitement over our new home and the business was all we could chat about as we bobbed around in the surf. The smile on Jim's face touched my heart. Renewed hope for our marriage, even without intimacy, briefly crossed my mind.

Two hours was all Jim could handle as we gathered up our things. He was so tired I didn't think he would make through the day without a nap. We had reservations for dinner at a little restaurant on the beach that Selina's cottage overlooked from the cliff. Unfortunately, we couldn't walk down the cliff and would need to take the car the short distance.

The doors on the passenger side of the jeep were closed when we approached. Jim insisted he left them open and I was sure he had. My first thought was some good Samaritan thought he was doing us a favor and closed them. Finding nothing out of order and the seats now dry; we drove back to the cottage.

Jim went straight for the bed and was snoring within three minutes. I took the couch and did the same. When I woke up first, two hours later, I cancelled our reservation and made sandwiches. We were both sun burned, still tired and needed a good night's sleep.

The following day we had a luncheon date with the sculptor who was participating in the Beleza Dentro grand opening. Having spent some time with Ken prior to Jim's arrival, I wanted them to meet. This was the first time I met his wife Josie.

Lunch was truly enjoyable as was the company. Josie was a sweetheart - very much a part of her husband's art business. They were our guests for lunch at the same place we were to have dinner the night before. Jim was very gracious in these matters and discreetly approached the bar to settle our bill. When he opened his wallet, it was empty.

Seldom, if ever, had I seen such a look of rage on Jim's face except maybe when he accused me of causing his heart attack. From across the grounds, Jim could be heard by everyone.

"Laura, what did you do with my money?"

I was so embarrassed I wanted to crawl under the table. My purse was back at the cottage and the bistro didn't accept credit cards which were still in Jim's wallet.

Ken quickly joined Jim at the bar, pulled out his wallet and paid for lunch. I was mortified while Jim insisted I took his money and was nearly out of control with rage. With the four of us now standing by the bar, Ken insisted we return to the table for a noon cap.

After we settled down, had a few gulps and began to relax, Ken put on his Sherlock hat and began an investigation.

Methodically he walked us through the past 24 hours. Jim had difficulty staying focused and continued to accuse me of taking money from his wallet – something I never did in all the years were were married. We had a rule that we both adhered to - wallets and purses were off limits.

"Jim, it's not the end of the world. So you lost a little money. Try to settle down and think this through."

"It wasn't a little money. I had close to $10,000 in my wallet."

All three of us choked on our drink when Jim made this revelation. I had no idea he was carrying that much cash.

"Jim, why in God's name were you walking around with that much money?"

"It was to pay the balance on our jeep but that didn't happen so I still had it on me."

"Then where the hell is it? We didn't go out last night. You must have left it at the cottage."

Jim and I were about to get into a heated argument when Ken intervened.

"Come on you two. Let's walk through this together. There has to be a simple answer and if we all calm down we will figure it out."

"Jim, what did you do after you took the jeep back to the deal?"

"Laura and I went to the beach."

"You took the money with you to the beach."

"Yes it was in me wallet in my left hand back pocket."

"Did you go swimming?"

"Yes, or course we did. That was the whole purpose of going to the beach." (sarcastically said)

"Did you wear your pants with wallet in the back pocket to go swimming? (sarcasm from Ken)

"Of course I didn't wear my pants in the water. I had my swimsuit on."

"Where were your pants while you were in the water Jim?"

"In the dam jeep."

"Jim, we left the car doors open to dry out the interior. Were you that stupid to leave that much money in an unlocked vehicle?"

"Oh shit."

"That's were it happened folks. You were robbed at the beach and you weren't the first and won't be the last."

"But the camera was still there and it was on the back seat too."

"These thieves can't get rid of a camera without getting caught. They were and always are after cash."

"But Ken, we never took our eyes off the jeep. I know I didn't."

"You said the doors were closed on one side when you returned to the jeep. Didn't that twig some suspicion?"

"I thought some good samaritan was trying to do us a favor."

"Not a chance."

"I do remember something now. Jim, remember the horses and the dog. Three horses with riders came along the beach at a fast gallop. Then this dog came out of nowhere and spooked the horses. It was pretty scary and our attention was diverted for a few seconds."

"I should have known. When I put my pants back on the wallet was in the left pocket. I always carry it in the right."

We reported the theft to the police as soon as we parted company with Josie and Ken. When we told the officers about the horses, they smiled - telling us the whole incident was well planned out and the dog well trained in his role. They hit the jackpot and there wasn't any hope in hell our money would be recovered.

We moved into our loaner house three days later after picking up our own jeep, paid for from reserves. It was total chaos with nothing familiar and our own treasures stored in containers until our house was ready.

On our second day in the house Jim dropped a soda bottle and before I could find a broom, he promptly stepped on a shard which lodged in the sole of his foot. I could have removed it but Jim was now a diabetic – to add to his many other ailments and I chose to take him to the clinic.

Despite everything, our time was relaxing although we kept busy with preparations for the gala. Jim read one book after another while I walked daily to the construction site to check on the progress.

Chapter Five
Baxter and Sam

or 13 years Jim and I argued over having a dog. I desperately wanted one but Jim wouldn't allow it. Now it was a necessity if we were going to be living fairly isolated half way up a mountain.. Our new home was at the highest elevation within the project. It would be some time before we had neighbors and I quite frankly hoped it would be never.

I didn't blame Jim for not wanting a dog. His children had several while they were growing up but it was Jim who scooped the poop after a long day's work or was awakened in the middle of the night to take the family mutt for a pee.

Jim noticed poster ads at some of the shops in town advertising Rottweiler puppies. Only a few months before leaving Canada, while doing my daily walk, I was attacked by one. No harm was done thanks to intervention by four big guys in a pick up truck. Jim knew I was frightened of this type of dog but assured me by getting a puppy we would train and love it, making it part of the family. I would not hear of any dog of mine being tied up outdoors day and night. Our dog was going to live in the house with us.

We drove to visit the dog farm to choose a puppy. It had to be a male and there was only one who was not yet four weeks old. I wanted so much to carry him home with me but he was too young to leave his mother and we were not able to even have a peek at him. We paid $500 US cash and left empty handed. Mr. James said he would call us as soon as the pup was ready to come home with us.

Once a week I drove to the far side of the island to buy fresh eggs from Mr. Tyson. He was a delightful man with a wide grin and eyes that sparkled with happiness. His eggs and fresh chicken supplied most of the island but I preferred to pick mine up at the farm.

On one such trip I noticed several nursing dogs in the yard and asked Mr. Tyson if he had any puppies. He grinned from ear to ear, put his fingers in his mouth and let out a whistle. Within seconds several puppies came running up to us as we stood beside my jeep outside the henhouse. They swirled around my feet chasing each other and yelping. One little scamp sat on my foot. His little neck and chin stretched upwards looking at me. I picked him up to cradle him in my arms like I would a baby. This little fellow liked being rocked. He just lay there with a look of contentment on his face.

The following week I returned again for more eggs when what I really wanted was to see the puppies. The scene was pretty much the same as the previous week. The same little guy came straight for me. He was by far the pick of the litter with personality and attitude. I fell in love with him.

I never discussed my visits to the farm with Jim. We already had a dog coming soon bit we had not heard from Mr. James since we paid him and I began to worry that we wouldn't. Jim assured me he would call when the dog was ready and until then I should be patient unless I was willing to breast or bottle feed him.

I wanted both dogs but didn't know quite how I was going to get this past my husband. We ate as many eggs as possible over the next few days necessitating a return to the farm four days earlier than normal. Jim questioned why we were having so many eggs for breakfast and lunch. I lied - telling him I was on a new diet.

Mr. Tyson came out to greet me as usual but he wasn't his jovial self and I felt as though I was being perceived as a pest.

"Wait here Mrs. Cassidy. I'll bring your eggs".

I wanted to see the pup but he made no mention of them. Disappointed, I waited for some time before Mr. Tyson came back. I didn't see or hear him approach because he came from another direction. My mind was made up to refrain from eating eggs for a few weeks before returning. By then the puppy would be gone.

"Mrs. Cassidy, I have your order for you."

He was carrying my puppy – both had smiles on their face.

"He's yours - take him home."

"Mr. Tyson I don't know what to say."

"Take good care of him and bring him back for a visit now and then."

"Thank you so much – what about my eggs"?

"You're eating too many eggs. Come back next week for more."

He walked away laughing.

Oh man was I going to be in trouble when I got home with this little guy. I stopped at the veterinary clinic because I felt it would have to be done sooner or later and I was stalling for time as I planned my arrival at home. I didn't have a clue what a dog needed but surely the vet would advise me. The first order of business was de-worming followed by injections for various things.

Jim smiled when I arrived home with a little brown ball tucked under my arm. He held him for a few minutes – rubbed his tummy then handed him back to me and said:

"Take him back to where ever you found him."

"Like hell I will. He's here to stay."

Jim never said another word. Within a few hours the dog was on his lap while I made every effort to control my jealousy. The poor little guy was terribly ill for the first 24 hours after his shots. I spent most of my time cleaning up after him or holding him. By morning he was tearing around the house, peeing and pooping on every mat. I had my work cut out for me. Jim sat back with a smirk on his face knowing full well what lay ahead for me with training two pups. Together we chose the name Baxter for him.

I drew a great deal of attention in banks and supermarkets as I carried Baxter around with me in my straw handbag. By the time I realized it was too late; the little devil found my teddy bear stash. Every bear was now missing eyes and a nose. Baxter was with us a week when Mr. James called.

I was so happy with Baxter that I now didn't care about the other dog but I dare not voice this to Jim. We picked Sam up that same day. He was three weeks younger than Baxter and three times the size. One look at him and I was in love with him also.

Any concerns Jim had over the dogs were quickly put out of his mind. Happily I did everything for them, never requesting anything of Jim other than to love them as I did.

It was a glorious day when we moved into our new home on the first of December. Baxter and Sam, now accomplished swimmers, went head first into the pool. They each had their own towel with their names sewn on. When they emerged from the pool they demanded to be towel dried. The only unhappy person was our pool service man.

The house came together in a matter of days. Our furniture looked terrific in the new surroundings. We hired a small crew to assemble things that required it and hang our art work. Furniture was re-located several times before I was finally happy with the look.

Gavin Brown came by every day with a small crew to finish up a few things. Another home was under construction not far from us. He was the job foreman and had to divide his time to do what had to be done for us as well as supervise the new construction. He often worked well past quitting time and either Jim or I drove him down the mountain at the end of the day.

I could see the new house being built from my pool veranda and was happy that our house remained at the highest elevation. The noise of pounding, cement trucks coming and going and noisy workers was not pleasant. We lived through the renovations of our first home, the construction of our second hom and the finishing touches on our third home. This was the last thing I wanted and I prayed the other vacant lots around us didn't sell.

Chapter Six
Beleza Dentro

The Beleza Dentro Art Show and Grand opening was a huge success. I could not have asked for anything more satisfying. Our guests arrived in evening attire - all dazzling with their striking jewelry and designer clothing. Everyone seemed to know everyone else. The atmosphere took on an immediate air of familiarity and warmth as guests greeted each other.

Selina and Beatrice volunteered to be greeters. They had difficulty moving guests past the receiving area where invitees were asked to sign a guest book and offered a glass of champagne. Many, having just returned to the island, were caught up renewing acquaintances they hadn't seen in several months.

They were a striking mix of people from all parts of the world and all were eager to meet me and Jim. I could have chatted with each and every one of them non stop but kept reminding myself I was the hostess and had to move on.

One couple in particular, Luke and Linda Diamond, caught my interest. They were beyond being called an attractive couple – they were both absolutely beautiful. Linda was 5 foot, 10 inches and weighed no more than 130 lbs. Her hair was blue black that set off her ivory complexion. Her large dark eyes were full of warmth as they introduced themselves to me.

Luke stood well over six feet and had the body of an athlete and was drop-dead gorgeous. He too had jet black hair with silver at the temples.

His face was bronzed from the sun - setting off pale blue eyes that made me want to swim in them.

Their interest was not in the art as much as it was in my decorating talent. I didn't' expect to solicit business with the opening but merely wanted to get my name and that of my business out front and center. They requested a consultation with me at my earliest convenience and invited Jim and I to join them for a drink at the pool bar after the show.

The evening came to an early end as is the way of life in the islands. After long hot days and socializing, people are ready for the quiet of their own homes early. The event was only three hours in duration but seemed more like ten. I wasn't sure which hurt more, my feet from standing or my tongue from talking.

We found the Diamonds at a pool side table after the doors were finally closed at the conference centre. Once again I was aware of their striking good looks. They sat at a pool side table facing the sea holding hands. These two were obviously in love. Jim didn't take in the romance between them as I did. His only comment was the age difference which struck me as odd when we were approximately the same ages as the couple. Whatever the Diamonds had between them - it was working. I felt the pangs of envy.

Luke's mother, now in her late eighties, lived in a flat in Scotland where Luke and Linda also still owned a flat. They travelled back and forth two or three times each year to spend time with his mom whose health was now failing. They built their home in St. Horatio four years previously but had not had the time to decorate and were now determined to get it done.

Luke was a retired detective from Scotland Yard; Linda a retired runway model. After marrying Luke ten years ago she abandoned her career to be with him.

After an hour with them we headed for home. I had my first booking for a consultation scheduled for the following day at their home and they had an invitation to our Boxing Day open house.

Christmas came two weeks after the show. We spent a quiet but busy Christmas day at home preparing for our open house the following day. I prepared numerous exotic dishes for our guests while Jim erected the Christmas tree and put mini twinkle lights on the verandas.

Over fifty people came to our party the following day, many of whom had helped us in one way or another since arriving on the island. The food I painstakingly prepared for three days was a huge success and the house looked fabulous in traditional Canadian style thanks to Jim's efforts.

Jason Dupree, his wife Jasmine and their two children were among the invited guests. The children discovered Baxter and Sam stashed away in our bedroom and spent the entire time playing with them. They took the bowl of shrimp with them. Jason was impressed with our home and asked me to consider doing consulting work for him. I happily accepted the offer.

Luke and Linda also loved our home. After our initial consultation following the opening they were pondering some of my suggestions but had not yet committed. When they saw our home, their enthusiasm to proceed with their own decorating was renewed. We made an appointment for another meeting after the New Year.

Their home was quite beautiful with a unique architecture that set it apart from any other I had seen on the island thus far. They really didn't need as much as they thought. A little color, a few pieces of art and some rearranging would do the trick and it wouldn't cost them much or take much time.

I met with them on January 3rd, 2005 and presented my ideas to them. Jason gave me the name of his best painter who I made arrangements with prior to meeting with the Diamonds. Linda and I flew to St. Martin to shop for art while the painting was being done. Three weeks later the work was completed and they were very happy.

The next few months flew by and with it came more clients. I did several consultations for Jason's new clients and found a few on my own.

My dogs never missed their walks twice a day and Jim and I found the time to take them to the beach when ever we could. I had little choice when it came to where I walked them and always had to pass by the construction site where Gavin Brown and his crew were working. A second house was now underway beside the one started shortly after we moved into ours. The entire area was one big construction site.

There was no further need for him to come to our house but he did drop in to say hello a few times a week and only stayed for more than five minutes if Jim wasn't home. Bumping into him daily could not be avoided but when his flirting resumed with greater intensity, I started to take the dogs north to a meadow. Gavin was never rude or suggestive but I was becoming uncomfortable although I basked in the glow of attention that my husband should have been providing.

Jim and I were getting along better than we had in years. This I attributed to his outings and outside interests. When we were home together we swam in our pool, watched TV or read and played with the dogs. He was no more loving than he had been in the past and I had no hopes for a change in that department.

I kept busy in the studio I had made as an afterthought that was built at the side of the garage on the lower level. Here is where I framed art work I purchased from local and other island starving artists. My office was on the main floor off the great room. An entire day could pass without seeing Jim.

In early February Jim developed an infection in his foot where the splinter of glass had been removed shortly after his arrival in St. Horatio. He was placed on antibiotics and given instructions which fell on me to perform. After ten days with no improvement, the prescriptions were renewed.

Jim took a lot of medication, most of which was life support. He arranged with a local doctor for regular visits and monitoring and or course he had to travel to Canada at least once a year to see his cardiologist and other specialists. He had his first trip scheduled for early April. The foot infection was a serious concern but when he made no further mention of it after finishing the second round of antibiotics; I assumed it was completely healed.

Jim's health gave me nightmares. I had done enough for him in the past ten years for which he never thanked me and I never recovered from his accusation over his heart attack. If anyone could have tried harder than I did to get him help, I would like to meet that person and put them in a room with Jim for a day. The last thing I wanted was another ten years of the same yet I felt there was something coming and it scared me to death.

He watched two things on the television – the news and commercials. We got calls weekly from the courier service to collect something he ordered. Always it was something to add ten years to his life or make him look ten years younger. He tried to take body cleansing remedies that would have killed him if I hadn't read the labels. I tossed it all in the trash. To get him into a shower with a bar of soap was like trying to get a dog to fly.

My only social activity was joining Seling, Beatrice and Linda for lunch and not all at the same time. I looked forward to these times but they were becoming fewer and less often. Everyone was busy with their own life and I was no exception.

On one such occasion when I was having lunch with Selina and Bea, a woman I had never seen before came to our table. We intentionally chose this spot at the far end of the patio close to the sandy beach and under a grouping of palm trees to prevent unwanted visitors. Selina was so well known it was impossible to have a lunch without several interruptions. She needed a break every now and then and deliberately asked for this table.

Bea moaned when she recognized the woman. I had never seen her before and Selina couldn't see her coming because her back was to her. She was wearing a large sun hat, Jackie O shades and a warm smile.

She spoke to Selina first before saying hello to Bea. She ignored me completely. I believed she wanted to join us but no invitation was forthcoming from either of my two companions. Within a matter of seconds the woman turned abruptly and left to sit at another table close by alone. My curiosity got the best of me.

"Selina, what was that all about?"

"Her name is Sheila and you don't want to know her."

Linda and I got together once or twice a week in the late afternoon for a glass of wine while Luke played a round of golf. She was a loner - claiming too many years in small dressing rooms with too many women made her this way.

Jim and I dined with them often in their home or ours. The Diamonds seldom went to restaurants or attend social functions. They didn't like crowds or small talk and preferred to be home alone or have guests of their own choosing in occasionally. Both Luke and Linda were extremely intelligent people with a world of experiences. Jim was a great conversationalist and intelligent as well. I was no dummy either and enjoyed our times with them. Luke was a fabulous cook while Linda couldn't boil an egg. Their agreement was he cooked and she cleaned up. This proved to be fun for me and Linda. We did the grunt work while Luke cooked and then we cleaned up while the men engaged in heavy chat on their own. When they were at our place, I cooked, Linda and I cleaned up and the men played chess. This gave us plenty of time for girl talk.

Chasing dogs and running all over the island with my new career was having a positive effect on my appearance. Slowing buy surely I was losing weight and feeling better about myself. Daily compliments and flirting from my friends and Gavin Brown didn't hurt the cause any either.

After dropping Jim at the clinic for a routine check of his anticoagulant medications, I made a fast spin to the supermarket to pick up a few things and ran into the Diamonds. Linda steered me into a corner near the dairy section and told Luke to get lost in the wine section for five minutes.

"Laura, there's a woman here who is driving us crazy. She will pass by and I want you to see if you know her."

Less than a minute later, the woman Linda was referring to came into the dairy section. She smiled and said hello to everyone yet she kept her eye on us. When she neared where we were standing, Linda turned her back until the woman moved on.

"Do you know who that woman is Laura?"

"She looks familiar but I can't say I know or have ever met her – why?"

"Her name is Sheila and she is nuts. She introduced herself to me a few weeks ago and hasn't stopped calling us since. She keeps me on the phone for twenty minutes and just talks and talks. She asks too many questions and keeps asking us to go out with her. I don't know how she got our number – it's not in the book. We had it changed and she is still calling us. How could she get our new number?"

"This is a small island. There is no such thing here as customer service or customer confidentiality. You should know that by now. Did you question her on how she got the number?"

"Yes and she said she had a good friend who worked at the telephone company. I told her we didn't give out our number and would file a complaint with the company. They had no right to give it out."

"See, I rest my case. Linda, it sounds to me like you handled it very well so what do you think she wants?"

"At first I thought she was just lonely and I didn't want to be rude but Luke believes she's stalking us or at least one of us."

"Well Luke was with the force and if anyone should know I would think it would be him. What does he plan on doing about it.?"

"Hell if I know. He doesn't have any status here with the force. I guess we could talk to the police but that is up to Luke."

"Why don't you and Luke have a drink or lunch with her?"

"Are you crazy Laura?"

"No I don't think so but if you did you might find out what her agenda is. Luke would know how to bleed that out of her. Give it some thought."

At that moment I remembered where I had seen her before.

"Linda I just remembered where I have seen her. She came by our table a few weeks ago when I was having lunch with Bea and Selina. They were not happy with the intrusion and literally sent her away. I think you should find out what's going on."

"I'll talk to Luke."

We parted company. I had to pick up Jim and was already behind schedule. Linda called me that evening to tell me she wanted no part of what I suggested but Luke liked the idea. She promised to let me know the outcome.

Chapter Seven
Family Visit

My daughter Samantha and son in law Guido came to visit us in mid March. Joseph now thirteen and Anna almost twelve years of age were on school break for two weeks. It had been almost eight months since I left Canada and I was due for some family time. I counted the days until their arrival and was disappointed when they missed their connection in Puerto Rico and had to stay in a hotel for one night.

Guido was having health issues of his own, most recently a single by-pass. He was only four years younger than I was and far too young to be having problems. I worried about him and his non stop smoking.

They loved the island and rented a small jeep far too small for a growing family. It was funny to watch them toot around with Joseph's head high above the windshield. They fried themselves to a crisp in the sun on the first day and moaned and groaned for the next two. Once healed, their days were spent at the beach close to a popular bar and under an umbrella or at home in the pool.

They came with back packs instead of suitcases as I had advised them to do. Why is it teenagers can be in water for twelve hours out of twenty four and still need two showers a day and how much can you cram into a back pack and still do five loads of laundry a day? A towel never gets used twice and they don't like anything that isn't fried or doesn't come in a bag with plenty of salt.

I ran out of water on their third day and paid handsomely to have some delivered. Guido was in charge of the barbeque that got used every night for two weeks. Jim and I bought it the year before we moved to the island and never used it. My son in law had to remove the tags before he set it ablaze.

Everyone had fun, including Jim who wasn't overly fond of any children. He taught the kids to play chess and paid a local boy to climb one of our coconut trees to cut some down. They took photos galore and wouldn't let the poor boy go home. They had never seen a Rastafarian before and were fascinated with him.

They wanted to catch a monkey but here we drew the line. They were cute to watch and pests when they got near any garden but we had no idea how vicious they might be and were not willing to risk it. They settled for more photos. Baxter and Sam were still small enough to go in the pool and that they did with the kids. By sunset both dogs were too tired to eat and our pool man threatened to quit.

Jim was leaving for Canada shortly after my family's visit and then my best friend Izzy and her two daughters, Debby and Chris, were coming for two weeks. I had so much to look forward to and too much to do. I regretted the short time my family would be with me but there would be other visits I hoped.

For the first time in a long time I was very happy. I had everything I wanted and ever dreamed of. I prayed it would last and family and friends would come often. To me the only disadvantage of living in the Caribbean was the distance between myself and those I loved most.

Samantha noticed Jim limping and being a nurse jumped right in to examine his foot. Although the wound looked healed she did suggest he have it checked again when he was in Canada. He should not be limping. I felt she was holding something back from me but she insisted she wasn't but the concern on her face did not escape me. Samantha was a darn good nurse and I was very proud of her. I wasn't going to disregard what I thought was a concern but she chose not to enlighten me.

It was a sad day when my family left. When would I see them again? For two days I was glued to the sofa on the pool veranda just thinking about them and looking at the photos we took – still in my camera. It was a wonderful time with them and yet I could not help but feel something was about to happen.

Every day I added something new to Jim's to do list when in Canada. Aside from his semi-annual checkup with his doctors, he now added foot doctor to the list. We called ahead to Jim's family physician to make an appointment. Then there was the shopping list of the many things we both wanted shipped down. Jim loved to shop even more than I did and would have no problem getting everything. Then of course he planned to visit his kids and a few friends. He would be away for at least eight weeks and I looked forward to it.

Less than a week after Samantha and her family left Jim fell when we were entering a restaurant. He claimed he had a stone in his shoe and went through the motions of removing it. We enjoyed a nice dinner and returned home. I stripped and jumped in the pool while Jim got ready for bed – he didn't like swimming at night.

His cry had me out of the pool in seconds. I found him on the bathroom floor with his foot raised up on the ledge. The smell was overwhelming when I entered and I nearly fainted when I saw his black foot.

"Oh my God Jim how long has this been going on?

He was crying like a baby; I could see and smell his fear. Somehow I managed to dress and get him into the car. The same words came out of the nurse's mouth when she saw his foot - "Oh my God."

They admitted him and immediately had him on IV of antibiotics. I left before the doctor arrived to go home and make some phone calls. I didn't need a doctor to tell me what was wrong and he was going to Canada as fast as I could get him there. Samantha was awakened by my call and agreed to make all the arrangements to meet him and have him admitted to her hospital as soon as he arrived.

I went back to the hospital where my suspicions were confirmed. They would have him ready and at the airport for his very early flight the following morning. We had insurance to cover travel assistance until he was safely in Samantha's care. I was not going with him.

Chapter Eight
Izzy

The next two weeks flew by. My days were busy preparing for Izzy and the girls as well as finishing up some jobs I was working on. I wasn't taking any new clients until I was guest free and Jim would not be returning until long after my guests left – giving me lots of time to get the ball rolling again. It was time for some real fun. I wasn't worried about being on the mountain alone. The house was secure and the phone worked. I loved my home more than any other I had ever lived in. Often I sat in the dark on the veranda in the early morning hours to mediate and give thanks for all the blessings in my life.

Samantha and I talked daily and Jim was coming along fine. He had severe cellulites and was high risk for gangrene. He would be in hospital for some time and was in good hands with my daughter in charge. I was worried about him after his discharge and would have preferred he forego visiting family and friends and get back home. He wasn't one to take care of himself and he ignored his own health too much.

I felt no guilt over not going to Canada with him. His condition didn't happen during dinner and if he had paid attention to his foot, this stint in hospital could have been avoided. I had enough of cleaning up after him to last me a lifetime. Let him go this one alone and maybe he would smarten up.

Izzy and the girls missed their San Juan connection for much the same reasons as Samantha and family. The connect time was to short and the airport was always in total chaos. The girls were on a tight budget and the hotel put a serious dent in their spending money. The welcome dinner I prepared a for their arrival went to the dogs.

They were exhausted when they arrived the following day but that didn't stop them from swinging into party mode right away. Once plied with local rum punch and a good meal, we turned on the music and danced, laughed, told jokes and reminisced over similar times long passed. It was well after two in the morning when we finally collapsed in our beds.

We seldom left my home over their two week visit other than for some beach time or to replenish our food supply. Bea had us over to her place for a luncheon barbeque and a swim in the Atlantic and several times she joined us at my home.

Izzy joined me each morning for my dog walk. Her daughters declined, preferring to sleep late or lounge in the pool. Not long before Jim's departure, I altered my route and climbed higher up the mountain to the meadow. This was too difficult for my out of shape friend. On the second day we went via the old route and ran into Gavin Brown. I didn't want him to know I was home alone after my guests left and cautioned Izzy not to mention Jim's absence.

I was sure he always saw me long before I saw him. Otherwise how could it be he was always close to the road when I passed by. After introductions and small chat we carried on our way. Izzy thought he was cute and I only grunted at the comment. Every day for the next two weeks, Gavin Brown - charming and flirtatious with both of us, was there to greet us and Izzy was talking too much to him.

Izzy was a charmer herself and was smitten with him as I was but she didn't have to live here and I wanted to get no closer to him than I already was. The less he knew about my life, the better.

"Laura he is so good looking and he wants you honey."

"Knock if off Izzy. I know he's flirting with me but all these men here are like that. I'm white and that is a trophy here."

"You're crazy Laura. Give him a tumble. Hell when was the last time you had a roll in the hay – what fifteen years at least?"

"I do enjoy the attention but that's all."

Izzy and I knew everything there was to know about each other. She wanted happiness for us both and had a marriage similar to my own. I was sure she never had an involvement with another man and maybe one day she would but she was not married to Jim. I would never get away with it and I didn't want to test out my theory.

I promised my guests a seafood night and tried for two days to find lobster. A client named Bob who was nothing short of a lunatic overheard me asking in the supermarket where I could get some.

"Laura, I will bring you lobster tonight. How many guests do you have?"

That was all I needed – Bob and his nutty wife Ginger at my dinner table but what could I do and I didn't trust that he would show up let alone come with lobster. I bought steaks instead.

We were having drinks on the veranda just as the sun was setting when the front door flew open and in walked Bob with an entourage. Two men carried in a box of lobster, a box of shrimp, a case of wine, and bags of other groceries. A fourth and very handsome younger man was our chef for the evening. The delivery men left and the chef threw me out of my own kitchen. Bob opened wine and sat with us with his own glass in hand. You could have knocked us over with a feather.

Francois was the name of our chef. He was no more than 30 and made himself right at home in my kitchen. The aromas emerging were heavenly. Having Bob for dinner was not in my plans but at least he left Ginger at home. We set a place for him since it appeared we had no choice in the matter. He was entertaining but I tired of him quickly because he never shut up. After one glass of wine he rose and left against our protests. He said he had other plans and would be back later to pick up the chef who became our entertainment the minute Bob was out of sight.

When Francois announced dinner was about to be served, we took our places at the table. He carried in trays of succulent food with Christine's help and promptly took the vacant seat beside her. He kept us in stitches throughout the entire meal which was wonderful.

Chris was very smitten with our chef as they flirted back and forth over the table. Christine was not happy in her second marriage and had one child. Debby was also married but very happy and had one daughter and was not nearly the daredevil her younger sister was.

When dessert was about to be presented, Francois got up and went to Christine and kissed her on the cheek. He whispered something in her ear that brought on a flush of blush. With a look of bewilderment, she burst out laughing as did Francois who made an exhibition of swinging his hips as he strutted back to the kitchen.

Bob returned shortly after nine to collect our chef. I was very thankful for Bob's generosity and felt guilty over the wicked thoughts I had earlier. After my guests returned home to Canada I planned to have him and Ginger over for dinner. Surely I could endure one evening with them at least.

Jim was discharged after twelve days in the hospital. He was staying with Samantha and Guido for a few days while he prepared for his road trip. Meanwhile Samantha laundered his clothes and packed a cooler with nourishing snacks and drinks for him to take with him. She asked him several times to make an itinerary of his plans and provide phone numbers where he could be reached. He never bothered to do it. I only spoke to him once to give him a report on my time with my guests. He sounded good and seemed happy and didn't ask any questions. He had arrangements made to rent a car and planned to get everything done although his return home would be delayed now.

After speaking to him, I remembered a few things that I should have mentioned. Rather than phone again, I sent an e-mail to my daughter. I knew his presence was stressful for them. They both worked long hours, had two teenagers and Jim could be demanding.

The night before his departure Samantha was preparing a special meal for him - at his request. While doing so he asked if he could use her computer. She neglected to sign off and he took the liberty of reading her e-mail messages, in particular the one from me even though she had given him a verbal accounting of the information I wanted passed on.

In my message, aside from giving her the information, I told her what a great time I was having with Izzy and the girls, about Bob's treat of the chef and the many other things we had been doing to entertain ourselves. I also told her I was glad Jim wasn't home to spoil the good time I was having and jokingly suggested Guido introduce Jim to his spinster aunt and hopefully they would fall in love and I would live happily ever after.

I thought it was funny and knew Samantha would see the humor intended as well but Jim went into a rage when he read the message and flew into Samantha's kitchen where his special meal was about to be served and spewed his anger at her. She was appalled that he went into her private mail and that he didn't see my message for the humor intended. She served dinner to Jim and her family and later claimed the tension at the table was thicker than her meatballs. Jim didn't say a word – cleaned his plate, got up from the table and went to his room. Sam was on the night shift and went to work shortly after dinner. When she returned at eight the next morning he was gone.

She went to bed as she normally did after working nights. At two in the afternoon she received a call from the hospital. They were trying to locate Jim. He didn't leave the itinerary as requested and she had no idea where he was. Jim's INR results taken just prior to his discharge, revealed a serious problem with his anticoagulant medication. He was in trouble if he didn't receive medical attention right away.

Samantha had no alternative but to call me. I didn't know his schedule but I did know his doctors in Toronto. It was during this conversation with her that she told me about the previous evening and the e-mail message.

My family had done enough and I couldn't ask them to take further responsibility for my irresponsible husband. My daughter sounded very tired and worn out and I was sure it was because of Jim. She visited him in the hospital almost every day and when she couldn't, Guido went to visit him. They took him home cooked foods because he complained so much about the lousy hospital food and did whatever else he requested of them.

"I'll take over from here honey. You get some rest and put Jim out of your mind. Thank you from the bottom of my heart for what you and Guido have done."

I telephoned his doctor's first and then his children. If I didn't hear back from any of them within twenty four hours, I planned to call the Ontario Provincial Police.

Izzy was by my side throughout the ordeal of tracking Jim down. If anyone understood the anguish the man put me through it was her. After the debacle with Stephanie and Mr. Nixon she almost convinced me to end the marriage. Here he was again, sucking the life out of me. Although I said I didn't care, I must have because I couldn't stop worrying about him.

Jim surfaced for a medical appointment and the crisis was averted. All that was required was an adjustment to his medication. His physician handled the problem and instructed him to contact his family who were frantically trying to locate him. He didn't bother to do so but his doctor did. He knew Jim better than I did. After I notified all who should be told that he was safe and the situation remedied; I put the bastard out of my mind and joined in with my friends to resume the party.

My last night with Izzy and her girls had to be a celebration and for the first time since their arrival we were going out to a local inn that featured a buffet dinner and live music. This was my treat.

Earlier that day we took our final walk together and of course ran into Gavin Brown. While chatting with him, Izzy made the grave error of telling him where we planned to spend our final night together. Izzy believed something was brewing between Gavin and me and she was wrong. I was happy with my fantasies about him and didn't plan on taking any further. I also didn't believe he was interested in me for anything other than sex.

We took great care and effort to look our absolute best for our night out.

I hadn't worn make up for several weeks nor had I worn a dress and high heeled sandals. I felt like a young girl - full of energy and mischief when we arrived at the already busy bar. The first person I noticed was Gavin sitting at the bar with several empty stools on either side of him. He was saving them for us which didn't please the bar staff when he told other customers they were reserved.

This was the first time I had seen him off construction sites. If I found him handsome before, he was absolutely gorgeous now. Christine and Debby swooned at their first sight of him.

The place was jumping and totally romantic. The bar and dance floor were no more than 30 feet from the sea shore. It was a breezy night but balmy. Palm trees swayed under a full moon in clear skies. Unanimously we decided we had the best seats in the place and took a pass on the buffet. We could have tuna sandwiches when we got home. I set up a tab with the bar to eliminate reaching into my handbag at every round.

Almost everyone hit the sand covered dance floor when the band started. Gavin took my hand and led me out with the rest of the mob. At first the music was fast but soon changed to romantic slow and sexy music and I was in his arms – check to cheek. He wasted no time before he kissed my ear first and then went for my mouth. I believed nobody noticed but boy was I wrong!

Izzy and the girls didn't lack for male attention as they danced with a variety of eager and probably not eligible men. They were having a good time and I was feeling as though I was in another time zone. Gavin and I went for a walk on the beach, leaving the dance floor hand in hand. The wind was so high we didn't get far with flying sand nearly blinding us.

My blonde hair was a mess when we returned to the dance floor to finish out the number that was playing. When we made our way back to our bar stools through the mounting crowd, Izzy and the girls greeted me with silly grins. I knew what they were thinking and didn't like it.

"Nothing happened on the beach so wipe those looks off your faces."

"Are you sure Laura" said Izzy steal wearing a stupid grin.

"Yes I am dam sure."

If they were thinking it then what were others thinking? Now I was worried.

When the evening came to an end I settled the bar tab. Gavin made no attempt to pay for his own drinks but he had done many favors for me and Jim and worked extra hours for which I was sure he was not compensation. I decided to leave the matter be.

The girls were leaving on an early morning flight and we were already later leaving than we planned. Gavin asked for a ride home which we really didn't have a choice. It was too late for him to find another way and it wasn't that much out of ours to drive him. Christine drove my jeep while I sat in the back with Izzy and Gavin. We all had far too much to drink with the exception of Chris who was now our designated driver.

Chapter Nine
Gavin Brown

It was an emotional farewell early the following morning. We all felt like dish rags after the previous night and I didn't envy them their long trip. I had far too much to drink and probably made a fool out of myself. The remorse I felt was overwhelming.

I made a pot of coffee when I returned from the airport and swallowed three Advil tablets before leashing the dogs for their morning walk. Before I could get out the door the phone rang. It was Beatrice. A call from her so early in the morning was unusual. Bea liked her sleep and one didn't dare call her before 9 a.m. It wasn't yet 8 o'clock. I braced myself for what I knew was coming.

"What were you up to last night Laura?"

"Oh Bea, I don't want to hear this."

You were still at the bar when I started getting phone calls from friends who were there. Who was this guy you were necking with on the dance floor?"

"His name is Gavin Brown. He works for Jason and is the job foreman that built my house and is now working on two other houses up here."

"Couldn't you find some old white man to take your frustrations out on? Shit Laura, you don't want to get involved with these guys. They are nothing but trouble."

"I know Bea and believe me I feel like a bag of shit right now and wish I had stayed home last night."

"Just lay low for a while. The gossip will pass as soon as some other idiot makes a wrong move for people to talk about. Just remember you live on a small island. People look to see what's in your grocery cart and then talk about the two bottles of wine in it. Be careful."

"Thanks Bea. I know you care and I was a fool and what more can I say."

"You don't have to justify yourself to me Laura. We have all been there and don't give it another thought. Just keep yourself invisible for a while. It will blow over and it's just gossip.

She was concerned and wanted to caution me. I felt so ashamed and as much as I loved Bea, I hated that she felt it necessary to call me. I drank too much and got caught up in the romance of the hour. Oh how I hated myself and Izzy was long gone for me to cry on.

I headed out with the dogs for their walk with many thoughts running through my foggy head. I appreciated Bea's call and knew she was right. She didn't tell me what I didn't already know but hearing it from a good friend made me feel worse.

Intentionally I headed for my familiar route. I wanted to see Gavin to tell him it had all been a mistake and to forget it ever happened. Then I planned to tell him to send a worker to my place if any further work needed to be done or if they needed to fill their drinking water jugs from my hose. I didn't want to see him again.

He came strolling out with a grin that spread from ear to ear while I looked like a bag of spent bullets. So much for my initiative; I invited him to come for dinner.

For the remainder of the day I played in the pool with the dogs and sat on veranda contemplating my life. As the hours passed I regretted inviting Gavin for dinner and yet I didn't do what I should have done and cancel. What was happening to me?

By mid afternoon I received another call, this time from Selina. Our conversation was much the same as the one with Bea. The whole island was talking about me. The damage was done and I hadn't really done anything. People would think what they wanted and there was nothing I could do about it. It was best to simply lay low as both my friends advised. Why then was I having Gavin for dinner? Was I using the excuse of gossip to justify not cancelling him? I didn't tell Selina he was coming for dinner.

Other than being very good looking Gavin had nothing that could possibly benefit me in any way. For the entire day I questioned myself. Was it sex, middle age crisis or something not quite registering in my lame brain?

When he arrived at 7 p.m. we had drinks on the pool deck while dinner cooked. I felt awkward while he exuded an abundance of charm and confidence. He talked about his homeland in Dominica and how he someday planned to return. I talked about Canada and my total lack of desire to ever return.

Gavin was living with a woman on the east side of the island. They had been together for six years but he was leaving her as soon as he could find a place of his own. That was a line I wasn't going to swallow no matter how numb was brain was at the moment.

Jim and I had driven him home once and dropped him at his front door, whereas when I dropped him off with Izzy and the girls he asked to be dropped at the end of the road. He claimed he owned and built the house himself and owned a small beach side snack shop which he pointed out to us – saying he owned it and his girlfriend worked it for him.

It didn't escape me when he mentioned finding a place of his own. If he indeed owned the house he claimed he built and owned the business, then why would he leave it? I had a pretty good idea what construction workers earned on the island and how most of them lived. Gavin wasn't telling me the truth or at the very least, not the whole truth. I learned much later he owned nothing. Everything belonged to his girlfriend.

We ended up in the bedroom shortly after dinner. This is what we both wanted – it was all that I wanted but I wasn't sure what Gavin had in mind. After thirteen years of celibacy, I felt clumsy and shy but Gavin was experienced, eager and moved quickly.

Any thoughts about the consequences were put on hold. The island was already talking so I wouldn't be any worse off than I already was. I felt desired and almost beautiful – feelings I had long ago forgotten. I was thirty pounds too heavy for my frame and fast approaching the golden years. Gavin didn't see my flaws or at least said he didn't and that was music I hadn't heard in a long time.

At 4 a.m. I awoke startled to see this man beside me. I shook him awake and told him to get dressed, - I was driving him home. He refused to leave saying I shouldn't be alone in the big house – he was going to stay with me.

How could I possibly sleep for the next two hours? With my eyes on the clock at the side of my bed, I counted the minutes until 6 a.m. I wasn't comfortable with Gavin in my house and wanted him out before workers started to arrive in the area. This was not how it was supposed to happen but I didn't think it through and apparently was not the one in control.

The workers were already reporting to work when Gavin snuck out early but not early enough. I sat on the veranda with my coffee watching heads turn as they passed on their way to work. They knew!

I went about my morning as usual by first changing the bed linen and then taking the dogs for their walk in the opposite direction to Gavin's work site. After a swim and some light housework, I was about to call a few clients when Gavin walked in the door. It was lunch time. Angry at first, I was quickly forgiving. He had no opportunity to get himself something to eat, didn't drive and we were half way up the mountain. He helped himself to a beer while I made him a sandwich and went back to work.

Promptly at 4 p.m. he returned and this I was not anticipating.

"Gavin last night was a mistake. You shouldn't be here."

"Laura Baby, I only want to stay with you to keep you safe. You can't be here alone at night."

"That's crap Gavin. I'm a big girl and will manage just fine on my own."

"There have been break-ins down below. These bandits watch the houses and will know soon that you are alone. What chance would you have if two or three guys broke in here in the middle of the night?"

"I'll give them what money I have and anything else they want."

"They will rape you Laura and then take your money. Can you handle that?"

"No, of course not but I can't have you living here. Jim will be home soon and this is our home – I am his wife. People on the island are already talking about us. How is it going to look to others and Jim will hear of it."

"I will be discreet so I'm not seen here but I can't leave you alone."

"What about the woman you are living with? Are you just going to forget her after six years together? You owe her more than that."

"I don't care about her; you are the one I want."

"Did you talk to her today? She must be frantic."

"She called but I didn't call her back."

"That's not a very nice thing to do Gavin – to anyone. You at least owe her some explanation."

"I don't owe her anything. She can stay in my house until I figure out what to do. That's all she cares about – having a nice home and working the shop. I will let her have both for now."

Lousy rationale influenced me to acquiesce to Gavin. What was the difference between one night and several? My life was about to change dramatically either way so why the hell not enjoy some pleasure before I had

84

to face my doom. The experience with Gavin did one very positive thing for me. I wanted out of my marriage but this was not the right way to go about it and for that I would pay a high price?

Jim did not deserve to be humiliated and he would find out. I had never lied to him in the past and wasn't going to start now. The only decent thing I could do was spare him further grief if I could. He had to know about indiscretion before he heard it from someone else.

Gavin stayed with me until two days before Jim's return. He made no attempt to be discreet as promised. Within days the workers were waving to him as he left my door step in the early morning and he made a show if it by sitting on the pool deck with a beer after work for all to see.

I felt renewed as a woman but the good feelings ended there. Shame, embarrassment, remorse and confusion were dominant emotions. I dreaded Jim's return yet I also welcomed it. It seemed the only way to get Gavin out of my house but it also meant moving on to the task of doing what I had to do and now suddenly I didn't want to do it. I loved my house and my life and here I was about to throw it all away. What lay ahead for me?

Linda invited me to lunch with her at the beach. We normally met only for a glass of wine in the late afternoon. Lunch was a nice change and an opportunity for a longer visit. I hadn't seen much of her recently – in fact I hadn't been off my property since Izzy left.

Wearing a sun dress, hat and looking good, I drove down the mountain on my way to meet her. Heads turned, people stared. Some seemed to be laughing at me or at least they were grinning – some even pointed to me while speaking to another. When I reached the main road, drivers in other cars, in particular white people, turned their heads to see me while others actually pulled over to watch me pass. When I pulled into the lane way that lead to the beach where I was to meet Linda, several cars pulled behind me. I called Linda from my cell phone who was five minutes behind me.

"Change of venue Linda. Meet me at my house." I turned around and went back home.

Tuna sandwiches and a bottle of wine was the best I could manage. Linda arrived the same time I did and buttered the bread. She was totally lost in a kitchen.

"How are you Laura?"

"You heard all the nasty stories I assume."

"Well yes, the whole island is buzzing. Do you actually have that man staying here with you?"

"Not by choice but that must sound lame. He insisted I shouldn't be alone up here and that is a pretty feeble explanation, but I figured I'm in a heap of trouble when Jim returns so what more did I have to lose by having some company and great sex for a few days?"

"You would have been better off to go someplace else, maybe a hotel."

"I couldn't leave the house abandoned and I have the dogs to think about."

"Laura you didn't have to stay all night at a hotel and the dogs would have been fine for a few hours."

"Linda, you sound like you are joining forces with the rest of the island."

"On the contrary; I care about you Laura and don't want you to dig yourself in so deep that you won't be able to climb back up to the surface."

"You're right and I feel so confused, ashamed, stupid and now scared."

"Did you and Gavin have sex on the beach the night that started the jungle drums beating?"

"Hell no; there were other people strolling the beach and I wasn't in that space at the time. I admit I was caught up with the romance of the hour – the moon, the sea and the tropical balmy everything. The wind was high. We had to turn back because sand was flying into our eyes and stinging like hell. Even Izzie teased me at the prospect of sex on the beach and I was angry with her for thinking that of me and now I'm upset that you are suggesting the same thing."

"Honey, I'm only trying to point out to you what others and thinking and saying. These are the stories that will eventually reach Jim's ears and you have to be prepared for the fall out when he does hear them."

"Linda, I don't want you or anyone else to think I'm some kind of tramp. I admit we have slept together but we didn't on the beach and I honestly don't know why it's important to me to care what people think."

"Laura don't' beat yourself up. You would be shocked if you knew half of what goes on in the bedrooms on this island."

"You don't know that for sure Linda – how could you?"

"You would be surprised what I know and I won't give out any names or details but let me tell you my sweet friend; you have nothing to be ashamed of. I have been having an affair for several years and Luke is aware of it."

"Linda I don't believe it. The two of you are so happy and in love."

"Yes we are and always have been and I hope always will be, but Luke has the same problem Jim has. He loves me enough to allow me to fulfill my needs elsewhere and I do. He never asks me anything but he does know that I have only one lover – the same one from the start. His name is John and his wife, who he loves very much, has been bed ridden for fifteen years. He finds with me what I do with him. There is nothing more to it than pure physical gratification and we are good friends."

I couldn't help but laugh. This revelation was the last thing I would ever expect from Linda.

"I don't know what to say other than I envy your marriage to Luke and am happy for all three of you."

Linda roared with laughter as she poured another glass of wine for us both. Although I didn't want to invade her privacy, I couldn't help myself.

"I don't want to be nosey but how did this affair of yours come about. Are you willing to share more with me?"

"I will tell you only that John does not live on the island and I only see him when I am in Scotland. We went to college together many moons ago. He is an accomplished individual who is kind and devoted to his family. I could not be with anyone who wasn't someone I respected and admired. I love him but I am not in love with him. Luke is the only man who I have ever totally been in love with."

"Jim would never go along with something like that. I wish he would or could but that is never going to happen. I have lived in a dead marriage for so long that having Gavin's arms around me knocked what little sense I might have had out the window.

"I know where you are coming from Laura. Luke and I have noticed Jim's possessiveness and his unhealthy attitude regarding your marriage. He is a very insecure man but he was that way when you met him. Luke is very mature and understanding. He once enjoyed intimacy and respects and understands that I have needs he can't fulfill and rather than lose me, he accepts our situation for what it is."

"Did you and Luke ever discuss or consider ending your marriage?"

"Never - I love that man with all my heart and would never willingly walk away from him. We hug, laugh and caress each other. The romance has always been with us and we both work very hard at keeping that alive. The difference between Jim and Luke is that your husband believes if he can't fuck, there is no point in loving you in other ways."

"Oh Linda, I'm in deep shit and don't know what I'm going to do."

"Whatever you decide to do Laura, Luke and I will be at your side to help you through it. Do you love Gavin?"

"No, not at all but I love the way he makes me feel."

"You have low self esteem and I don't blame you one bit. Gavin is the wrong person for you to be with. He's an opportunist and a peasant. You can do better Laura."

"He is the least of my worries. I hear what you are saying and it didn't need to be said. Already I see him in the light you are suggesting. I was once a very successful independent woman. The last thing I want is a man who will suck me dry."

"And that my dear is exactly what he will do."

"Where do I go from here?"

"I'm not going to give you advice Laura. That would be wrong but I am going to tell you what I think to help you put things in perspective."

"O-k, I'm listening."

"As long as Gavin is in the picture, you have an on-going problem. The gossip will not end until the two of you do."

"You are right. Tell me more."

"You might want to consider a strategy but first you must decide if you really want to end your marriage. Jim will hear about it but do you want him to find out over a bridge game?"

"I have already thought about that and I don't want to humiliate him in any way."

"Then you have to be the one to tell him before he hears it from someone else. Do you agree?"

"Yes, and I was planning on telling him."

"Do you know for sure what you want?"

"Yes, I don't want to be in this marriage anymore."

"Then you have to have a plan to get out."

"I thought I would wait to see what his reaction is and take it from there."

"That is not a plan at all Laura and the wrong thing to do. You would be putting yourself at his mercy and subjecting yourself to the decisions he will make and make quickly. He will be angry and want revenge. You have to think this through more carefully. It's like saying 'I'm leaving you' and not having a place to go."

"What do you suggest?"

"Find a place of your own and don't include Gavin. He has nothing to offer you and he will want you to grab what you can from the house and your bank accounts. As long as you are seeing him, it would be like rubbing Jim's nose in it."

"I have been on this island a lot longer than you have. You are not the first and won't be the last. I can send you to at least four women I know who were in the same situation you are now in. They lost everything and ended up being beaten by a local man and had to run for their lives. They now live in squalor and are broken in more ways than one."

"Linda, what do you honestly think is going to happen?"

"Laura my dear friend, I hoped we wouldn't get to this level but since you asked, I have to tell you what Luke and I think will happen. I'm sorry that we have been discussing you but we love you and are worried."

"I love you too Linda but I can't think straight and need all the help I can get."

"Jim will crucify you."

My time with Linda was well spent. I loved the woman so much and appreciated our very candid conversation. She made me think of things I hadn't even considered.

Gavin found an apartment or rather a dump with a toilet, not far from the construction site in a village close by. I was so anxious to get him out of my house that I donated some furnishings we had stored in the garage that were going to the trash site as soon as I could arrange it anyway. He found a friend with a pick up truck who did it for free. I killed two birds with one stone – cleaned out the garage and my bed.

I told him not to call me – it was over. Jim was due back within two days and I had to focus on myself and the future. Selina began the search to find me other living accommodations but the task was heavier than I anticipated. An apartment was out of the question with two dogs and I wasn't willing to leave them behind. Houses were more than I could afford unless I was prepared to lower my standard of living and take something in one of the villages. This, I was not willing to do. She kept searching but warned me it was not going to be easy. I either had to give up my puppies or find the means for something more up-scale.

New rumors came to light regarding the woman Gavin had spent the last six years of his life with. She cleaned out their joint bank accounts leaving with nothing. She packed up his clothes and had them delivered by bus to his new residence. Where I once felt pity for the woman who I believed was being tossed aside, I now had great admiration for her. She owned the house and the snack shop and without abandon put Gavin where he belonged – in the gutter of poverty.

I wasn't sure what time Jim was arriving until he telephoned me the night before. He was curt and efficient before ending our short conversation. His attitude didn't help matters any but then it never did. I spent the entire day cleaning the house, brought in some groceries and tried to set a mood of welcoming and home for him. So many times I was placed in the position of smooching him to keep the peace and here I was again doing the same thing. I prayed he would eat the light dinner I prepare and go to bed early. I didn't want to get into an argument with him on his first night home.

Although I had concerns over a place to live, no money for much and worried about the past ten days with Gavin in my home, I was still determined to get out of my marriage. But after my time with Linda, I did give much thought to other things. This was one time I couldn't fly by the seat of my pants and I needed a plan. Nothing was coming together and I wasn't the most patient person on the planet. I had to put my faith in God for all to work out and hold my ground until then.

He settled into his favorite chair on the veranda while I unloaded the car. There was tension between us from the very minute he hobbled off the airplane. He wasted no time mentioning the e-mail and like a child, it was all about him. All I could think about as I listened to him rant was how selfish he was. He twisted and turned everything to suit himself. There was a time when he admired my humor but now he used it to his own advantage.

When he made a verbal attack on my daughter, I got angry.

"How dare you criticize Samantha when she did so much for you? What's wrong with you Jim?" Where were your kids when you needed help? They are always too busy unless they want something from us. Did they even visit you in the hospital? Stop this nonsense right now - I refuse to listen to you. You are a greedy nasty old man who expects everyone to stop their own lives to help you save your own, and it's my family who were there for you. They put their lives on hold for you and that was a great sacrifice but they love you and wanted to help."

"I didn't ask for their help. You were the one who brought them into it. I could have managed on my own."

"If it wasn't for me and my family you would have been dead years ago. You can't tie your own shoe laces without help. It wasn't enough what we did for you and then you disappeared without leaving an itinerary and we spent close to twenty four hours trying to track you down to save your live again."

"How can you be so cavalier about this Jim when everyone stopped what they were doing to find you and the expense of phone calls, time off work and whatever else you put us through? Are you so selfish that you are incapable of appreciation?"

"It wasn't a big deal Laura – why make a mountain out of a hill?"

"It was a mountain Jim. You have been having your I.N.R. tests weekly for several years and know how important it is. You had one just before leaving the hospital and didn't bother to get the results."

"That was the doctor's fault. I shouldn't have to wait around while the lab does their work and he should have called with the results before I left Samantha's house."

"You always cast blame on the other person. Well when I lower you into your gave, I will blame the boys with the shovels for not digging it deep enough. That should make you happy!"

Within his luggage was a large box containing a wide assortment of medical supplies. The dressing on his foot had to be changed daily and as it had been over twenty four hours since the last change, it had to be done right away. There was no option other than for me to do it.

After preparing the instruments and setting them on a tray with a sterile sheet of gauze under them, he removed his shoes and socks to reveal a big job ahead of me and smelly feet. Somehow I managed to get through it with Jim issuing instructions along the way. I suggested we consult the hospital the next day to see if it could be done there or perhaps pay a nurse off duty to come to the house. He said no – I could do it for him. Well surprise for you buddy, I'm not doing it again.

I served the light supper I prepared earlier that day. He didn't want to move to the dining table so I gave it to him on his lap. My appetite was gone the minute I looked at his foot. I wasn't' hungry and had a glass of wine while I watched him eat. I somehow felt it was going to be a very long night.

He wasn't home three hours yet already my gut felt sick. I didn't want to live like this. Jim was totally incapable of compassion – life was all about him and his needs and now I knew that my needs were as real as his and needed taking care of.

With Baxter and Sam at my feet and guilt heavy in my soul I made the decision there and then. What was the point in waiting?

"Jim, there is something I need to discuss with you. I was going to wait a few days but I see no point now in putting off the inevitable. I want a separation."

"Who is he?"

"Is that so important to you Jim? You don't seem at all upset that I want out of our marriage."

"Did you have sex with him?"

"I'm not going to discuss that with you Jim. There was someone else but he is not the reason I want to leave. I should have done this years' ago."

I got up to go to another area of the house. This was going into the danger zone.

"Sit down Laura. You are not going anywhere until I have some answers. Tell me who you've been fucking around with and when and where."

I'm not answering any of your questions. I am not your property and this property is jointly owned by the two of us. You will not tell me what I can and can't do here or anywhere else and I will no longer be held accountable to you when you have done so much to hurt me with your spying and lies and treachery. I'm going to bed and you will use the guest room from now on."

"I knew this would happen – for years I've worried about it and you lived up to my expectations. Dam you Laura."

I left him sitting on the veranda and went to my room. How I hated him at that moment. Any other man would have cried or shown some emotion to indicate sadness, but not Jim.

During the night when I was in the deepest of sleep, I had a dream. My body was being caressed in a very passionate way. I felt hands on my most private parts. The yearning in me was intense, my mind on Gavin. The man in my dreams was talking to me.

"What's my name? Who am I?"

Still thinking I was in a dream I laughed and called Gavin's name.

The hands were suddenly gone and I awoke to see Jim leering over me in my bed. The moon light gave the bedroom a soft glow, enough that I could clearly see the expression on his face. He was grinning now that he knew the identity of my lover. Gloom and doom were on the horizon for me.

With words befitting a trucker, I threw him out of my room - locking the door behind him. He could wait until morning. Not once in our marriage had I been dishonest with him and I wasn't about to start. He wanted the whole story – he deserved the whole story and he would get it when I was ready to give it.

Morning started off with a roar. I berated him for his nasty ways while he wore a smug face.

"Even in my sleep I can't escape you Jim. You don't own me or my soul and I hate you after last night."

"You're the one fucking around, not me. I should hate you for being a whore."

"I don't think too many people would blame me if they knew you for what you really are Jim."

"What's it like fucking a black man Laura? I hear once you go black you never go back."

"You are disgusting Jim."

"You're the whore – not me."

"You really are a nasty man. I've known it for years. Why did it take you this long to show yourself for what you really are?"

"Tell me Laura is it true black men have a big bamboo? Mine wasn't good enough for you so you got yourself a nigger."

"Yours wasn't good enough for me. I haven't seen it in thirteen years. Are you living in the space zone Jim?'

"You could have had it anytime you wanted."

You fuck head. It doesn't work and you told me many years ago you were not interested – or have you now conveniently forgotten that?"

"Why a black man Laura? Are whites not good enough for you?"

"I don't see color Jim. I see a man for what he is, not how God painted him. We all have the same color blood, we all have feelings, a heart and soul and I would never have thought you were a racist. What a disappointment."

"I might have forgiven you if it had been anyone else Laura."

"You might have forgiven me. Who are you trying to kid? You don't have an ounce of forgiveness in your body and I am not asking for it. And what you really mean to say Jim is if it had been a white man. Would that have been easier for you to accept? Frankly, I doubt it because you are a monster, a racist and a greedy pig. But I will amend what I said about wanting a separation. What I really meant was a divorce."

My only regret was Gavin. He was now a third party in this equation and that didn't sit well with me. Jim could and would be cruel. Gavin was a big boy and could take care of himself. What worried me most was my own situation. No court in the Caribbean would chastise me or be swayed in Jim's favor because I chose a man who was a different color. Let Jim try to blow that one by a judge. Regardless, Linda was right; he was going to crucify me and I prayed for mercy from a system that was totally foreign to me.

Jim repeatedly asked me what my future plans were and wouldn't let up on asking questions about Gavin. How could I tell him what I did not know? I walked away when he brought Gavin into it.

Things settled down after a few days and we at least managed to be civilized with each other. We agreed to sell the house and signed the necessary papers with Selina. We were joint owners on the house and all that was left to divide was the furniture. Everything else had been liquidated before we left Canada. Our joint accounts would remain intact until the house was sold.

Gavin called me over the next few weeks but we didn't see each other. He pledged love for me and wanted me to move in with him. That would have been suicide and I didn't want to live in squalor.

I carried on with my life as though nothing happened. I kept my clients to a minimum and went about my life as usual with the exception of being seen any more than necessary.

While shopping for groceries not long after we put the house on the market, I ran into Sheila. Linda had not mentioned her when we last met and I was desperate for some company. I agreed to have lunch with her.

She was a fox if ever there was one. Full of questions, albeit it subtle, she managed to extract my current situation. I really didn't care. If she didn't' already know what was happening in the Cassidy household, she soon would and I need to vent – what harm could come of it?

She bragged about her life with her last husband, Dr. Sturgess. They had separated a year earlier and were already divorced. Their magnificent home, not far from my own, left her with over a half million in U.S. dollars. She currently lived in an apartment she wasn't happy with and was looking for something better.

Jim changed almost overnight. He was happy and helpful as we went through all that we had. He left the house many times and always came back with a glow. It hurt me to think he was so happy over the end of our marriage. Why did I wait so long to do this and how could I have been so blind? The man was nothing like what I believed him to be. He was a greedy self serving monster. He got boxes for me to pack but I had no plans to leave.

He was overly eager for me to move on – I felt I was being pushed out.

"I'm not leaving Jim until the house is sold. I don't have the money and neither do you so let's just face the fact that we are stuck together until then."

"We can't stay here together. One of us has to go and it should be you Laura."

"Not a chance Jim."

It was off season and not likely the house would sell quickly. Selina was confident the market would pick up in a few months but then the economy took a dive and that spelled disaster for property in the Caribbean.

Why should I have to be the one to leave and why was Jim so eager to get me out? His behavior become even stranger and had I thought about it in the proper light and remembered how he was when we first dated; I would have seen what was going on.

Gavin's calls became more frequent, he was desperate to see me. I needed some warmth and company but was afraid to be seen with him. A few times I walked the dogs to his apartment in the early evening but never stayed more than an hour. I put nothing past Jim and was well aware he would twist any situation to his benefit. I had to be careful.

"Move in with me Laura. You can't stay in that house with him."

"No Gavin, that is what he's waiting for and he will crucify me. Can't you see what a bastard he is?"

"How can he crucify you? You own half of everything and will get it in time."

"I'm not going to add fuel to an already out of control fire. I don't know what he can do but I don't trust him and can't take that chance. I also have my dogs to think about."

"Alright but if you need a place, you know I'm here waiting for you."

The last thing I wanted was to move in with Gavin and live in a roach infested dump. I also knew that once I moved out of my house I could be charged with desertion and I wasn't taking that chance. The Horatio courts were based on old English law. Desertion could cost me everything.

Jim was bad mouthing me all over the island. I couldn't go into town without encountering someone who either snubbed me or said something vile to my face. I tried to take it all in stride but it was very difficult.

I believed what Linda told me and since then others had as well. I wasn't the first woman to have an affair on the island but what I couldn't understand was why Jim was coming out of this with a halo over his head while I was being treated like a harlot. I refused to believe it had anything to do with color. Jim was a racist but the people who were offending me were not. Was life so dull that my own had to be the main source of entertainment?

Jim continued to attend Sunday service while I stayed home. I couldn't bare the idea of being seen and being seen with him. He joined the Sunday morning brunch club and asked for my help when he prepared his food contributions the night before.. Jim couldn't cook worth a dam and now all of a sudden he wanted to be the galloping gourmet.

I continued to see Gavin occasionally and always at his apartment. Jim was going out so much we had to develop a schedule for the sharing of the jeep. I was home most of and every day to take care of the dogs and the house. I continued to prepare meals for Jim and do his laundry.

Gavin asked me to take a trip with him to Dominica and I needed to get away from everything. Jim agreed to take care of the dogs during my absence. Something was going on with Jim. I made him sign a letter and had

Linda and Luke be my witnesses. I was taking a short vacation and would be returning to our home within six weeks. He agreed to care for our dogs, our home and handle our affairs during my absence. I was covering my ass.

The only friends I saw were Linda, Selina and Bea. Linda and Luke were no longer bothered by Sheila and they did have one lunch with her. She had a new a new man in her life and was over the hill about it. She bragged about his beautiful home and their plan to marry. I didn't bother to tell them I had a lunch with her. As far as we were all concerned, she was a non entity.

There were a few showings of our house but nothing came of it. Without proceeds from the sale I could not move forward. This was the only thing that Jim understood and accommodated. Once my business was shut down I had no income. Jim and I discussed many possibilities. He was over eager and volunteered to take a small apartment if the house didn't sell by Christmas.

Chapter Ten
Dominica

*g*avin and I left for Dominica on June 1st. With money owed to me by clients, I paid for our flights and the apartment we secured for our stay. Had it not been for that we would not have been able to make the trip. Gavin had big ideas and made plans without a penny of his own going toward anything and I was too willing to cover the expenses.

"What do you do with your wages Gavin? You can't expect me to pick up the tab for everything."

"Jason hasn't been making payroll for the last four weeks and I had to pay my rent and buy food with what little I had."

He was lying.

I wanted to see another island and heard many wonderful things about Dominica. Even when I had my half from the sale of my home, I would not be able to afford St. Horatio. I was determined to stay in the Caribbean and one island was as good as the next. Jim received a good pension and would live well even with half of what we had. I wasn't so fortunate and had a ways to go before I could access my own retirement funds. Ironic how my dream was now Jim's life! Here I was fighting to survive with not much hope and travelling with man who was nothing short of a parasite.

Gavin's family welcomed me to Dominica but when they put their hand out for greetings, they were palms up. Gavin played the big shot and gave them money – mine of course. I was nothing more to them than a sugar mamma. I tried to focus on the bigger picture. I wanted to see all there was to see and what better person to show me than someone like Gavin?

His relatives hung out at our apartment from morning until night. They expected to be fed and rum watered and Gavin was happy to accommodate them. I had a rental car and refused to carry his family and friends around. It was small and I wasn't a taxi service. The few times when we did take a few family members with us on a day trip, it was me who paid for their lunches and snacks along the way and they had no qualms about asking for things. It was Gavin who was seeking the glory while I was simply trying to keep my money in my bag.

For several days we planned to travel to the south end of the island and possibly stay overnight. Only minutes before we were about to set out, Gavin told me his sister, her husband and two sons were coming with us. I said no, the car wasn't big enough and I didn't want to take them. He told me to get a bigger vehicle. I refused and we didn't take the trip.

When we did managed to have time alone we went for swims in the river or to local eateries and bars. Often we just took walks. I enjoyed these times with Gavin who was always loving and attentive. He knew the island well, its history and some special secret places that few tourists managed to find.

Dominica was the most beautiful island in the West Indies. Although a poor country, the warmth of the people made up for it. It broke my heart to see such poverty while at the same time my heart was warmed with joy with many facets of the culture. It was nothing like St. Horatio although I loved that island equally as well.

Gavin claimed he loved me more than he had any other woman and wanted a lifetime with me. Although I enjoyed the attention he showed me and the romance, I knew I could never be happy with him. There was a side to him that was slowing exposing itself and I didn't like it.

The cost of living in Dominica was much lower than St. Horatio. The price of land was ridiculously low for a Caribbean island and there was plenty of it available. I looked seriously at Dominica as my future home. I couldn't afford to buy a home and had no means to support myself but I could afford to buy a piece of land. If nothing else, it was an investment that would show a good return one day.

I began to make inquires and looked at several pieces of land. Before I left the island five weeks later, I owned an acre.

Gavin was excited over my purchase and believed it was ours. He bragged to family, friends and anyone else who would stand still long enough to listen, that he owned a piece of property. With every new telling, the acre grew as did the price I paid.

I let him have his hey day. There was no harm in bragging and lying to people. Let them believe what they wanted. The property belonged to me and it would be a long time before I could build anything on it; that is if I chose to when the time came. It was strictly an investment in not only property but also to establish myself with the government as an owner of something. Immigration papers would be much easier to obtain when I made the final move if I owned property.

Gavin was not a smart man. In fact he was totally ignorant and a liar. He prided himself as being the patriarch of the family. His many nephews thought he was a joke and a loser. They saw him for what he was and it was them who opened my eyes to many things I needed to see.

We returned to St. Horatio the second week of July. Baxter and Sam were on top of me before I got in the door. Jim was a totally new man with a glow I hadn't seen since we were engaged. Maybe he had another woman already – well good for him and too bad for her.

There had been no showings of our house during my absence and it wasn't looking good for the next few months. I settled back in to my routine and went about living life as though nothing had happened.

Gavin didn't call for three days and when he did he told me he resigned from his job and was returning to Dominica to build a house on our land.

"How can you build a house Gavin? Do you have money for that?"

"Give me twenty thousand Laura and I will get the foundation started and send for you."

"I don't have that kind of money and even if I did, I'm not ready to build anything yet."

"Borrow it from Jim. Tell him we will pay him back."

"No Gavin, that's now how it works. My house has to sell first and then I will have my own money and I'm not sure what I want to do yet."

"Lend me the money to go back please. I will find us a house to rent and then you can join me."

"No Gavin, pay your own way this time."

He left two weeks later. He could do nothing on my land and had no means to put stakes in the ground let along start building. I wasn't worried but I did want to go back but not because I wanted to be with him. I wanted a new beginning and Dominica was where it was going to happen.

I cashed in a few bonds I had in Canada and flew to Dominica a month later. Gavin and I were in touch the entire time. He couldn't find a place for us to live and he couldn't find work. It was all hog wash. I would find a way to support myself. Jim agreed to fly the dogs to me once I had a place and he promised to keep me informed on the sale of our house.

Jim helped me pack and arranged for overseas freight. He was a changed man and happy. By now I figured he had someone else in his life and was happy for him. I hoped for his sake he would be a better partner with her than he had been with me and I prayed for his health.

Three days before my scheduled flight, I was served with divorce papers. Jim wasn't wasting any time. I retained a lawyer of my own and cross petitioned on the grounds of mental cruelty and impotence. My attorney, Ms. Cartier, wasn't taking any chances when I told her my story. She believed this was going to be a messy divorce and she was right. Jim was setting me up for the crucifixion and he wasn't smart enough to do it alone. He had help.

Carrying fifty thousand in cash on my person, I returned to Dominica on August 1st with a heavy heart. Leaving Baxter and Sam behind was more difficult than leaving my beautiful home and I was more than aware that Jim was up to no good. I never thought I would see the day when I would learn just how devious and nasty he was capable of being.

It started with the divorce petition that his lawyer, Mr. Henry, should have been ashamed to submit to the courts. It wasn't enough to name me as an adulterer. The detail that I got fucked in the matrimonial bed, was a drunk, a whore, contributed nothing throughout the marriage and that I deserted him, was all listed in sordid detail and in a language that no decent lawyer would willingly sign his name to.

Jim was claiming to be my sole provider for fifteen years, a loving and caring husband who was also an ordained Untied Church Minister. He was crushed by my sordid behavior, humiliated in the community and saddened to the point of suffering health issues.

Gavin was an hour late meeting my plane. His last call before I left St. Horatio was to tell me he couldn't find a place for me to live and I should not come. I wasn't falling for that line. When he did finally show up, he was warm but different – very different.

I booked a room at a seaside motel not far from the village of Glanvilla where we stayed the first time. When he learned of this on the ride from the airport, he suddenly had a place for us to stay. It was the same apartment we had on our first trip and just that morning the tenant moved our and he moved in. I also had a jeep reserved and asked our driver to drop me at the rental agency to pick it up.

Gavin wanted my land and not me. With me out of the country, who would challenge him if he did build a house on it? I may have been Irish but I wasn't green.

He carried my suitcases into the small apartment and didn't have them both on the floor before he asked me for money.

"We are not on vacation now Gavin. This is new a new life beginning for me and my money isn't going to be the gravy it was the last time we were here."

"My boss couldn't make payroll again today. I'm brokes Laura."

"I went to my purse to give him twenty dollars. He claimed he had to go somewhere right away and needed to take a bus. I would have driven him but he didn't ask.

"I couldn't pay the rent Laura. Will you take care of it while I'm gone?"

I had my wallet in my hand when he made this second request. He grabbed it from me and pulled out my stash.

"What are you doing carrying this much money with you. Anyone could rob you. I'll hold it for you."

Rage took over me as I tore the wallet from his hands. He hit me several times and I fought back with all my might, finally giving him a knee in the balls that brought the bastard to the floor. With his pockets empty he left the apartment.

This was hardly the way I was expecting my first night in my new country to be but at least I had a roof over my head. I could have gone to the motel but I was already here, it was late and I was hungry. I went to see Irma the landlady and gave her two weeks rent and told her I was the tenant, not Gavin.

"But he's been here for almost a month and hasn't paid me. He said he was waiting for you to come with his money."

"Irma, if you believed that then you shouldn't be operating a business."

She gave me fresh linen and cleaning supplies. The apartment was a mess and Gavin hadn't been living there alone. Who ever she was, she moved out that day and in a hurry. She left behind things I never would have and Gavin left his condoms in a dresser drawer.

Less than a week later I found a two-bedroom apartment on the upper floor of a two storey building. Below was a vacant commercial space that inspired me to look at some possibilities to earn a living. The landlord agreed to rent it to me for a very low rent and was agreeable to me renovating for a small restaurant and bar.

Gavin came and went when it suited him while I was staying at Irma's guest house. When he learned of my new venture, he was eager to reconcile and assist. I needed help from someone. Every electrician or carpenter I sought out wanted three times the going rate. At least Gavin got me good workers for honest wages and they did a great job.

The next two weeks were very busy. My container arrived and the construction was underway full tilt boogie. When I was turned down for a liquor license because I had no residence status, I had no choice but to put the license in Gavin's name. I didn't know another soul on the island other than his family who were all unemployed and beggars.

My restaurant opened on September 16th, 2005. My apartment was too small for all that my container held but it fit nicely into the restaurant and made it a place of charm and elegance.

He pleaded with me to give him another chance – saying he was sorry for being such an ass. He promised never to hit me again and to keep his pecker in his pants. He was living with one of his nephews – sleeping on the floor. He wanted to help me run the restaurant and didn't feel comfortable with a white woman in the Portsmouth area running a bar alone. My brain cells must have been hibernating; I agreed to take him back.

"You need protection running a business like that in this area Laura and I will be with you all the time. I will keep the bar open very late because that is when the bars bring in the most money. You can be upstairs by then if you want."..

He did keep the business open late but the take didn't support the cost of electricity. Gavin was an idiot with no sense of business. If he had two drunks sitting at the bar drinking Cass rum – the cheapest available; he kept the place open. He played music so loud the neighbors complained. He allowed groups for freeloaders to come in and dance without buying drinks.

I couldn't get it through to him we were better of closed than open but he just didn't get it and argued to the point of hitting me when I wouldn't see things his way.

"I'm the man. This is my place and I make the decisions.'

The restaurant and bar did well during the day when I was alone. He claimed he was working on a construction job but he never brought any money in and had the same old feeble excuse. The boss couldn't make payroll and this was a different job than the one he had previously.

The success of the restaurant necessitated the hiring of two cooks. I couldn't keep up with the cooking and tending the bar. Gavin showed up when it suited him and usually played Mr. Ambassador with the customers. It was amusing to listen to him boast about his restaurant and how pleased he was with the hired help – me in particular. He was quite the liar and boaster and often I saw the expressions on the faces of those who listened to him. They didn't believe a word he said. He was always there for the late night shift on his own where there really wasn't any business worth keeping open for but I was upstairs in my bed and didn't give a dam what he was doing. I also knew that what sales he did get was going into his pockets.

It was a happy day for me when Baxter and Sam arrived. I spoke to Jim only briefly when he called to give their flight information.

"Any interest on the house yet Jim?"

"I took the house off the market. I plan to live here quite comfortably for a few years." He hung up without another word.

My lawyer said she would file for a court order to sell at the time of the divorce hearing which would be in December.

"Ancillary matters have to be dealt with at that time Laura. There is nothing we can do before then and it's only two months from now."

I was sure Gavin had another woman and I didn't care. My priority was to get my business established and making a profit. I could always hire a bartender once I got rid of Gavin but he was right that I couldn't run the bar alone at night. Locals were not a nice lot to deal with at night when they were drunk.

Everything was in my name with the exception of the liquor permit. Once established and with a few months residency under my belt, I should be able to get one on my own. If not, I would find another sponsor. I was meeting people every day and some were possible candidates.

Luke or Linda and Selina called me often. They were worried over the choice I made and repeatedly reassured me to come to them at any sign of trouble. I couldn't tell them of the abuse I was suffering - not yet, but Luke wasn't so easily fooled and often called me when Linda wasn't around. He didn't want her to worry anymore than she already did but he told me he had learned some things about Gavin which was why he wanted to stay close to me.

Gavin never got over his fear of my dogs. This was a blessing. He never went upstairs to the apartment unless I was there and he would never dare to strike me around the dogs. I also felt safe when one of my cooks was in the restaurant but many times I was alone between shifts. This became Gavin's venue for hitting me when there were no customers.

The land I owned was foremost on Gavin's agenda. He wanted to build a house with no money and even if I did have any, I wasn't going to build a house. He had it cleared with profits from the restaurant and planted crops. When the plants began to produce and he sold and kept the proceeds, I hired a man to rip everything out.

He came tearing into the restaurant full of rage when he discovered what I had done. He was about to beat up on me when a customer and one of my cooks intervened but not before I took a few blows.

On the advice of my cook Randy, I spun a story to Gavin that defused the current situation. I told him I had a buyer for the land and would make a handsome profit. I also lied and told him the bank manager convinced me to invest the money in a one year term deposit that would pay a high interest rate. At the end of the year we would have enough money to buy something better.

"We should have looked more before we bought Gavin. There is property available on the beach and a place that is huge and abandoned for two years now. We could have a much larger restaurant; live on the upper level until we can build a separate home on the same property. We can put in a dock and set up a small marina with laundry and a canteen for yachts. We can provide services for emptying their holding tanks; supply them with fresh water and fuel and dingy taxi for the larger boats that have to moor out. The possibilities are endless."

He fell for it and within a day was bragging to customers about his plans. He was a walking talking joke.

My cooks, Randy and Donah were sick over my continuous black eyes and bruised face. Finally, Randy put the closed sign on the restaurant one afternoon and sat me down for a little chat. Not only did Gavin have another woman with whom he shared an apartment since the day I arrived, she was a prostitute which explained why he never saw her at night. His so called construction job was non-existent. He spent his afternoons with her, taking her into town in public - holding hands and shopping for food. Randy also told me of the many times he took large quantities of food from the freezers and late at night when he was tending the bar, the woman was there with him while I was asleep upstairs.

Randy and I talked most of the afternoon, taking her from her kitchen duties. I enjoyed the few hours of visiting with her but when she left and I realized she hadn't prepared food for the dinner hour; I went into high speed to prepare food and tend bar. People were arriving for dinner and I was alone.

Gavin showed up shortly after six. This was early for him but I needed his help or I wouldn't be able to cope. It was mid week and not normally this busy. This was the only night of the week when both cooks were off.

He had the usual scowl on his face and didn't say a word to me. When I walked past him from the bar to the kitchen he slapped me on the side of my face so hard I fell over. I got up stunned and got another slap on the other side. I ran upstairs and locked the doors.

The kitchen was a mess the following morning. Food and garbage covered most of the floor. Sinks could not be accessed with stacks of dishes blocking the taps - It had been a busy night. I kept the closed sign hanging in the window for three hours while I cleaned up. The ice packs from the previous night did little good. I had two black eyes and a perfect hand mark on my face. When Randy arrived she took one look and went back out again to get the Dominican cure for bruises – orange butter.

The previous day's receipts were long gone with Gavin. I had to keep the restaurant open with or without black eyes. Randy and I got the day's menu together and got things cooking. We traded jobs that day. She became hostess and bartender while I did her work and hid in the kitchen.

Randy offered to move in with me for a while. Gavin was crazy and becoming more abusive.

"The only way you're going to get him out Laura is to push him out. He won't come around if I'm here all the time."

Gavin didn't show his face for the next few days and Randy couldn't move in until she got her own affairs in order. At best it would be two weeks. . We were so busy I barely had time to tend to the dogs or think about my problems. The cooks worked overtime and hung around to cover those gaps between their shifts.

Selina called to talk to me about the house. She had interested buyers but couldn't get in to show the house. She knew the sign was down but hadn't been told it was no longer for sale.

"Didn't Jim talk to you Selina?

"I can't get through to Jim. His girlfriend is the one who answers the phone and when I went there a few times, she wouldn't let me in."

"What girlfriend? I didn't know he had someone in the house but he did tell me he wasn't selling but that's not his choice entirely – I have a say in my home too. The divorce hearing is in December and we will get a court order to sell it. Just leave it until then - we really don't have much choice. Who is the girlfriend?"

"The dragon lady herself – Sheila. He couldn't have made a worse choice. This is going to be messy Laura. I know this woman and she's evil."

"I don't care who he has there. We own the house jointly. "

Carnival was in full swing on the island. The restaurant was crowded every night making it necessary to purchase more seating. My cooks were run off their feet as was I with serving and tending bar. My savings account was growing with the money coming in and Gavin not around to steal it before it got deposited. Randy still hadn't moved in.

Gavin came and went but I closed the restaurant early now. He was only stealing what was coming in and playing the big shot with customers. When he learned Randy was planning to move in he threatened to cancel the liquor license in his name and report me for working without a work permit. He didn't have the balls make good either of his threats and if he did, I would find a way around it.

One rainy miserable day we had more customers at one time than ever before. We ran out of food early and Randy couldn't stay after her shift to help me prepare more. Donah was well past her arrival time and customers kept coming. She was never late and didn't call to say she would be. I could not handle this myself and would have to close if she didn't show up soon. Money was pouring in faster than I could count it. I was running from kitchen to bar to waiting tables. I stashed money in my apron pocket. I didn't dare leave it under the bar with the mob that I had and Gavin could easily slip in without me seeing him. This was going to be my best night ever if it kept up. This was the one night I didn't want to close and would keep it open late if the people kept coming and spending the way they were. Somehow I would manage and if one of my better customers came in, I would hire him to tend bar for me.

Two male customers sat at the bar for most of the afternoon. They were drinking heavily and running a tab. I had never seen them before but they were pleasant and conversing over some business venture. These were the type of customers I wanted. They were still there when Gavin walked in at six o'clock.

The dogs had been alone in the apartment all day without a pee break or food. There was plenty of prepared food ready in the kitchen to fill orders – things were under control. I asked Gavin to cover for me while I went upstairs for half an hour. I also wanted to empty the money form my pockets. I didn't want him around but I also did not want to turn away business. I kept looking for Dave, one of my regulars who normally came in around this time and always alone. He would happily take the bar for me and I could get Gavin out from behind it but he hadn't shown up yet.

There was still no sign of Donah and I couldn't reach her on the cell phone. I wasn't happy with her no show.

I returned to the restaurant twenty minutes later to find the two men about to leave. There stood Gavin with pen and paper asking them what they had to drink. I quickly pulled their tab from under the bar and handed it them.

Both men went berserk over the $34 tab claiming they had not had that much to drink and calling me a cheating white bitch. I politely went over the bill with them or attempted to when one of the men grabbed my hand and bent my pinky finger back to the point of fracture.

Gavin told them to pay what they wanted and pushed me aside. I was not going to tolerate this and demanded they pay or I would call the police. One of the men rushed to come behind the bar where I stood and I went to meet him head on as he threatened to bash in my white head.

Gavin was quickly on my heels and I believed he was coming to my defense.

"Get upstairs to your fucking dogs. I'll take care of this."

"Like hell you will. They owe $34 and that's what they're going to pay."

"This is my place. Get upstairs now."

"This is not your place mister. You steal from my investment and my efforts.

Gavin hit me, knocking me to the floor and continued to order me out of the restaurant. He was putting on a show for the customers who were enjoying it all. I stood my ground and got knocked down again. The battle had begun and I was ready, or so I thought.

Once I was back on my feet he kept hitting me while I kicked and clawed at him. When I was down on the floor for the third time he kicked me several times in the head and stomach, all the while saying:

"You're in my country now. This is my place - you will do as I say."

By this time there were no less than 10 men in the bar, possibly 12 or more. They made no attempt to help me and cheered Gavin on.

He pulled my hair and pulled my shirt off – anything for the show. I had to get out of there but the door was blocked by customers and people in the street to see what was going on. I got a glimpse of Dave trying to get in the door.

"Dave, help me Dave please."

The machete was in the kitchen – if only I could get to it. Gavin knew it was there also and blocked me from the kitchen. He knew I would use it if I could get my hands on it and with the rage I was in – I would have taken his head off.

When Gavin picked up the boom and started hitting me in the head and back with it, Dave went insane and broke through the barrier with some help from a few friends. He was on top of Gavin in an instant.

"You no good mother fucker - leave her alone.

Instantly I saw the fear in Gavin.

"Take it easy bro. Have a drink on the house while I teach this bitch a lesson."

"Over my dead body Gavin - back away from her now or I'll kill you."

The two of them were now fighting while Gavin kept trying to hit me in between. Dave went down once – giving Gavin the chance to drag me out the back door with Dave hot on his tail. Gavin began hitting me again when Dave got him by the throat from behind. A few good punches to the head and Gavin was running. I seized the opportunity and ran for the apartment but not before I heard Dave's last words to Gavin as he ran.

"You ever touch her again and I'll kill you and I'll come with back up next time."

I grabbed my purse, leashed the dogs and went back to the bar. It was the only way out. There was no sign of Gavin and the customers were helping themselves to the bar. When I ordered them to get out, they didn't move and threatened to kill my dogs. I unleashed them.

I locked the doors and ran with my boys to the police station two blocks away in the pouring rain. They refused to allow me access because of the dogs. I wasn't leaving them outside and I wasn't leaving without filing charges. They parted as I entered, Baxter and Sam on either side of me.

Finally an officer took me to a small interview room with my dogs where I told him what happened. He seemed docile or had been drinking. Either way my visit woke him up. In any other country officers would have been dispatched immediately to the scene but not so in this case.

The officer took well over an hour to methodically write down everything - asking me to repeat the same information at least three times. I used my cell phone to call the one and only white person I knew. We met by chance at the bank and become casual friends.

I was making a bank transaction when the teller insister I show her my Dominican passport.

"I don't have a Dominican passport. I'm a Canadian."

"No, you have a passport. We have a copy in your file."

"What file? Why would you have a file on me?"

Irritated, she asked me to wait while she went to the other side of the bank to pull out a file. She stood there talking to the bank manager while they looked through my file – looked at me and then looked at the file again. Finally she sauntered over at her own slow pace and slammed the file down on the counter for me.

I picked up the huge file to see on the first sheet a copy of the so called passport belonging to someone else. However, the resemblance between me and the woman in the photo was uncanny. Who ever this person was, she was a big investor in the bank. All her personal papers, loan applications, investment documents and other papers were handed over to me without a second thought by a very stupid clerk.

With the folder still in my hand, I told the clerk I wanted to see the manager right away. With a roll of the eyes, she slowly wandered to his office. He came out as far as the doorway and looked at me. I raised the file and waved my finger at him to come hither.

"What can I do for you Miss?"

"I came into this bank to do a simple transaction and was told I had to produce a passport which I do not have. This clerk insisted I did have one when I know darn well I don't and you should also know that sir because I have met with you several times when I bought my land here."

"Please forgive me but I still do not see what the problem is."

"I could have walked out of this bank carrying a file with very personal information that belongs to someone else."

"What do you mean someone else?"

"This file belongs to a woman named Winnie Taylor. I am Laura Cassidy and that information was given to the clerk and noted on my deposit slip."

The manager snatched the file from my hand before I knew what he was doing.

"I come into this bank at least three times a week. If I look like someone else and I admit, it appears Ms. Taylor and I do look alike, then the name should have been referred to before assuming I was someone I was not. Do you agree sir?"

The man, although black, was scarlet with embarrassment.

"This was an honest mistake. I hope you understand Mrs. Cassidy."

"No sir I do not understand and this is not acceptable. If I was Ms. Taylor I would have your job. Every personal financial record of hers is in this file. This is an unforgivable violation of privacy and trust on the part of this bank."

"Clerks in any business have no right in making assumptions. She had my name and that should have been enough. She questioned my ability to properly identify myself and rather than pursue it she took it upon herself to assume she knew better than I was who I am and violated another customer by doing what she did."

"But you look so much alike and she owns her own restaurant in the same area."

"No wonder your clerks don't know what they are doing. You are worse than they are. Don't make excuses for incompetence. Fix it or I will take my business elsewhere and I will advise Ms. Taylor of this incident. She has a right to know."

I saw enough in the file to learn the name of the restaurant Winnie owned – The Tomato. It wasn't far from the bank. I didn't have a vehicle and didn't care to hop on a bus. I went to a snack bar beside the bank and called her. She came right away to meet me and we could have been twins. We hit it off right away and visited each other's restaurant whenever we were within range of one another.

She wasn't happy when I told her what happened and she was grateful that I made some noise at the bank.

Winnie came immediately and raised holy hell with the cops. She had lived in Dominica for many years, was well respected and appeared to have some clout. After telling him to get off his ass and do something, he quickly snapped out of his docile mode and got with the tour. He asked for Gavin's cell phone number and put in a call. His opening comment was, "Hey brother where you be?"

We were not going to get anywhere with the police. They gave me a form to take to the hospital where I was to be examined. I was badly bruised and sore all over but nothing was broken and I refused to stay overnight for observation. Winnie stayed with me – the dogs were safe in her SUV. She drove us home to find the place in darkness. We checked every room in the apartment to make sure he wasn't there and proceeded to do the same in the restaurant, keeping the dogs with us while he checked.

We took two bottles of wine from the cooler, some cigarettes for Winnie and went back upstairs. Gavin wouldn't come around – he knew the police were involved.

Winnie and I threw Gavin's clothes over the balcony to the street below. We laughed and drank the wine in a hurry and went back to the restaurant to get more. She was determined to cheer me up and wasn't leaving until I was ready.

I watched her leave at 4 a.m. from the balcony. Already Gavin's clothes had been picked over by drunks and beggars. Oddly enough I felt calm and relieved knowing Gavin was out of my life for good now. I took two Advils for my aching body and smoked my first cigarette in many years from the pack Winnie left behind. With Baxter and Sam in bed with me, I slept like the dead.

Randy was in the street below the following morning with several others. I looked over the balcony to see what the commotion was and was called names by some of the women I recognized from the neighborhood. Gavin was there with two police officers who insisted they be allowed up to get his things.

"He has nothing here belonging to him."

"Let us come up to see for ourselves."

Like a fool I allowed them to come up. Gavin went into the bedroom without pause and came out within seconds and left. He had something hidden right under my nose and I had no doubt it was money and the cops got a share.

Randy was hollering at the women in the street – telling them to go to their own homes and leave me alone. She then came upstairs to keep me company. We took the dogs for a good run in the park and went to the police station where I filed formal charges. We returned to my place and put on a pot of coffee. I told her what happened the previous night and my decision to sell everything and leave the country. She agreed to stay on with me for pay to help me shut everything down.

We placed signs all over town advertising my big sale. Donah came on board to help as we carried all but what I absolutely needed to the lower floor. People came in droves and fought over my beautiful possessions. It broke my heart to see my things being carried away by strangers but I needed the money. Within three days everything was gone. I had my bed, two plastic chairs, a lamp and nothing else left to my name.

It wasn't until the trauma and drama subsided a few days after that horrible night that I remembered Donah's absence from work on the night when I needed her most.

"Gavin told me not to come to work. He passed by my house as I was going out the door for work and told me you were sick and the place was going to be closed."

I checked with the police every day but other than being served a summons to face the charges in court, they were doing nothing. Gavin didn't show up for court – he left the island. The angry judge asked the officers why he wasn't there when he had been served.

"He wasn't served Your Honor – he was already gone when we went to serve him."

What bull shit this was. He was warned by the police.

A handsome man named Lincoln Powell bought many of my things and came and went over the several days I was selling out. I liked him and he took a personal interest in my safety. He was an electrician who lived less than three blocks from my place. He took charge of hiring a crew to dismantle the restaurant for me

Most of the wood was sold and what wasn't Lincoln agreed to store for me until I found a buyer. Everyone worked fast, all wanting to get out of there quickly. It was already well past dark and the men had already worked a full day at their regular jobs.

They were throwing the lumber in piles on the floor while Donah and I tossed it into the back of the pick up truck. The wood was heavy and the nails were not being removed. For every piece I tossed, Donah tossed four. I should have quit when I realized it was too much for my little body but I wanted to help and continued. I picked up a piece that was bigger than I anticipated and was buried under another at one end which I didn't see. I couldn't hold it and promptly dropped it on my foot.

I stood there frozen as activity continued around me. Lincoln stayed close by me and tried to convince me to leave the work to them. He looked at me – glance away to say something to one of the men and then looked back at me.

We stood there staring at each other for several seconds when his eyes went down my body to my foot and then back up again to meet my eyes that were surely glazed over.

"OH SHIT – EVERYBODY FREEZE NOW."

I was nailed to the floor.

Pain seared through my foot and up my leg. Nobody moved – everyone stood still except for Lincoln and Donah who rushed to my side. No words came from their mouths as they stood staring at me.

O-k, now everybody listen to me. Donah get on the floor and hold my foot perfectly still. Don't let my foot move at all no matter what happens. Lincoln, pick up that board and pull it strait up very slowly."

"Laura, are you sure?"

"YES I'M SURE. Get that dam thing out of my foot fast and one of you guys get over here behind to catch me."

Lincoln's hands were shaking – sweat poured down his face but he did exactly what had to be done. The nails came out smoothly. I fell forward instead of backward. Lincoln caught me and carried me to a chair. I didn't pass out but came close. He put my head between my legs for a few minutes until the nausea passed and then I started to shake uncontrollably.

"She's in shock; we got to get her to the hospital."

I don't know who carried me to the truck. I only remember Lincoln's cursing at the men.

"You dumb bastards – I told you to take the nails out before you tossed the wood. Mother of God, the woman was nailed to the frigging floor."

My search for accommodations anywhere in the West Indies was not going well. I could have moved back into my house but Jim had Sheila living there and I did not want to interfere with his new relationship. He deserved happiness and although many thought his choice was wrong, it was his life and not my business.

My nights were lonely and long. I went no where but stayed in my sparsely furnished apartment the entire day with the exception only of walking the dogs in the park and trips to the cyber café. I had no idea what would come of my life.

Lincoln called me every day to make sure I was alright. He never came up to see me and often when I sat in the dark on my balcony in the early morning hours, I saw him slowly drive by. I told him I saw him and he said he was only checking to make sure I was o-k. When he had to go away for a few days, he had a friend patrolling around my place.

He took me for Chinese food on my birthday and bought me a small gift. It wasn't a date – just a good friend looking after another. Christmas was two weeks after my birthday and I dreaded being alone.

I heard nothing from my lawyer and had to assume court would be recessed until the New Year. Until suitable housing could be found I had no choice but to stay where I was. My landlord was sympathetic and came around often to see me. He told me not to worry about paying rent – to just get myself feeling better and move on when I was ready.

Winnie came daily to bring me something to eat from her own restaurant. She knew I wasn't taking care of myself and feeding me became her primary objective. Since arriving in Dominica my weight had plummeted to an all time low. Any other time I would have glowed with the slimmer me, but I was beyond slim now and it wasn't attractive.

Chapter Eleven
Calibishie

Winnie showed up one morning of December 15th with her cooler and picnic basket.

"Laura, you need to get out of here for a few hours. Get your swim suit and what the dogs will need and let's go have some fun."

We drank beer as she drove north. The dogs were happy the minute they were in her jeep and I was soon after. The scenery was beautiful – how had I missed this part of the island that was so close to where I had been? We sang songs and stopped for more beer along the way. Winnie was a lot of fun to be with and I was thankful for the day trip.

We arrived at the Village of Calibishie before noon. Along the way Winnie told me about the village and in particular her friend Carol Ann Watson, who owned a beach bar bistro named Kokonutz. The place was closed until December 21st when Carol Ann returned from her annual visit home in Vancouver Canada. Winnie was Canadian also – from the east coast.

"There's no reason we can't use the beach at the back of the bar. There's great shade there under the Almond Trees and the area is quiet. You will love it Laura."

Kokonutz was post card perfect. I loved the place and the village the minute we arrived. I had never seen Almond trees before and these were magnificent if pruned properly as these were. They are nature's umbrellas on sunny days.

We spent the entire day in the village eating chicken from sidewalk snack stands and drinking more beer from local merchants. We walked with the dogs on the beach and through the village. The people were friendly and welcoming. We swam in the sea and lazed under the trees for hours. We were exhausted when we returned to my apartment after sunset.

I returned to Calibishie on the bus with Randy the next day. Within a few hours I had a house to rent across the street from Kokonutz. It was a furnished three bedroom heritage home with cheap rent. I moved in on December 20th 2005 and met Carol Ann a day later.

A voluptuous Irish bubble is how I describe her even now. She greeted me with a hug not knowing my name yet or how I came to be in Calibishie. She opened her place the following day and invited me to come for drinks on the house. She was warm and vivacious woman with a mass of red curly hair that bounced when she breathed. I liked her instantly - we became good friends.

She invited me to a Christmas dinner she had been planning for months - to be held on the very beach where Winnie and I spent our wonderful day. This was a private party. Her bar would not be open for business on Christmas day. All invited guests were required to bring a dish which she organized to prevent the arrival of ten salads and no meat, and we were to bring our own drinks.

I bought and cooked a large ham and helped Carol Ann set up the tables end to end on the beach. There were twenty one of us for a wonderful Christmas dinner. Winnie and Ron were among the guests. A full moon and lanterns provided the evening light while the gentle surf provided the music. I met many new and wonderful people that Christmas, many of whom are now friends. It was a Christmas I will remember fondly for many years.

SCOOPS Ice Cream Parlor opened for business on January 16. Using the wood from the restaurant I had in storage and my chest freezer that did not sell, I had all I needed to get set up. My shop was directly across the street from Kokonutz and two doors from my house. I hired a young man to paint it in stripes of blue, yellow and pink and made my own signs. I was off and running at long last.

I hired a young Rasta boy named Coffy to work in the parlor at night. The days were long and exhausting. At night the village changed into a party alley. With Reggae music blaring and crowds of people roaming up and down the street, I was quite happy to walk the dogs after dinner and stay home.

At ten in the evening I closed the shop and crossed the street to Kokonutz to help Carol Ann close up. Nicky was her boyfriend and partner. They worked the business together during the day but at closing time he headed for the boys in the village before going home while she closed up and went home to her two dogs. They had been together four years and worked hard at the bistro. Carol Ann was on a mission. She wanted to build her business to the point of sale for a good profit and then build a home for herself. She was almost there with the most successful eatery in the village.

My dream was much the same. I wanted a little Caribbean house of my own and to find something of interest to work at and enjoy. I didn't want to scoop ice cream for the rest of my days. Everything was almost perfect in my life and at last I was feeling happy and settled. The only exception was I had heard nothing from St. Horatio.

Chapter Twelve
Sheila

Linda and Luke called me in late January. Once again they spent Christmas in Scotland with Luke's mother who was still holding strong and living on her own. They congratulated me on my divorce and I nearly fell off my chair.

"I have not had the divorce yet. Where did you hear that?"

"Laura, the whole island is talking about it. Are you sure?"

"Well I think if I was divorced I would be the first to know and I have been waiting for the call to attend court."

"Check it out with your lawyer. Luke was in the court house and said it was posted in early December to be heard. He can't remember what day it was but he is not mistaken, it was your case."

"Have you heard anything about Jim and Sheila?"

"Oh yes, we have heard plenty. We were having lunch at our favorite spot when Sheila came in alone. We invited her to join us. She was already drunk and I just kept filling her glass. The more she drank the more she talked and boasted about what she had – mainly your house Laura.

"Luke you know darn well she doesn't own my house. Who does she think she's kidding?"

"Well there's more to it than that my girl. She knows where you are and about Scoops. Someone is feeding her information and she's obsessed with you. She said Jim was madly in love with her and would give her anything she wanted and promised her the house once they got rid of you. She laughed at her own words and called Jim pathetic."

"Surely Luke you don't believe her. She crazy – everyone knows that and Jim is too if he can't see through her. Why would he promise her the house if it's not his to give away?"

"She is definitely crazy but I don't know about Jim. He seems to have disappeared – no one has seen him for some time."

"Laura let me give you a word of caution. I have worked with people like her before. She's psychotic and therefore dangerous. I'm trying to find out where Jim is and will let you know but in the meantime, watch your back. Someone is keeping this woman informed about you. I also know for a fact, something she herself confirmed after I heard it elsewhere; their meeting was no coincidence. Sheila targeted Jim. She knew you were leaving him and set out to snare him."

"Lots of women, especially her age, would leap at an opportunity to have a companion and a home. But remember she is a psychopath and a drunk and has a reputation. Jim wasn't the first man she went after. He's just the first man that fell for it when other slammed the door in her face and she's still looking for Jim's replacement."

"Then she will move on eventually."

"Not until she has been rewarded. Her type won't walk away with nothing. In her mind she believes she should be compensated for the time she has invested in Jim and her price is your house."

"Luke are you sure about all this?"

"Without a doubt my girl; she moved into your house three days after you left."

"Then she was seeing him while I was still there. I thought he was too happy for a man about to lose half of everything."

"Laura, I'm going to tell you something I probably shouldn't. Jim is naïve and needy. He's old and sick and doesn't want to be alone. I believe he sees Sheila for what she is but he chooses to have anything rather than nothing and because of that I am almost as worried about him as I am about you."

"Do you think he is in any danger?"

" ... "

My conversation with Luke had me worried and especially so when he didn't answer my last question. I wasn't sure what to think but now I remembered something that I had not given much though to at the time.

I had only been living in Calibishie a few days when a police officer came to see me. He had been assigned to the Portsmouth detachment when I had my troubles with Gavin and was transferred to Calibishie just a few days before I moved there.

He knew I was there and put his guard up when he took a call from a woman claiming to represent a law firm in the United States. She wanted to confirm the whereabouts of Laura Cassidy. When asked why, she said I was wanted in the U.S. for heavy debt and fraud.

The officer knew I was Canadian – not American and asked for the woman's name so he could call her back. She fumbled with the question and refused to give it. He then asked for the name of the firm she represented. Again she refused and promptly hung up. He claimed he gave her no information because that was police procedure until authenticity was verified. He also believed the call was suspicious from the onset. He was able to determine after the call terminated that it came from an island in the West Indies and not the U.S.

"Do you think Gavin is trying to find me?"

"No, he's a Dominican and could find out whatever he wanted by having someone look for you. That would be very easy to do here."

"Then what do you think it was about?"

"I'm not sure and we have nothing to go on. I just wanted to let you know and thought maybe you could shed some light on it."

"I don't have a clue. I have never done any business at all in the United States so that was definitely bogus but other than Gavin I can't imagine who would go to such lengths to find me."

Just be careful Laura. Something is going on and it's not Gavin. He will never hurt you again."

"How can you be so sure about that?"

"We will deal with him our way. He's already had one shake down and if it's necessary we will deal with him more severely next time, if there is a next time. Not everything is settled in court."

"What do you mean?"

"It's best we don't discuss this any further Laura."

Not long after my conversation with Luke, four immigration officers arrived at my door at dawn. I was still in my night gown when I answered my door. They wanted to check my passport and immigration stamps. All was in order and they left but not before telling me they received an anonymous tip I was in the country illegally. I walked to the local station to let the officer know and then called Luke.

It took a while before I put two and two together and there was no proof it was Sheila but as Luke pointed out; she could have had someone else make the calls. He was convinced she was behind it but to what end remained a mystery to us both or he wasn't willing to tell me what he was thinking.

Ms. Cartier assured me the divorce had not been called when I finally reached her in March. I asked her to check it out anyway. Selina had reported the same rumor and this was no coincidence. I never heard back from the lawyer.

Chapter Thirteen
Ms. Cartier

Ms. Cartier was not a good lawyer. She never responded to my calls or e-mails and when I didn't hear from her again after we did speak, I assumed the rumors were false. My cross petition could not be ignored – she had to know what she was doing. Divorces are not that complicated.

Three months later on June 17th her assistant called me to advise I had to be in court on the 19th for the hearing. I flew to St. Horatio the following day.

From the airport I went directly to Ms. Cartier's office where she awaited my arrival. After reviewing my petition she assured me the hearing would be a walk in the park. I was instructed to meet her the next morning at the courthouse at 8:45.

I arrived at the courthouse on schedule only to find my lawyer not there. Two minutes before court was called to order, a harried Ms. Cartier literally ran into the courtroom. When she opened her briefcase, the contents scattered over the floor.

She was flushed when she quickly came over to where I was sitting.

"Laura, I'm so sorry but I just learned that the rumors you heard were accurate. Today's hearing is Jim's application for the decree absolute. You don't even need to be here."

I wanted to rip her throat out

"I'm not leaving because there were two divorce petitions and mine hasn't been before the court yet.

We were the first case heard and called into chambers for the hearing. Mr. Henry, Jim's lawyer and his two assistants were the only ones present other than myself and Ms. Cartier.

"Mrs. Cassidy's presence is not required for this hearing Your Honor. The divorce has been already been granted to my client."

"Your Honor, Mrs. Cassidy cross petitioned the divorce and has not had her side heard before the court. We were not advised of the hearing held on December 8th."

"You lie Ms. Cartier. You were in court that morning – we discussed the case that was to be heard within minutes. You were served with notice of the hearing by the courts and by my office and you could have checked the schedule posted on the courtroom wall. I watched you pack up your briefcase and leave the court minutes after we spoke and you did not return."

Well that statement explained the rumors I was hearing. Any member of the community could check the court schedule that was posted in the administration offices.

Ms. Cartier vehemently denied any knowledge of the hearing and didn't recall having any such conversation with Mr. Henry.

I couldn't believe what I was hearing and felt pity for Ms. Cartier as she continued to make a fool of herself. She was incompetent and I was likely going to pay the price for it.

The judge denied Jim's application and asked if I wanted to have my petition dealt with then and there. I said no – not at this time. I was so angry and confused and needed to know how this could have happened, what damage may have been done to my case and whether or not Ms. Cartier was capable of properly representing my interests.

In the court garden afterwards, I challenged her. Again she denied having any knowledge about the divorce. When I reminded her that I had specifically asked her to check in March, her cheeks flushed as she claimed having no recollection of my request. She swore she would get to the bottom of it. Her assistants might have received and misplaced the documents. I knew she was covering her ass, but I didn't want to beat her to death in a public park outside the courthouse.

What a waste of time and money. I had come to St. Horatio for nothing and now was stuck here until this matter was settled. I couldn't afford such luxury and had no place to stay. My return ticket was for two days hence and now that would cost me as well to change it.

I decided to take a trip to my house to have a little chat with Jim. There was no reason why he should not talk to me and I certainly needed some answers. I couldn't blame him for the mess up but he did know of the cross petition and I suspected his lawyer took advantage of my lawyer's incompetence. There was more to this than a divorce. There was property to be dealt with and that appeared to have been swept under the carpet. Conspiracy was in the air. I had to rely on my own resources and be the client, the attorney, the detective and God only knew what else if I wanted to come out of this alive.

Two cars were parked in front when I arrived. One was Jim's and mine, the other I assumed was Sheila's. No one answered after several knocks but I knew they were there. I walked to the back veranda and knocked on the inside French doors and again no response. The TV was on in the bedroom and the bed unmade - It was only 10 a.m. There were no signs of activity and I could see clearly into almost every room from the many windows on the veranda. The only suspicious observation was the closed door to the office.

I called his name.

"Jim, don't be such a coward. You have to talk to me sooner or later. I own half this house. Let me in."

Keeping my eyes on the inside of the house, I sat on the sofa and lit a cigarette. This new bad habit would send Jim off his rocker. Hopefully the offensive smell would lure him from his hiding place.

More than an hour passed when at last I saw the office door open a crack. Thinking it was Jim, I said:

"I see you Jim, don't be such a coward. Let me in so we can talk."

Sheila came through the door looking like something the cat dragged in. Her hair was in disarray; she was ghostly pale and was wearing a ragged looking T-shirt nightgown. Her breasts sagged almost to her waist – she was sweating profusely.

Slowly as if she was in a trance, she walked toward the French doors but stopped five feet short.

"Open the door Sheila; I want to talk to my husband."

She shrugged her shoulders in the gesture of not knowing.

"I know he's in there, open up now or I will break in."

Again the same gesture with no words

"Back away from the door Sheila."

She stood there mute and made no effort to move away from the door. I picked up a heavy metal vase and swung to the opposite door away from the French doors that led to the kitchen. I didn't want to hurt her – my business was with Jim, not her.

The window pane closest to the handle broke easily. I reached in and opened the door and entered my house.

Sheila continued to remain standing in the same spot while I went from room to room looking for Jim. He wasn't there. I demanded to know where Jim was and again she only made stupid body gestures but never uttered a word. I sat down on the sofa and advised her I was not moving a muscle until I had some answers.

She went into the bedroom closing the door behind her. I heard her speaking which could only mean she was using the telephone. When she reappeared five minutes later she was dressed. She sat on the chair opposite to where I was now sitting and spoke for the first time.

"Jim's not here. He's in the hospital in Canada."

"How long has he been in the hospital? What is wrong with him?"

"I don't know."

"Don't give me that crap Sheila. What are you doing in my house?"

"I'm in charge."

"Pack your things Sheila and get out. This is my house and if Jim's not here then I will be the one in charge."

A commotion at the front door brought Sheila to her feet as she ran to allow entry to two police officers. Mr. Jacob Sylvester, Superintendent of Police and his deputy were both dressed in full uniform. They came into the great room where I was sitting

I sat quietly as Sheila took Mr. Sylvester, a man of admirable presence, by the arm and led him to the kitchen where she pointed to the broken glass and the door where I had gained entry. Again she did not say a word to the officer – only pointed.

He came into the room where I was sitting and asked:

"Why did you break the window?"

"This is my house and I can break whatever I want."

"You are Jim's wife Laura."

"Yes sir I am and this woman refused to let me in so I had no alternative."

He put out his hand to shake mine and introduce himself and then he asked Sheila to join us in the grouping of chairs where I was sitting. His deputy stood off to the side. He turned to me as if he wanted further information to which I complied.

"I was in court this morning and surprised Jim was not there. I came her speak with him and was refused entry. Sheila has informed me that Jim is in the hospital in Canada and that is all I know. I asked her to leave but she doesn't appear willing to do that."

He then turned to Sheila.

"Why would you refuse entry to Mrs. Cassidy when you know she owns this house?"

"Jim left me in charge."

"When is he expected back?"

She shrugged.

"How long has he been gone?"

"Seven months."

"Mrs. Cassidy has asked you to leave and she has that right."

"He left me in charge and I'm not leaving."

My patience was nearing the end. I told Mr. Sylvester I wanted Sheila removed from my house immediately. He turned and asked her to leave. She repeated she was not leaving.

"Jim cannot refuse access to his wife and given he is not here, she has every right to assume responsibility for the house. I will take you to a friend or a hotel."

Sheila got up and went into the bedroom to use the phone. Several minutes later she summoned Superintendant Sylvester to come to the phone to speak to Jim. When he returned he presented Jim's offer to me to stay in a hotel at his expense for the night until things could be sorted out.

I refused and asked the officer to remove Sheila immediately now that she had a hotel paid for by Jim.

She responded with the now familiar shrug, a hand gesture and a cynical grin.

"My loyalties are to Jim. He left me in charge and I'm not leaving. He has offered to put his wife up in a hotel at his expense and if she doesn't want to accept that she can go to hell."

Mr. Sylvester stood up and asked me to join him on the pool veranda for a private talk. When Sheila attempted to follow us, he very firmly told her to remain with the other officer until we were finished. He gestured to the officer to keep her at a distance from us.

Once we were seated on the veranda I told him I was not leaving my house and demanded he remove her physically if he had to. He agreed that I was within my rights but he wanted me to hear him out first.

Until the day I die, I will believe this was a turning point in my life. If I had not listened to the officer, things would have turned out quite differently. I have always respected the police and have had, on occasion, called on them for help and was never disappointed. This was my first encounter with the law in St. Horatio. My experience wit the law in Dominica was a fiasco and a disappointment. But Mr. Sylvester was nothing like the officers I dealt with there. His position alone dictated compliance and respect and until he proved unworthy of either, I was willing to give him both.

"May I call you Laura?"

"Please do."

"Trust me Laura. I want you to leave the house with me. I will bring you back tomorrow morning with your luggage but for now, it is best you leave."

"You must be joking. Why would I leave my own house? I have no place to stay and can't afford a hotel and I won't let Jim have his way here."

I was emotional and angry and saw he was trying to calm me by chatting with me. We covered many things before I felt calmed down but not before I told him why I left Jim and the events leading up to my arrival at my house.

"That sound all pretty sneaky on everyone's part and you have been railroaded from the sounds of it but it is the courts now that will have to sort it out."

"Laura, as a personal favor to me, come away with me now. We will find you a place to stay for one night and I will bring you back first thing in the morning."

"I don't like this one bit and why should I do you a favor?"

"Is there someone you can call?"

"Yes my friend Selina but why should I?"

"Let's get you settled. I have unfinished business here but I need you settled first. I will come see you tonight and explain more."

Reluctantly I left with the officers and watched Sheila gloat as we made our exit. This was ludicrous and I felt this cop better know what he was doing or I would have his head.

He drove me to Selina's place after I called her to let her know I was coming. She was on the way to the airport and left the keys for me. Mr. Sylvester and I exchanged cell phone numbers before he left me with a promise to return later with more information.

At 9 p.m. he arrived at Selina's place. His appearance was quite unlike the official uniform I had met earlier. He was wearing a red knit muscle shirt and shorts which revealed more muscle than I have ever seen on one man. His head was shaved and he was gorgeous. He was perhaps in his late forties and was as gentle as a lamb with the presence of a lion.

He accepted a glass of wine and sat on the sofa. I prayed he was worthy of my trust. Little did either of us know just how much my life was hanging by a thread and it would be a matter of a few months before he became my protector, a good friend and the man who kept me alive.

"Call me Jacob when I'm not in uniform Laura."

"I promised you an explanation and now I'm going to give you one. Sheila was very drunk this morning and I had to get you out of there."

"That is a lousy excuse Jacob Sir. Why didn't you arrest her? She was the trespasser and with Jim gone seven months, she has no rights at all where my house is concerned. Jim can't dictate what he wants when we both own the house."

"I agree with you. Jim is totally under her influence and has a relationship with her. You have been off the island for a long time. You can't deny he had the right to re-build his life."

"I'm actually happy for Jim to have found someone else even though I think his choice was poor. I should not have left the house this morning Jacob. She was the one who should have been removed."

"She would have returned and likely much drunker and you would have been alone on top of a mountain with no vehicle. Even if you managed to call the police it would take too much time over the mountain road to get to you."

"How did you get there so fast this morning? Were sitting in the back driveway waiting for the call?"

Laughing - "No, I just happened to be in the area."

"What you are saying Jacob is not an acceptable explanation. The green jeep in the front of the house still belongs to me and Jim. You could have taken the keys from her. I would not have been stranded. If she did return drunk, I would have dealt with it. I ran a bar for a few months in Dominica. I'm sure I could have handled little old lady."

"No Laura, you would not have been able to handle Sheila. I know her – you don't and I don't say these words lightly."

"Jacob you had several good reasons to take her out of my house this morning. Why didn't you?"

"She didn't commit any crime and was only doing what Jim asked her to do. If she had committed a criminal act I would have arrested her in a minute, but she hadn't and calculated such into her plan. Sheila is very cunning - even when she's drunk."

I'm trying to be fair to all parties Laura and I spoke to Jim myself as you know. He didn't want Sheila removed from the house and I had to take his wishes into consideration and come to a temporary solution almost instantly. I think I've done the right thing here. You will be back in your house tomorrow."

"And she will still be there unless Jim says it is o-k to put her out. Are you prepared to remover her based on what I want or are you a politician looking to keep everyone at bay?"

"I was aware Sheila was living in the house. She was the one who called me to arrange to have all the locks changed shortly after you left. She told me she was the housekeeper and had Jim's authorization to make changes. I saw him later that same day and he confirmed he had given her permission."

I tried to talk to him in private which is not easy with Sheila around. That's how she operates – keep him away from those who might influence him and there are many on this island who have tried to get to Jim for exactly that reason and with no success."

"I am still concerned for Jim. He has no idea what Sheila is capable of and has played right into her hands by leaving her in charge of everything. He could have any number of people look after the house for him during his absence but he chose Sheila and he had every right to do what he wanted even if the rest of us didn't like it.."

"This woman is no stranger to me. Many times the police were called to her home when she was married to Dr. Sturgess. I barely knew Jim but was concerned. I waited for an opportunity to see him alone and did when I saw Sheila go into the beauty salon in town. That's usually good for an hour.

"How was Jim when you saw him alone?"

"He seemed o-k physically. I told him I was checking the locks. He offered me a bottle of water and walked around with me. I couldn't reveal to him what I knew about Sheila and I don't think he would have listened anyway. I spent a good hour with him and tried to caution him on letting Sheila have too much authority over his home."

"Jim did say things like she was already costing him a lot of money with all the changes she wanted done and buying things he didn't need or want. I got the impression he was concerned about that."

"Jim shouldn't let her do that. Already I noticed all the colors have been changed. That house was just painted less than a year ago and didn't need new paint. She's putting her own stamp on things. She's not the housekeeper Jacob so why the pretense?"

"I believe that is Sheila's doing, not Jims and I'm not sure why."

"I think I might know the reason. Some friends told me Sheila was still looking for Mr. Right with lots of money. She would have to conceal that she was anything more than an employee of Jim's."

"That is quite possible Laura. When I visited Jim, it was you he talked about most. He missed you Laura and was still angry over losing you."

"That's a load of crap Jacob. Jim practically drove me out and has been up to no good it seems since I left. I heard Sheila moved in only a few days after I left. That hardly sounds as though he was pining away for me."

"I know what you're saying but we all make mistakes and maybe he regretted those final months or weeks with you. Anger makes us act badly and time makes us see our mistakes. I think also Jim is the type of man who can't be alone. Some men are like that."

"Jacob you have hit the nail on the head. Jim has replaced the women in his life with the bat of an eye and then finds himself in the wrong relationship. What you say is true and I think Sheila had that figured out from the start."

"You and Jim might have reconciled Laura. You made a mistake going with Gavin but it appears you got yourself out of that quickly for which I am very glad."

"Jim and I would not have reconciled. My life was hell with him and he was impotent after the honeymoon and remained that way. I would not have come back to him."

"Are you telling me you and Jim had no sex throughout your marriage?"

"None - absolutely nada and Gavin was the first and only man I was with since marrying Jim."

With eyebrows raised "This puts an entirely different perspective on the situation and now I am very concerned."

"Why would that information give you more concern?"

"It confirms what it is Sheila wants."

"I could have told you what she wants Jacob. She wants to live in luxury and spend Jim's money."

"Yes, that is part of it but not all."

"Am I missing something here Jacob?"

"She wants your house Laura."

True to his promise, Jacob picked me up the next morning. We arrived to find Sheila a totally different woman from the previous day. She was wearing a very short black mini summer dress, high heels, too much make up, plenty of jewelry and was sober.

She greeted us with the arrogance of queen of the manor – laughing and joking with Jacob in too friendly a manner for my tastes. They were more familiar with each other than the previous day but then she was drunk and he was had a deputy with him. Sheila called him by his first name and kept touching him on the arm or back when she spoke to him. Jacob did not seem uncomfortable or embarrassed with her behavior. Was this an act put on for my benefit?

There were no signs of Sheila preparing to leave my house and Jacob did not bring the subject up. She was polite to me and told me I could use the guestroom. I waited for Jacob to say something but nothing was forthcoming.

Jacob was out the door when I returned from putting my things in the guest room. I wasn't happy with his sudden departure and here I was now sharing space with Sheila. I phoned him for an explanation and guidance on what to do now.

"Laura this is a matter for the courts. Talk to your lawyer and get the ball rolling. There is nothing I can do about this situation but I will take care of you. I don't want you to eat or drink anything in that house."

"Well I don't have the keys to the car so how am I supposed to eat?"

"I will call you later and take you out for something and we can decide how we are going to keep you fed after that."

Ms. Cartier was unavailable when I tried to contact her and it was now going into the weekend. I had to think this through. Why would Jacob warn me not to eat or drink anything? There was only one answer to that.

I came to St. Horatio to attend a court hearing – nothing more. It was never my plan to take over my house. Finding Jim ill and in Canada was unexpected. He had every right to have a person of his choice living with him and I had no business interfering with this, but given his lengthy absence, I should have the right to re-claim what was mine.

Finding Sheila should not have upset me but it did. Perhaps it was her behavior upon my arrival and Jacob Sylvester really didn't help my situation much and I wasn't sure what his agenda was. Was I right or wrong to want to take my house back when I found she had been living in it for several months alone while I was struggling in Dominica?

What if Jim didn't return? She could not stay in my house if Jim was dead and did his long absence indicate his illness was serious. Sheila claimed she did not know much about his problems but she was not telling the truth. Was that a cover up to protect herself?

I had no choice but to stay where I was until I made contact with my lawyer and I wasn't sure what to make of the Superintendant of Police. Whose side was he on?

With little choice in the matter I settled into the guest room, grabbed a book from the library and went out to the pool. Sheila couldn't have been more accommodating – treating me like a visiting relative. It was Friday and I had a long miserable weekend ahead of me with her for company.

I spent the day around my pool reading. If I didn't eat something soon, I was going to pass out. Had I known this would be how my day would be I would have chowed down before arriving. I prayed Jacob would not forget me.

Around 4 p.m. Sheila left without the house without saying a word and returned two hours later with Jim.

Using a walker he shuffled his way to the pool veranda where I now sitting. Upon entering his opening remark, delivered with considerable sarcasm was:

"We are divorced sweetie."

The shock of seeing him so feeble left me speechless. Sheila must have known he was arriving and I suspected Jacob did as well. That explained why he dropped me off and left so quickly earlier in the day.

"I'm afraid not Jimmie. You should talk to your lawyer more often - your motion for absolute was denied."

The shock of my retort had a visible affect on him but even more so on Sheila. Both stood speechless before Jim finally laughed and sat down beside me and asked how I was doing.

Sheila was in her element calling him darling and honey to which I had a response.

"Nice talk for the housekeeper"

With a red face she retreated to the kitchen to prepare something to eat. Crackers, smoked canned salmon spread and juice was the best she could offer Jim, who was probably starving and would never have accepted that as a meal if I was the one in an apron. I could touch nothing and sat with my tummy rumbling.

Sheila talked non stop when we were all seated on the veranda sofa. She reported on her children and grandchildren and all that she planned to have done to _her_ house or had already had done to _her_ house. I watched her body language more than I heard her words.

She reminded me of she-wolf – taking every opportunity to establish her territory. It wouldn't have surprised me if she urinated on the various pieces of furniture as she pointed out to Jim what had been re-upholstered or was about to be. Ignoring her was easy for me and from the responses coming from Jim, he was ignoring her too. Every sentence began with I or My.

Jim was a very knowledgeable man in so many ways. He was highly educated, well read and wise. However he lacked in areas that dealt with human behavior. I was always an open book and wore my heart and head on my sleeve. I never lied. I loved life and people and gave my all to whatever I set my mind to. He admired those qualities in me and often said I was unique and he was proud of my passion for life.

He had a good relationship with his children now and for this he gave me credit for bringing a broken family together again. We had many people come and go in our life and thought nothing of giving someone a place to stay with us when they had troubles. Our kitchen was a hub of activity at all times and our workers shared many meals with us at the family table.

As I sat there watching and listening to Sheila, I could not help but wonder what happened to Jim. This was not a person he would have been attracted to and would have in fact, not welcomed her into our home if I was the one who introduced her. Why couldn't he see what was going on?

Jim had a Master's degree in psychology but that only meant he aced his exams to earn the degree. He was also an ordained minister and yet when his children grieved over the death of their mother, he had nothing to offer them in terms of healing support. Maybe this explained why Sheila was getting away with what she was and why I never really knew the man I once wanted to spend the rest of my life with.

Jim tired of listening to Sheila and let her know it. I had never known him to be rude to anyone and what he was now doing was beyond poor manners. She irritated him – in fact I thought he didn't even like her at times. If I hadn't been sitting there, I'm sure they would have had an argument.

Jim wanted to talk to me – to learn how my life had been over the past several months. I chose to believe he cared and gave him honest answers to his many questions. I had no designs on reuniting with him and was no threat to Sheila but that was not how she was seeing the situation.

My life was not what I wanted it to be and I worried about my future. Nothing had worked out for me since I left St. Horatio and here I was now a guest in my own home and not liking what I was feeling. Jim and I were always good at communication – both of us appreciated the knowledge of the other. But now that Sheila was part of the equation and given the sneaky way in which he removed our house from the market, obtained a divorce and was about to have it finalized – all without my knowledge; I had to wonder if he wasn't a good match for Sheila after all.

Jim knew a great deal about my life in Dominica – information I had not shared with him. When he asked me about Scoops, I was totally taken aback.

"How did you know about my ice cream parlor Jim"

"Sheila you told me. How did you know?"

"I can't remember Jim. I heard it somewhere on the island."

She was lying and she knew I knew it. It went totally over Jim's head. The more Jim and I talked, the more her body language spoke of defeat as she physically re-coiled as a snake would when the prey was taken away. She was very easy to read. I only wished Jim could see and feel what I did.

Shortly before nine he excused himself to retire. Sheila turned off the lights, locked the doors and went into the bedroom with him. I turned everything back on and phoned Jacob. I was hungry.

We agreed to meet at the top of the road. It was best they didn't know who I was seeing. I carried a knife as I walked in the dark to meet him. He didn't show surprise when he learned Jim was home which confirmed my suspicion he knew all along Jim was on his way. Jacob wanted us to sort it out ourselves, and I had no problem with that. This really wasn't a police matter and he did his best to keep the peace until Jim returned. But I didn't like being deceived the way I apparently was.

Jim never came out of his bedroom after that first night. Sheila took him a tray with coffee and muffins in the morning and at 4 o'clock made him a fruit smoothie in the blender. For a diabetic this seemed hardly healthy and nourishing for a man who needed good food to heal.

I saw Sheila for what she was over the next few days - a sneak and a liar. Jim was under her control and was either too weak, too stupid or didn't care enough to do anything about it. I witnessed her writing cheques from his book and taking cash from his wallet. She left the house at least once a day and came back tipsy and carrying a large metallic thermos that was filled with booze. I could smell it.

She schemed and played out her tricks on me. She started arguments and then ran crying to Jim that I was doing this or that and it displeased her. I never heard his comments but I did hear her fake crying and tell him lies one after the other.

Two weeks passed and I still could not reach my lawyer. I wanted to speak with Jim to get a few things settled so I could get on my way home but Sheila prevented that from happening. Jim was always sleeping or not feeling well. It was all crap and I should have just burst into that room and demanded his attention but I didn't. I honestly believed he was where he chose to be because he was happy but I should have been more aggressive and taken matters into my own hands. I will forever regret that I didn't.

I overheard her refer to the house as hers too many times and enlightened her as to the joint ownership and watched her turn pale. Even with a divorce, the property would remain jointly owned until it sold and I was more than willing to split it with Jim. If one of us died in the interim, the survivor would own the house exclusively and only then. Now I knew what her agenda was.

"What do you mean you still own the house? It belongs to Jim. You deserted him.

"No I didn't desert him Sheila. Our separation was a mutual decision and it wouldn't matter if I did desert him, I still own the house jointly with Jim.

Sheila's mother was reputed to have befriended three frail elderly and very wealthy men. Her foothold into their lives was gained by becoming their housekeeper/caregiver just as Sheila was now presenting herself with Jim. In each case she eventually married all three men who died within months of the nuptials leaving the widow with everything. Sheila's mistake - one her mother never made, was going after a man with a living wife.

She grabbed a glass from my hand as I was filling it from the fridge dispenser:

"That's my glass."

I walked to the stove where she was cooking chicken for her dogs and turned it off and took another glass from the shelf – turned to Sheila and said:

"This is my kitchen."

When it was necessary for me to leave the house I planted dental floss and strands of my own hair around the door knob to my room. Each time I returned I found my traps sprung. She kept keys to every room on her person at all times, including my room. When I asked for keys to the outer doors, she only laughed.

My bathroom had a Jacuzzi tub which I longed to use. My routine has always been to enter the tub, then turn on the motor. I was about to do so when the hair on the back of my neck stood up and my flesh became prickly. I altered my routine and switched the Jacuzzi on first. It shorted out.

I reported this and many other bizarre incidents to Jacob. His concern was mounting and with his encouragement I tried to find another lawyer.

My friends kept me supplied with packaged foods that I prepared in the microwave and ate in my room. I didn't want to be around Sheila under any circumstances and Jim had yet to come out of his room. When in town, I treated myself to a decent meal, often paid for by one of my friends.

After several attempts to replace Ms. Cartier it became abundantly clear no other lawyer was willing to take my case once they learned of Sheila's involvement. She was well known on the island after having gone through several lawyers herself, none of whom ever received their fee. I was stuck with Ms. Cartier.

A very angry gardener arrived unexpectedly one afternoon. He was in a roar over money owed to him. Sheila was in the bedroom with Jim when she overheard me talking to him. I knew the man who was happy to see me and with a gleam in his eye asked if I had come home to stay. From the window she yelled before proceeding to come down.

"I'll take care of this Laura. He's my gardener now."

I seized the moment and went into the room where Jim was laying with his back to the door. I could hear Sheila outside fighting with the man and refusing to pay. He angrily told her he wasn't leaving until she did. She threatened to call the police if he didn't leave the property. He handed her his cell phone.

"Hi, Sweetie" Jim said when her heard me come in.

Believing he thought I was Sheila returning, I told him it was me but it wasn't necessary

"You are the only sweetie in my life Laura."

"May I sit with you for a while Jim?

He looked terrible and said he felt terrible. The noise coming from the ground below was upsetting him.

"I have to listen to this all the time. She fights with everyone and they all hate her."

"Why do you put up with her Jim? If you owe the man money then pay him. For God's sake these people work hard and deserve their wages."

"I have no problem paying anyone. Sheila has the money for him but she's a greedy woman and screws everyone but when it's my money, I don't like it."

I came around to sit on the side of the bed close to him. He told me the gangrene in his leg was an on-going threat. Several toes had been amputated while he was in Canada and he feared he would lose his leg soon.

"Well Jim, you never were a good dancer anyway and losing the leg is a lot better than losing your life."

"Laura, you always see the sunshine. I have missed that so much."

"So what happens now Jim?

"I honestly don't know sweetie. They have had me in an experimental program that kept me in Canada for several months. Look at what she's done to this house. I didn't even recognize it when I got back. You had this place looking so nice and now these ghastly colors on the walls and all her crap everywhere. The things I treasured like Mom's trunk that you had sanded and re-varnished has just disappeared. When I question where things are she says you must have taken it and I know you didn't"

I can't move freely in this dam house now with this bad leg for fear I'll knock something over and she's on my back all the time about being careful"

"What is going to happen with this procedure now?"

"We won't know if it worked for a few months." him.

"Is that all that's troubling you Jim? What are we going to do about our house?"

He didn't answer me.

"Jim you should not have come back – you should have stayed and finished with your treatment and waited there for the results. Things here will work out eventually. I only came because I thought the divorce was being heard and then I came up here to see you. I was never told about the hearing in December. My lawyer doesn't know what she's doing and I was frightened."

"I was shocked to see the changes in the house and Sheila was shit faced drunk at ten in the morning when I arrived. It didn't make me feel good at all to hear her claim it was her house now, she was in charge and ordering me out like an intruder. This is still my home too Jim."

"Laura, I don't know what to say. I didn't know you were coming and I don't know what would have happened differently if I did."

"Jim, let's just forget it for now and get you well. You look terrible but on the night you arrived you looked really good. Are you taking sleeping pills or sedatives? Your eyes are glazed and the pupils are dilated. You jeopardized your health to come home to this nonsense."

I'm not taking anything like that Laura. We both know I can't with my other medications and I wouldn't take that stuff anyway."

"Jim, do you think Sheila could be giving you something like a sedative without your knowledge?" I've never seen you like this before – even when you had your surgery.

"How could she? She doesn't make meals for me."

"She brings you a fruit smoothie every afternoon and in the morning you drink coffee she makes."

I started to cry and for a brief moment he held me in his arms. I was crying for him. How could I help him now with her in the house?

"Jim I made a mistake by leaving you. All I can say now is I'm sorry to have put you through this."

"I'm sorry to honey but the damage is done now isn't it?"

At that moment Sheila came barging into the room.

"Well isn't this cozy. Get out Laura. I'm taking care of Jim and he needs his rest."

When Jim made no attempt to counter command her, I left the room but of one thing I was absolutely certain - she was drugging him.

When Sheila finally emerged from the room I was waiting for her.

"I'm not even going to ask Sheila because you're a fucking liar and I have my answer already. You won't get away with it, and read my lips if you don't want to hear my roar. This is not your house and it never will be. Jim and I own it jointly. When it sells, we each get half and that won't be enough for you. Start looking for another man while you still can and if anything happens to Jim, I will promise you one thing girl. I will come after you."

Jim overheard my conversation with Sheila but made no attempt to leave his bed. I wanted desperately for him to take a stand even if he had to yell from his bed but nothing came out of him. He was weak and frightened for his life. For that I could only feel compassion for him but how was I to help him?

I went to see Jacob. The least I could do was tell him of my suspicions and set off a few alarm bells.

"Jacob, if his doctor did a simple blood test we could find out if she is giving him something. I went to see the man before I came here and he practically threw me out of his office, but you could talk to him please. He hasn't been out of that bed in almost three weeks. I don't think he has a clue what she's up to."

Jim came out of his room the next day – dressed nicely and alert. He wasn't drugged but I still believed he had been and wasn't going to give up on him just yet. They went to town to do some errands. Now why didn't Sheila take care of this herself?

I went to town myself to do some business of my own. Jacob wasn't in his office when I dropped in and he wasn't answering his cell phone. I topped up my own phone, had something to eat and arrived for my scheduled appointment with Ms. Cartier. We had spoken earlier in the day and agreed to meet in her office at 3 p.m. I waited for over an hour and once again she didn't appear and couldn't be reached.

I arrived home to find Jim and Sheila drinking juice on the veranda. Jim was totally alert having just recently returned from town. He greeted me warmly and asked me to join him. Sheila was even more smug than usual – something that caught my immediate attention.

We remained on the veranda for some time. It was good to see Jim in good spirits and alert but Sheila was jovial to the point of being high which kept distracting me. Had she been drinking and maybe still was with something in her glass of juice?

Again she prepared no dinner for him but kept replenishing his glass of juice. He waved her off saying he had enough and would be up all night peeing if he drank more, but she persisted. I watched Jim with the eye of an eagle. She wanted him to drink the juice and finally he gulped it and slammed his glass on the table..

"Are you happy now Mommy?"

Within minutes Jim changed. His pupils dilated, his eyelids grew heavy and his head started bobbing around. Sheila helped him up to take him to his bed.

"Did you give him a double dose in the juice Sheila?"

She laughed like a hyena.

I heard nothing back from Jacob and was too depressed and worried to call him again. Sleep escaped me for the entire night. I had to do something to help Jim. How could a grown and intelligent man be so blind?

I called former friends the next day but not a soul wanted to get involved. With some I pleaded but got nowhere. Many had tried, as I was told by a few, to visit Jim when they first learned Sheila had moved into the house. They were not successful to even reach Jim by phone because Sheila never let them speak with him. Several men came to the house to see him but were denied access by Sheila once again. They eventually gave up and forgot about Jim.

Chapter Fourteen
Lionel Sturgess

Nervously I made one last call to Sheila's former husband, Dr. Lionel Sturgess. I didn't know the man at all and wouldn't blame him if he hung up on me. From what I heard about the troubles he had before divorcing her, I suspected the last thing he would want was to have any further involvement in anything concerning her – but I had to try.

"Hello Dr. Sturgess, I'm sorry to bother you but I was hoping to have a few minutes of your time. I am in a situation and at my wit's end and reaching for any available straw. My name is Laura Cassidy."

"Laura Cassidy – I know who you are. What can I do for you?"

"If it's not too much of an inconvenience could we meet for a coffee?"

We met the following afternoon at a small restaurant near the ferry dock in town. Dr. Sturgess was still wearing his scrubs but I recognized him from church. He greeted me warmly and ordered two coffees.

"I cleared the rest of my day Laura. What's on your mind?"

"I recognize you from church but I had no idea you were Sheila's ex husband."

Dr. Sturgess was a tall good looking man with thick white hair. He exuded warmth – I was immediately at ease with him and found it difficult to conceive he was once married to Sheila. Like a race horse, I came flying out of the gate.

"I don't know what to do Dr. Sturgess. I didn't know where to turn. I've been to the police and called people Jim and I once associated with and even tried to see his doctor. I went to see Father Antonio but no one seems to care. I'm sure she's drugging him. I've only seen him once in nearly three weeks and the three of us are in the same house together. She's a nasty greedy woman and Jim doesn't have a clue what's going on. I don't know if it's his illness, the drugs she's giving him or..."

"Slow down Laura and call me Lionel."

He took my hand and ordered two beers.

"Take your time Laura and start at the beginning Laura – I'm here to help you if I can."

Lionel laughed when I finished telling him my life story. I wanted him to hear all there was to know about me from my own mouth and I didn't want him to think I as a flake or anything like his former wife. My concern was solely for Jim and that message was sincere.

"I was glad when the gossip turned to you. That's how it works here – they chew on smut like vultures but that's entertainment on a small island. Then when the next one comes along they forget the one before it. We're all sinners in one way or another so I wouldn't worry about it if I were you. You took the heat off me so I should be grateful but I know hard this has been for you."

He handed me a napkin to mop up the tears running down my face.

"Of course I heard all the rumors about you Laura as did everyone else but when Sheila moved in with Jim not long after you left the island, people began to re-think their opinion of you. Many people from the church told me you were a very nice lady and I can see for myself they were right. You made a mistake Laura when you chose to run off with the wrong man but you had good reason from what you have told me. Who gives a dam what other people think? They didn't live with Jim and it's none of anyone's business. Your mistake is worthy of forgiveness but you don't need that from me or anyone else. You have to forgive yourself, if there is anything to forgive, and I don't think there is other than poor taste in your choice of men - that's all that matters."

"I'm going to tell you about my life with Sheila. Tit for tat – you told me your story so now I will tell you mine. At least it will give you a perspective of what you're up against. I meant it when I said I would help you in any way and you are going to need help from anyone willing to give it to you. By the time I'm finished you will need a lot more napkins."

"I was with that bitch for close to 20 years and it was a living hell. Sheila is a no good worthless drunk who uses men to get what she wants. She's a pathological liar, devious beyond hell and she will get rid of anything that gets in her way. She tried to kill me more than once and I couldn't' begin to count how many times police were called to my home because of her drunken rages.

"Why did you stay with her all those years Lionel?"

"The absolute truth is she was terrific in bed and I'm a horny old fart. What healthy man walks away from that easily? But even that wasn't enough to justify living in hell after a while."

"Sheila is an alcoholic . I didn't see it in the beginning because we were both heavy drinkers but then she got to the point where she couldn't stop until she dropped. I knew she was in trouble and tried to help her but then she started closet drinking and chewing gum was the give away. She chews her gum like a cow chews its cud. Have you noticed her chewing gum? Whenever I see her driving her car or bump into her at the supermarket, I always notice the gum and then I run like hell because that's a dead give away she's been drinking."

"You're so right. She's always chewing gum."

"Of course she is and she also carries a large thermos type mug with a lid on it. The only one she's fooling is herself. The mug is supposed to send the message there is coffee in it. Have you seen that at all?"

"Yes, when she leaves the house she comes back with it. I thought it was coffee and wondered where she could get a decent cup of coffee on this island."

"You can't get a decent cup of coffee on this island and she doesn't drink it anyway – she never has. I know the place she goes to get her tank filled. It's on the beach not far from Sunshine's. I think he threw her out of there long ago and this new place will take a while before they toss her out on her ass too. Everyone on the island jokes about her coffee mug."

"Tell me about how you met her and your life before she came along."

"We met back in the states where I had my first practice. I was married with a family and I thought I was happy at the time, and then she came along. Sheila was quite beautiful in those days and was like a size zero with great boobs. Before I knew what hit me I was in bed with her. She chased me – came into my office almost daily and wouldn't let up until I finally lost my family. I suspect she had a lot more to do with that than I was aware of at the time. My first wife still won't speak to me to this day and because of Sheila I lost contact with my kids and my sister. Everyone tried to warn me about her but I was too in lust to listen."

"What I don't understand Lionel is why Jim puts up with it. He is very anti drinking and if I even got the slightest bit tipsy, he was on my case about it."

"That's why she's giving him his a daily dose of happy juice. Once she starts drinking she doesn't stop until she passes out or someone ties her down and she does stupid and dangerous things when she's a conscious zombie."

"She was been dried out a few times - in treatment centers but she never volunteered to go. I threatened her with divorce if she didn't get herself cleaned up and her kids also pushed her in a paid the fees to get her well. She came out dry every time but what choice did she have? As soon as she was back at home she started drinking again but she also had another addiction that she picked up at these rehab centers – barbiturates."

"Why would a clinic give her drugs when she is an addictive personality? My first job out of college was with the Addiction Research Foundation in Ontario. I know a little about this sort of thing and to give barbiturates to an alcoholic is unheard of."

"You're not telling me what I don't already know but I wasn't with her in the rehab center and don't know what went down there. I had no contact with her when she was confined and I was not in communication with the medical staff. The first time she was in I called to find out how she was. They had no record of her until we established she was there under another name. When I told them I was her husband and wanted information, they refused because she claimed on her admission papers, she wasn't married."

"How does she get pills now?"

"Your guess is as good as mine Laura but I think it would be very easy here. When we were still together I did discover she was taking some from my own dispensary but I quickly moved them to another location and secured them. She probably gets them from the states when she goes back for visits and has several doctors here who keep her supplied. It's not their fault. This is a third world country without the technology we are used to from our own home territory. Nothing is cross reference and she would lie to any doctor to get what she wanted. Our medicine cabinet was full of more pills that I have in stock at the office. Sheila will go to ten doctors with none of them connecting the dots. It would be easy for her because she's a pathological liar and when she wants something she flashes those boobs in low cut tops and flirts with her supplier. Like I said she was once a very beautiful woman but she's not anymore but she thinks she still is and these dumb asses fall for her every time."

"Lionel, I'm sure she's slipping something to Jim. I saw his pupils dilated and after a glass of juice, he's in the twilight zone. Do you agree with me or could it be something else?"

"Don't second guess yourself Laura. You're a smart woman and saw it right away. If anyone would it would be you. You lived with him all those years and know him better than anyone else Trust your instincts. Does she make him smoothies?"

"She makes him one every day around 4 o'clock and I haven't seen her cook him a meal yet."

"After one of her smoothies, the last thing you would want is to eat. She pulled that on me many times and for a while it worked but I'm a doctor whereas Jim would not clue into it as quickly as I did and he is in a weakened condition to begin with."

"What was her purpose in sedating you? Jim's a nice guy and would tolerate a lot more than most men."

"Sheila loves one person in this world and that's herself. She likes her own company and has a good time alone as long as she can drink herself blind. She sedated me to put me to sleep and out of her way. She's doing the same with Jim. You said he was anti drinking and he has probably given her some grief over her drinking. She won't tolerate anyone telling her what she can and can't do so she puts them to sleep and parties on her own."

"She doesn't want Jim and never did. She wants only what she can get out of him and it sounds like she's getting away with it now. As long as she can be stupid drunk she's happy listening to her music, doing her nails and talking to herself. She has a bad habit of phoning people when she's drinking. Many times she phoned people she hardly knew and talked with them as though she was their best friend. When they hung up on her, she was furious at their rudeness and vowed to get even."

"I know some people who have had that experience with her already and didn't quite know what to make of it or how to deal with her."

"That doesn't surprise me but the sad part is that often she didn't remember calling these people."

"I had to take the car keys from her and hide them when she drank. It always ended with world war three but that was better than her going out and killing some innocent in an accident."

"My God Lionel; did this happen often?"

"Almost every night; I'm surprised she's still walking around and functioning to some degree. She should have been put away a long time ago. I'm not saying this as an ex-husband with deep hatred for the woman. I say this as a medical practitioner. The woman is crazy and should be put away.

"Was she ever in trouble with the law?"

"I covered up for her for the first ten years and after that I started calling the police myself when she chased me around the house with a knife. Here in the island the cops just try to defuse the situation and walk away from it without doing anything. They don't care if they have to come to your house several times a week. What they don't want to do is throw a white person in jail, especially a woman."

"Why not?"

"The prisons here are not like those in the U.S. or Canada. A man might make it through but a woman wouldn't. Can you see the headlines in one of our papers? White woman dies in prison, etc. etc. Can you imagine what that would do to the tourism trade and international politics?"

"Do you know Jacob Sylvester?"

"He's a good friend and I can't count the number of time he pulled that bitch off of me. Often he took the car keys so neither one of us could drive but he always brought them back the next day. I can remember a few times when he had to come back to my house after already being there. There was no way Sheila would settle down until she was ready to. One time after Jacob had been there and took the car keys, she found the spare set and drove the car through the house intentionally. She's nuts!"

"What made you finally end the marriage?"

"I just couldn't take anymore. She was an embarrassment to me and my practice. She used to do the books for me until I caught on to her stealing. She must have been doing it for years before I got wise to her. She lied to everyone and anyone – thinks she's a queen or a descendant from royalty and above everyone else.. Where she got some of her stores from is anyone's guess. She lives in a world of fantasy. Have you noticed any paintings or sketches in your house that bear a resemblance to her?"

"Yes I have and she claimed they are all of her but I know a little bit about art and she is not the subject although she wanted me to think she was. I can see she has a very unreal imagination and opinion of herself."

"Drunk or sober – Sheila is crazy and she's mean. We rented the same unit for several years on the island of Anguilla. The last time we rented it, the landlord jacked up the rent but not much. I was happy to pay him – he was always good to us and after several years with no increase, I thought it was long overdue and fair. Sheila was furious and argued with the man until I finally dragged her away. The day we left she dropped her pants and pissed on all the sofas and laughed the whole time.

"Why didn't you stop her?"

"By the time I realized what she was doing, it was too late. The cost to clean the furniture, if he could get it cleaned, would have been far more than a month's rent. She's a nasty vicious person who doesn't like to pay or be crossed. For a long time I thought it was the booze but it wasn't the reason for her insanity. She's totally psychotic and should be locked away someplace. The booze is secondary to her primary problem. You are not dealing with a drunkard Laura. You are dealing with a drunken psychopath."

"Was she ever in therapy of any sort other than the rehab facilities"

"She was seeing a shrink for years back in the states before we moved to the tropics."

"Why did she stop?"

"She said they were nuts and she also went to Alcoholics Anonymous and came home after the first meeting and told me she wasn't going back because they were all a bunch of drunks."

"Oh Lionel, you had such a bad time of it. I'm glad you're finally free of such a mess."

"So am I Laura – so am I! When I couldn't take it anymore I just told her to take whatever she wanted and go. She took everything we had including my pre marital investments by forging my signature. She lied in court, on affidavits, to friends, family - police – everyone. It cost me a bundle to beat her at that one but I still came out with almost nothing. "

"You must feel relieved now that it's over Lionel."

"It's not over Laura. She's a greedy bitch. She took me for everything I had, almost ruined my practice by trying to extort from my patients and now she is still trying to squeeze any dime she can get from me. I lost my home because I had to sell to give her half. I had no problem with that because she was entitled to half but she didn't even leave me with a fork." She walked away from our marriage with a half million in U.S. dollars and she's still trying to suck my blood."

"Sheila had a long history of court activity. She sued members of her own family and neighbors in various areas where we lived when we were in the states. We had to keep moving to avoid angry neighbors. She changed lawyers as often as her underwear so she could get away without paying her bill. She didn't like to part with her money and didn't. The woman was skilled at cheating people and thinks nothing of leaving unpaid debts and broken people in her wake."

Once we exhausted ourselves Lionel ordered another round of beer. We took a break and talked about other things while I mopped up with more napkins. Lionel's story made me cry and I wanted to hug him. We were both feeling drained and had a long way to go still. Lionel was a beautiful man with a big heart. I hoped this was not our first and last meeting. I needed a friend like him.

Lionel started to laugh and shake his head. We watched sea gulls dive for their food and ferry boats, loaded with passenger, coming and going from the pier. It was close to the end of the business day on the island and neither one of us was anxious to part company.

"Let's get back to work Laura, we have a lot more to talk about."

"What I am going to tell you now Laura - I say with sincerity. I've vented my anger and cleared my chest and now I'm all yours. I prayed for God to grant me one wish and he didn't give me what I asked for but He did hear my prayers and gave me what I needed. I can now get a good night's sleep and live a stress free life. What more can I ask for except to erase the memories of her?"

"She doesn't give a dam about Jim. She wants your house Laura and she will get it if you don't get down and dirty with her. Jim's being a fool but he's needy from what you've told me and is not well. He's frightened to be alone right now. It's all up to you to protect both yourself and Jim and what you worked hard for."

"You told me something earlier that now has me even more concerned. Sheila couldn't have known you owned the house jointly with Jim. She was counting on getting him to will it to her because she knows he's not going to live much longer and she might even help him on his journey. Her mother did it three times but she wasn't stupid enough to get involved with a man who was in the middle of a divorce with property owned equally by a wife. You have ruined Sheila's plan."

"I know I'm frightening you Laura and I'm sorry to be so candid. You are not safe. She already has Jim where she wants him but you are an entirely different matter and she has to get you out of her way to get what she's after. You have to be one step ahead of her at all times and keep your back covered. You seem to have a solid relationship with Jacob Sylvester – stay close to him Laura and don't hesitate to call him or any of the precincts if you are afraid or feel there could be danger lurking. "

"There was a time when I couldn't look a cop in the face thinking he might be the one who pulled that drunken bitch off me the previous night. I can't begin to count how many times I had to call the police and after a while it was always Jacob who took the calls and came to my house himself. There isn't a cop on this island who isn't aware of what you are up against. They are your friends – especially Jacob. Don't hesitate to call them if you have to. God bless them all."

As Lionel told me this and more, the picture in my head of what was going on in my own home became a frightening reality. Some of what he said I now saw as clues that I had overlooked. I didn't doubt any of what he told me and didn't think he exaggerated in the slightest. I was living in the same hell that took him years to escape. I hung on to every thing he said and sought clarification when I was unsure or confused by his meaning. More than anything I needed to understand how Sheila's mind worked. That was my starting point. From Lionel I was learning how to interpret her moods, habits and reactions and already I was ahead of the game with my ability to interpret her body language.

"Lionel, why would Sheila keep Jim sedated?"

"For two good reasons and maybe more; the first is so she doesn't have to deal with him. She doesn't want him as a mate and never did. He's a means to an end and nothing more. He's a prime sucker and that's all there is to it and he was very vulnerable and probably still is. Just look at what she has already accomplished in such a short time. She's running the show and enjoying Jim's money while he's merely fighting for his life. She can do what she wants with the house, his money and herself if he's not coherent enough to either know or care."

The second reason is you Laura. Jim still has feelings for you and visa versa. You may not believe you're a fighter and you probably don't fight for yourself nearly as much as you will fight for someone you care about and you do care about Jim and Sheila knows it. "

"Sheila is intimidated by you Laura. You are younger than she is and very good looking. You're also smart and accomplished. Sheila never did anything in her life to speak about. She uses people and tells tall tales about how she did many successful things when the truth is she could never hold a job for more than week without getting thrown out on her ass. She thinks she's the cats meow but she's not and she knows it. You had the life she always dreamed of and you are the woman she always longed to be. This is bigger than you realize. She wants to be you.

"How can she be me?"

"She already is in her mind. Sheila walked right into your shoes the minute you left."

"Did I mention Lionel that I am the irrevocable benefactor to Jim's pensions – even if divorced?"

"Oh shit Laura, this is getting scarier by the minute. If Sheila is aware of this and I'm sure by now she is, then you are definitely in danger. What happens if you are dead before Jim? Would Sheila get the pensions then?

"I don't know but I can check it out with a phone call. If she is eligible if I'm no longer around and I don't see why she wouldn't be, then I am really worried not too."

"But Lionel what can I do - how do I fight her, where do I start?"

"You're already off to a good start. It took courage for you to contact me and I'm glad you did. Stay in the house and make her life miserable. She's a dirty fighter and will come at you from behind when you least expect it. Learn to anticipate her. She's not that smart but she is cunning. Always have a few aces up your sleeve and don't wait for things to happen – make things happen. The ones who snooze, will loose!"

"Beat her at her own game. I know you're not a fighter but you have to learn. Sheila is dangerous to Jim and now you and I'm not talking about just your worldly goods; I'm talking about your lives."

"I can't thank you enough Lionel. You have opened my eyes to what I needed to know and do. Thank you."

"You are very welcome and if there is anything I can do for you, I will. Stay close to Jacob Sylvester; he is on your side. The enemy of my enemy is my friend!"

"What does that mean?"

"You are my friend."

We parted with a hug and a promise to stay in touch and I knew in my heart Lionel would be a friend for life.

Chapter Fifteen
Homelesss

Many things happened over the next week. Sheila's harassment toward me was escalating and as such, she was making grave mistakes. Everything she did was a show for Jim's benefit. Although he continued to remain in his room, she now often left the door open so he could hear what was going on. When things didn't go the way she planned, she closed his door or went into him crying with a barrel full of lies that I overheard.

Had I not spent an afternoon with Lionel, I would have missed much of what her game was. I'm not a particularly foxy person and tend to look at things from the surface. To do this with Sheila was dangerous.

Soon I came to see that everything Sheila said or did was all part of the charade. She wanted me out but couldn't succeed without Jim's help and it was him she was working on – not me. I had no control over him and resented that I felt I had to play her game but she was the one who snuggled up beside him at night and a few caresses would go a long way with Jim.

Sheila was setting me up for something but I could not see what was coming. I wanted to leave and go home but first I needed to have some resolution to our property settlement. I wasn't about to leave with everything hanging in the air. It would only mean I would have to return and go through the same thing again. At least now I was in my house and thought I had some leverage.

Sheila didn't lift a finger to do anything domestic other than cook food for her dogs. Her housekeeper came three times a week. She did the laundry and the ironing – all of which was Sheila's clothing. She d scrubbed everything including the outer railings to the pool which is something I would never expect a cleaning woman to do. We had a power washer in the garage and could easily hose down the outside of the house or have the groundskeeper do it.

Jim was paying for it all but as Lionel had mentioned, Sheila didn't lift a finger and thought nothing of having a cleaning lady in daily which is something Jim would not have tolerated. I always did my own cleaning – even when I was working. I only hired someone to help when the work demanded someone taller than I was or if I was so far behind that I couldn't see the light of day.

Babette, Sheila's housekeeper, was a woman I wasn't familiar with. She was pleasant enough but kept her distance from me. She was instructed not to clean my suite and not to speak to me but when Sheila wasn't around, as she often was not when the house was being cleaned, Babette did talk to me. She was a lovely young woman with several small children to feed. She always had a smile and a warm greeting for me. I knew she was nervous around me when her demeanor changed once Sheila was back on the premises. She was frightened of Sheila who never offered the woman a glass of water or lunch.

I did have a housekeeper when Jim and I first moved into the house. Her name was Audrey and she couldn't clean worth a dam in spite of the many times I showed her what I wanted done and how to do it. If I wanted my house cleaned to my standards, I had to work alongside her to get it done right.

Audrey was a bit simple minded but was trying her best to please me. Raising two small sons on her own and living in squalor; I kept her on because it was the only way to help the woman without humiliating her. I paid her twice what she was worth, did most of the work myself and sent her home with a full day's wage and take-outs from my fridge and pantry.

Sheila had no respect for other people and once she got her pint of blood from them, she discarded them without a second thought. I was sure Babette was making less than minimum wage and was struggling in her own life. She was frightened of Sheila but needed the work and put up with the abuse.

Sheila called the police when I called her a freeloader - telling them I threatened her life but when they arrived at the door the best she could do was call me names and wave her hands around while saying everything in the house belonged to her. The police only laughed when I told them what actually transpired and Sheila had no comment when they asked her to elaborate on the threat. The woman was a demon in a dress.

Efforts to get my lawyer to do anything were in vain and I grew more worried with each new day. Three of us living in the same house could not continue and I couldn't get into the room to speak to Jim who I came to realize was not part of the equation. This war was between me and Sheila. She already had him where she wanted him.

No law could keep me out of my own home, or so I believed and I was still legally married to Jim. We had to work this out together and Sheila was not and should not be in the picture until we did. Yet Jim chose to listen to whatever lies she told him and she was filling him with plenty. She was really in control and there was no way I could reach him.

The police arrived early in the morning only a few days after my meeting with Lionel. They had a court order to remove me – grounds were I threatened to kill both Jim and Sheila and both signed a sworn affidavit claiming I made such a threat. Echoes of Lionel's words about false affidavits – lies and treachery stung my brain cells and I didn't have my back covered.

I could not believe this was happening and called Jacob Sylvester while two officers waited for me to pack my things. He told me he just learned of the court order himself and was working on it - to leave with the officers to avoid arrest and let him know where I was. I didn't have to pack because Sheila, wearing a smile, had done it for me. When I got off the phone she handed me my suitcase and a plastic bag containing my food. Jim stayed in his room while I was being evicted from my home.

The police waited outside with me until Beatrice arrived. I had no place else to go and was grateful she offered me her guest room. There was no way I was going to be chauffeured around the island in a police car and at that moment in my life I hated Jim with all my being.

Ms. Cartier kept her appointment with me the following day. Bea came along to chauffeur me and to be present in the meeting – I wanted a witness. Ms. Cartier was preparing a petition for the court to have the injunction overturned – she was sure we would be in court within twenty four hours and we were but good old Mr. Henry was always one step ahead of Ms. Cartier and was prepared himself with medical reports to substantiate Jim's state of health required he be allowed to remain in our home with his care-giver and that my presence was stressful and harmful to his health. The death threat allegation was thrown out but once again Jim and Sheila won the day.

Had my lawyer done her homework she could have won the day for me but as always, she was not prepared and too willing to accept whatever went down. I pointed out one of the medical reports was signed by Jim's own son in law in Canada but Mr. Henry created enough of a diversion for my news to fall on deaf ears and Ms. Cartier was not polished enough to resurrect the issue.

Mr. Henry – Jim's Lawyer stated for the record that Sheila was Jim's caregiver and as such was required to reside in the house. She had no qualifications other than being a hostess at a restaurant many years earlier but again Ms. Cartier let that slide over her head. Mr. Henry also pleaded with the court for Jim to have full access of the house without interference from me for as long as necessary to heal from a serious illness. Why didn't my lawyer seek compensation for me? The very next morning Jim returned to Canada alone while Sheila remained in the house and had every window and access door boarded up. Then she hired a life in body guard.

When the judge asked me if I had anything to say before our case was dismissed; I stood to speak. Ms. Cartier was stunned as this seldom happens and Mr. Henry rose to protest. He didn't want to hear what I had to say.

"It's a travesty of justice when anyone can swear an affidavit on the Holy Bible based on lies with no proof to validate the false claim and an innocent person, who has equal rights to the property being disputed here is unjustly crucified."

I walked out of the courtroom.

Residents on the island were shocked over my eviction but what good would that do me? I was the victim of a vicious scheme to take away what was rightfully mine and Jim was as much to blame, if not even more so than Sheila was. I didn't to hear about anyone's anger; I wanted to see picket signs outside the courthouse but that would never happen.

It was time for me to get down on my knees and pray. I had nothing left.

Lionel was out of his mind with anger when I called him with my latest news.

"I told you Laura – I warned you. She convinced Jim to do this. You have had no contact with him – he's going on what she's telling him and he's a fucking idiot whether sedated or not. J.H. C. – I'm so mad I could spit nails."

Jacob had nothing to say about the incident other than it was a court matter and the only place where it would be resolved. That was fine for him to say but I was the one who had a useless lawyer and no money to find a replacement.

Ms. Cartier drove by my house to see for herself it was indeed boarded up. Sheila was on the inside calling friends who reported to other friends and none of whom were her friends, that she was frightened for her life – how I tried to kill her and several more green bags full of garbage. Luke and Linda were not on the island and I don't know what help Luke might have given if he was but I wished anyway they were around. If anything he could have exposed the façade of threat – boarding up the house and the lover body guard.

I couldn't stay with Bea forever and needed to get back to Dominica. I was out of money and had a life of my own to re-build. On my last visit with Ms. Cartier before leaving her advice was to pack my things in Dominica and return to St. Horatio.

"It's your house Laura and no one can keep you out, especially now when Jim left for Canada the day after the hearing. We don't even have to provide proof they lied – we simply get proof from immigration he left within twenty four hours of the hearing. The courts will not be made a fool of – I can guarantee you that. I don't know your husband but I can tell you he is no better than Sheila to do this to you when you are co-owner and he is trying to take it all away from you and keep his girlfriend living well while you struggle to eat."

"I can't just move back in – what about the court order? "

"We'll deal with it at the time. Get back as fast as you can and take over your property."

Using borrowed money I returned to Dominica and sold what little I had left and returned five days later with Baxter, Sam and one suitcase.

Money was slipping through my hands faster than the speed of light. An unexpected expense with the airlines for the dogs' overweight kennels ate up a thousand dollars at the airport in one toss. On top of that I was charged double for a vet to meet us for inspection Before clearing customs and the hired help to get us to the ferry boat.

I hired four hired men from the pier to accompany me home. The boards had to be removed in order for me to gain entry and I wasn't sure what I was going to find once inside. No one was really sure where Sheila was as she hadn't been seen for some time and rumor had it that she wasn't living in the house at all. There were so many rumors flying around I didn't know what to believe but I did suspect she wasn't far from the house if indeed she had even left. I did know she was not in Canada with Jim.

Regardless, it was my house, Jim wasn't there and lied to the courts through his lawyer and I would stake my claim and fight it out with the courts but I planned to live in my house no matter what. Sheila could join Jim in Canada if she was his true care-giver but she was not going to put me out of my home again. Like a fool I put my faith in what Ms. Cartier told me. Their lies would be established and I would be restored to my rightful place. She also doubted, as did I, that Jim would discharge himself from hospital again to play Sheila's knight in shining armor and that, I was counting on.

I called Jacob from the taxi as we climbed the nasty road upwards. He nearly had a coronary when I told him where I was and where I was going. He tried to convince me to turn back but I wasn't going to listen to him or anyone else. I was fed up with people running my life for me and not doing a very good job. I hung up on him.

It saddened me to see my home boarded up and my lawns and gardens over gown in such a beautiful area. In all likelihood the pool had probably turned to skunk by now too. With no money to hire help I would take care of myself. I was not a stranger to hard work and for many years cut my own lawns and cleaned the pool I once owned in a previous marriage. I would find work —take in laundry or clean houses for other people if I had to. I considered renting out the guest room to a student as another possibility to earn a little cash.

My hired men went right to work removing the large sheets of plywood blocking the front entrance. Baxter and Sam excitedly headed into the house once I opened their kennels. They knew they were home when they aimed for the spot where their feeding dishes had been at one time. The flight home was hard on them as was the ferry boat ride. They were hungry and confused.

As I was hauling in my luggage, an unfamiliar dog came running out. It was a small Rottweiler that hadn't been there on my previous visit. Sheila had a Doberman that I befriended and no sooner did the first dog scamper away when the second one appeared.

He remembered me and went willingly when I took him by the collar to the pool veranda. The men would be frightened of any dog and I didn't want the dog frightened also.

As I was closing the veranda door I saw Sheila - stark naked run from the pool and along the veranda to the master suite. When I looked back to the pool I saw a man who was trying to hide below the lip of the pool. Noise coming from the men distracted me for a few seconds – the man in the pool was gone when I looked back, and that's when Sheila, now dressed and carrying a phone, came screaming into the great room.

"You get out of here Laura. This is my house and I'm in charge."

"This is not your house Sheila, never was and never will be. As you can see, I'm moving in and you are getting the hell out."

The men were working fast taking down the boards on the front veranda but they were making too much noise and would damage things if there weren't more careful. I went to join them when there was a commotion coming from the living room where one of the men was about to tackle the boards on the back veranda. I heard an agonizing scream – followed by yet another when I turned to see Sheila coming at me with a can of pepper spray.

Two of the men rushed past me and out the front door while another was thrashing around – bouncing from wall to wall knocking things over. His face was totally red as he tried to wipe away the heavy dose of liquid oozing from his eyes and down his face.

She got me square in the face with the brutal spray. Only one of the men was still with me but he was covered with spray and hurting badly. The burning in my eyes and face was like nothing I could have ever imagined - as though gasoline had been set afire and sprayed at me. Somehow I managed to keep my eyes open and grabbed her by the hair. The look on her face will be with me until the day I die. She was grinning, gritting her teeth with eyes ablaze. She wanted to kill me. I held onto her hair as we flipped and flopped around the room. At one point I managed to pull her head down low enough to ram my knee into her face. I felt weak, that my blow didn't have the impact intended. She was much stronger than I was in spite of the years of youth I had on her. Everything was in slow motion.

When handfuls of her hair came out in my hands, I grabbed more from another location on her head. She broke free for an instant, freeing my right hand from her hair. Seizing the opportunity, I hit her in the face several times but she kept going. The can of spray was long ago emptied, later to be confiscated by the police as evidence but as expected it was never used for anything other than a paper weight.

One of my men came from behind and tried to pull her off me. Between the two of us we couldn't take her down. She was winning the battle and I was nearly blind. I was swinging madly at her and at one time had her in a grip and tried to push her out the door with the help of the helper but the two of us couldn't manage it. I wanted to vomit or pass out and feared what would happen if I did.

I had to get to water and found my way to the kitchen sink, threw up and then put my entire head under running water. My back was burning which I noticed for the first time. Had she put a knife in it? I pulled my shirt off and used the sprayer to rinse my back. The more water I used, the more my skin burned.

Strange voices and gallons of cold soothing water and I didn't know how much later; brought me back to consciousness. Someone was stroking my arms while another held my head back to rinse my eyes under a forceful fountain. Who were these strangers? It was cold and I was sitting on a cement floor.

"Laura – Mrs. Cassidy - you're safe now. We carried you out. You will be fine, just let us keep washing you off. We won't hurt you."

They were my former work crew who were working on a new home beside my own when they heard the commotion. All five of them ran into the house and found me unconscious on the kitchen floor. They carried me to the garage in the new home where the only a source of water was located. I had no idea where my dogs or the hired men were and neither did the workers.

One of the men loaned me a dirty t-shirt before they escorted me back to the front gate of my property where Sheila had not only locked the gate to keep me out but also where a crowd had gathered along with the police. The crowd had been summoned by Sheila to watch the show. None of them were from the immediate area and none were familiar to me. Oh she was good – calling in the audience to witness how she was attacked in her own home. Those were here words as she pranced around the yard taking pictures with my camera.

Sam was wimping beside his kennel when I arrived at the gate. He came rushing when he saw me but had to be put back into his kennel by order of the police officer who was unpleasant and repeatedly waved a stick at me as he spoke.

I demanded he help me find Baxter who was somewhere inside the locked property. Sheila reluctantly opened the gate to allow us to search. Knowing exactly where Baxter would hide, I walked to the far end of the property where there were dense shrubs. He came immediately when he saw me and happily took refuge in his kennel.

Sheila put on quite a show as she entertained the curious crowd from behind the gate – now locked again. She called me names and took pictures of me sitting on the grass. One man, a respectable member of the community for many years – in fact a leader on the island, came over to me to offer support.

"For what it's worth Mrs. Cassidy, I was summoned here by Sheila's frantic phone call and I have yet to figure out why other than to see this ridiculous circus."

The cop cited me the riot act - violation of a court order – but he didn't seem to know what to do or was waiting for back-up – after all I was a dangerous criminal. I borrowed a cell phone to call Ms. Cartier who was unavailable. My second call was to Jacob.

"Are you alright Laura?"

"No Jacob I am not alright. I've been pepper sprayed and bamboozled once again and I have this stupid cop standing over me waving a stick at me."

"Put him on the phone."

He refused to take the cell phone from me and wanted to know what I was up to.

"Your boss wants to speak to you officer."

"Officer James speaking – who is this? Yes sir, I understand sir – yes sir."

"See to it that Mrs. Cassidy is taken care of. She's not the offender here – the other one is but the courts have to sort this out. Get medical attention for Mrs. Cassidy – she's the rightful owner of the property, show her respect but it is safer for her to leave for now and bring that can of spray in to the precinct as evidence."

"Yes Sir."

Only one of my men - Ken was there with me. The driver took off at the first sign of trouble while another officer, the partner of the first, took the other two to the hospital and later returned. I called a friend with a pick up truck to come for me and my dog. I had no idea where to go but Ken offered to help. He knew of a place where we could go for a short time.

After more eye flushing and a few stitches to my right arm from a wound I had no recollection of, my friend dropped Ken and me off at a vacant shack in a small village on the other side of the island. By this time I was going into shock and felt detached from reality. Here I was in some dirty shack with no furniture, a man I didn't know, no money worth counting and no future in sight while that wretched woman was living in luxury in my house.

With literally no choice I made a list of what my immediate needs were and sent Ken to the supermarket to get food for ourselves and the dogs. Ken offered to stay the night with us and given I didn't know where I was, was afraid of where I might be and not looking forward to sleeping on a cement floor, I agreed he could. Tomorrow had to be a better day!

We sat on the floor with the door open to eat our food after which Ken took them for a run. They snuggled beside me and fell within minutes while Ken and I sat smoking cigarettes and drinking rum until I could no longer hold my head up. I fell asleep using Sam's backside as my pillow.

Feeling no better in the morning than I did the night before I at least had come to some realization of what I had to do and fast. First order of business was finding a place to stay. Ken walked the dogs and cared for them while I walked into town. I had five hundred dollars to my name and the one thing I wasn't going to waste any more money on was cell phone calls to Ms. Cartier. We were finished.

I hired a guy to drive me to a few places and ended up renting an end unit at a closed down resort on the beach for $45 a night. The new manager had only recently purchased the place and had plans to renovate and re-open before high season. Fresh linen was available if I picked it up when he was on the property but there were no other services available. I bought food and bottled water and settled in with my dogs. We were the only residents in a deserted inn on a lonely stretch of beach.

For the first week I saw and heard from no one. Daily I saw the inn manager who was always nice to me. When I told him my story and the state of my finances, he told me to forget paying rent. I could stay as long as I needed.

Four weeks passed and I wasn't healing emotionally. I was no closer to knowing what I was going to do than I was the first day I moved in. I walked the dogs on the sandy beach several times a day and played with them in my room until I was tired enough to sleep. I went into town on the bus only to get food for them. I ate raw vegetables and fruit purchased at a little stand not far from the inn.

My good friend Kit, my sister Mary and Samantha sent a little money. They pleaded with me to come home but I simply didn't want to. I wasn't leaving my dogs behind nor would I let Jim and Sheila get away with their treachery.

At the end of my fifth week I forced myself to face reality. I had to find a place for the dogs and return to Canada. When no one was willing to take either one of my dogs, there was only one other option and it broke my heart to even consider it but there was no other way. I was getting weaker by the day and needed to take care of myself and the only place where I would heal was in Canada.

We were romping on the beach when my cell phone rang. It was my sister.

"Hi Mary – is that you?"

"Laura how are you and where are you now?"

""Oh Mary it's so good to hear your voice. I'm on the beach with the dogs for a run. I'm still in St. Horatio and no closer to a solution than I was five weeks ago."

"I'm sending you money today through Western Union. Can you get to pick it up?"

"Mary thanks but you've already sent me money, I can't expect you to support me. Things will work out – I just need a little more time. I have to find a place for the dogs first and it's not looking very promising. I may have to put them to sleep."

"Oh Laura honey, I'm so sorry to bring bad news to you but you have to come home now. Guido died this morning."

I collapsed on the sand sobbing in agony. I was so angry at life and at God. What would happen to my daughter Samantha – my daughter – my little girl and my grandchildren now? Dam you God – why them? Haven't I had enough? Why didn't you take me instead of him? They need him – they don't need me. I'm just a burden to everyone. What do I have to live for?

Mary's sobbing brought me back to reality as we resumed talking to each other between sobs.

"I will be there as fast as I can Mary."

After picking up the money Mary sent I flew to Dominica with Baxter and Sam. They would be safe there.

My good friend Teddy owned a small bed and breakfast in Calibishie. It was off season and the place was empty. She opened her doors and arms for me and did everything imaginable to make me and the dogs comfortable while she helped me find homes for them.

Teddy fed us until I thought we would burst. In the evenings we sat on her veranda on the sea talking. At night I laid awake petting my dogs or just watching them sleep. With the help of another friend – Sandra, we were at the brink of saying good bye to Baxter and Sam. It was heart wrenching for me but at least were going to good homes, one of which was Sandra's. On our third day, I cried when she drove off with my Bax. He was going to Sandra's seven acre property where he could roam and swim in the stream than ran through her land – he would be happy there.

On the fourth day Sandra and I took Sam to his new home in the countryside where he too had acres to roam. We were greeted warmly by the owners who fell in love with Sam at first sight. They were dog loves and had several others to keep Sam entertained.

My emotions got the better of me as I was about to leave. I couldn't control my sobs and neither could Sandra as we tried to tear ourselves away. I did not want to do this. Oh Dear God why do I have to give up my dogs? I bent to give Sam one last hug and kiss and for the first time, he licked my mouth as if giving me a kiss. Sandra gently pulled my arm to leave and handed me a tissue. The lady of the manor was also crying.

....I didn't look back as we got into the car but I knew Sam was on the veranda watching me. As we drove down the long driveway heading toward the main road, I heard his mournful yelp and then the howl that would haunt me for the months to follow.

Chapter Sixteen
Canada

As my plane left the ground in Dominica and flew over the areas where my dogs now lived, I let out a sob that drew attention from other passengers. This was the final farewell to two beautiful animals I loved more than life and to a country I had once called home. Thanks to my family and friends I was on my way - a final journey for a very long time. I didn't make it in time for Guido's funeral.

Samantha's home was like a funeral parlor with dozens of floral arrangements and more arriving every day. People came and went constantly to bring trays of home cooking and baked goods. Most of my day was spent serving guests and doing dishes and at first sign of a wilting flower, I discarded the entire arrangement. At the end of three weeks the children returned to school and Samantha went back to work. At night I could hear the kids crawl into bed with her – their sobs were heart wrenching.

Life slowly returned to normal but my life was in limbo. I kept busy doing the laundry, cleaning house and preparing meals. I was alone most of the day with nothing else to do but think about what I had just come through and of course, Baxter and Sam were forever in my thoughts.

For the first time in months I began to sleep through the night, was eating properly and feeling healthy. I could have a good life if I stayed in Canada but I didn't want to live in a granny suite in my daughter's basement or have to rely of family to take care of me.

I heard from friends Jim was still in Canada and could have contacted him but I didn't. He wasn't gracious enough to send condolences to my family and after what he put me through, I hated him.

Several visits to doctors for routine health checks and to an optometrist kept me busy. I was told my eyes were scarred from the pepper spray and would never be the same again. Samantha treated me to facials, pedicures and massage therapy at spas and often treated herself to a little spoiling.

I spent hours on the computer researching case studies of separations and divorce – those that were controversial and similar to my situation. I chatted on line with legal professionals and a few times paid for the consultations. It was all coming together.

Former employers easily provided me with a complete history of my earnings for the previous fifteen years or more. I travelled to the cities where Jim and I owned property and got copies of all the records showing joint ownership. I went to several banks and investment companies where we did our business and obtained all that I needed. Friends and former work colleagues provided me with letters of recommendation speaking to my integrity and financial acumen and sworn statements where I thought it might prove beneficial. What to do with all my efforts proved to be the biggest challenge.

I celebrated my 55th birthday in those first few months and celebrated again shortly afterward when I received my first cheque from my retirement pension funded from my severance package. Before long I had money in the bank and a brighter future to look forward to.

Selina knew what I was up to and supported my initiative.

"Don't give up Laura – fight for what is yours. I know a lawyer who does a lot of work for me and told him about your situation. He was excited and said he wanted to represent you."

"How can he be excited when he doesn't even know me?"

"Are you kidding Laura? Every lawyer on this island is watching your case and everyone else is talking about it."

Mr. Roman Jeffery called me two days later and agreed he wanted to take my case. The man actually sounded excited. I could hardly wait to meet the man who lifted my spirits with his jovial manner and confidence.

"I will start the papers right away. We're going for a court order to sell your house. Forget about living there again – let's just get it sold and get some money for you. Fedex that bundle of papers you have been so busy collecting. Selina told me what you have been up to and that was very smart of you. Send them to me right away. "

Sheila continued to live in my house with a man who no one seemed to know anything about. Jim had not returned to St. Horatio. She was often seen out at local bars and was reputed to have made advances at two men of Jim's age who had recently become widowed. She was looking for Jim's replacement.

Two more family birthdays and Christmas brought joy and sadness into my daughter's home. We went overboard on gifts and parties and wearing my gift from the kids, a granny apron, I took charge of Christmas dinner for twenty one people. Samantha was invited to something almost every night and I went along with her. The kids no longer cried as they had done when I arrived. They were flourishing in school and had many friends who were always around and Joseph had his beginner's driving permit.

Samantha drew the night shift for New Year's Eve and the kids were staying over with friends. I chose to decline an invitation to celebrate the New Year with friends and stayed home alone to solidify my plan.

On January 4th, 2007 I flew home to Dominica.

Chapter Seventeen
New Beginnings

What a glorious day it was for me to find Carol Ann and Teddy waiting for me at the airport in Marigot. Forgetting the temperature difference between Canada and the tropics, I broke into a sweat before I was in the car.

"We found a house for you to rent Laura. It's not far from the village and high on the ridge. The rent is within the range you gave us and it's all yours if you like it. We're going there now to meet the owner who is waiting."

"The house was perfect although it didn't have a kitchen. We had to laugh about the concept of no kitchen but it wouldn't cost much for me to put in a sink and a bit of counter space and I wasn't planning on dinner parties in the near future.

While in Canada I cleaned out many of the papers I left in Samantha's care. I found my American Express credit card that had not yet reached the expiry date. It was actually my spousal card in Jim's name and one we never used much. He cancelled all my other cards but I wasn't sure if this one escaped his nasty ways.

With nothing to lose, I went shopping. Thirty five thousand dollars later, I had furniture for my little house and a car. What I wouldn't give to see the expression on Jim's face when he got the bill. He was living the good life in half of what was mine and had not a care in the world for anyone other than himself and Sheila. I was entitled to something but I had one regret; I should have kept on shopping.

My new jeep would never have passed a Canadian inspection but it worked and did get approval from the Department of Motor Vehicles in Dominica.

Mr. Jeffery kept in touch regularly and gave me the encouragement I needed. We would be in court within a few months and I had to be ready to fly with little notice. I kept money aside to pay for my flight and hopefully come back from St. Horatio with the promise of more. More than anything I wanted to buy or build a small Caribbean cottage and make a new life and Dominica was where I planned to do just that.

Sandra and I bumped into each other almost every day in the village. She gave me good reports on Baxter. I had no plans to see him or interfere with his new life. As long as he was doing well – that was all that mattered.

I couldn't get any news of Sam and I longed to see him. His mournful cry when I drove away from him and that little kiss he gave me were as fresh in my heart as they had been five months earlier. After a few weeks, now settled in my house with all that I needed, I took a ride to visit him. As I got closer to his new home, I questioned the wisdom of seeing him. The last thing I wanted was to hear another mournful cry when I left him for the second time but I had to be sure he was happy.

The sound of my jeep arriving brought a pack of ten or more dogs running to greet me. The first dog, in the lead, was Sam. The owners were not far behind the now frenzied pack.

Sam was in the jeep the minute I opened the door and I got what I longed for – another kiss. I was invited to come in for a glass of juice and Sam was allowed to be with me. He was long ago relocated to the barn with the rest of the dogs, none of which were allowed in the house. Today was an exception for Sam.

He sat at my feet watching my every move. It wasn't going to be easy to leave him behind this time and I wasn't sure I could. I gave my dog to these kind people; how could I ask for him back? My selfishness with this visit would cause sorrow for everyone and most of all Sam.

"When you left him with us Laura, Sam cried for weeks. We kept him in the house with us until we felt he was ready to be with the other dogs. He settled in fine and until today I would have said he was happy but seeing him with you now, I don't believe he ever was really happy.

I was fighting back my tears.

"Gemma, I thought about Sam every day that I was without him.

"That dog belongs with you Laura."

"Can I take him home with me Gemma - please?

"Of course, he wouldn't let you out of here without him anyway. Take him, he is your dog."

Before leaving she gave me enough food for Sam until I could shop for him. His bowl, toys and bed were packed up and loaded into my jeep where Sam already waited.

Sam and I settled into a nice routine. We walked miles each day and drove to the beach almost as often. He never left my side, didn't need to be leashed and was obedient to all my commands. At night he slept on the floor beside my bed. When the landlady came around, I hid him in my room. Sam weighed more than I did and scared the poop out of everyone.

Chapter Eighteen
Court

Mr. Jeffery called me to St. Horatio for the hearing in April. I rushed to get there in time and had to get someone to stay in my house to care for Sam. I met Roman Jeffery for the first time in the park across from the court house. He was as nice in person as he was on the phone. He was very handsome, very professional and had a contagious smile. We quickly discussed what his agenda was and went into the courtroom together with confidence.

Much to my surprise Jim was present. He was going for everything. His lawyer, Mr. Henry, put on quite a show when he tried to convince the judge I contributed nothing in all the years Jim and I were together. I couldn't believe what I was hearing while Jim could not look me in the face.

Mr. Jeffery was well prepared and worth his weight in gold when he countered every allegation made by Mr. Henry and then backed it up with proof – all that I had collected in Canada.

"Your honor, I submit to this court notarized copies of Mrs. Cassidy's payroll records for the past fifteen years as exhibit A. I also submit exhibit B which shows direct bank deposits of Mrs. Cassidy's earnings into the joint account in the names of James and Laura Cassidy."

"Exhibit C Your Honor is notarized copies of three homes jointly owned by Mr. and Mrs. Cassidy and Exhibit D, is the original copy of the deed to their jointly owned property here in St. Horatio."

Mr. Jeffery continued for the next forty minutes producing financial statements, sworn affidavits, testimonials, joint business venture and investments documents all jointly owned. Mr. Henry sat motionless except for the tapping of his pencil on the table.

Mr. Jeffery also spoke to the court of the care I provided to Jim through his many illnesses, of how I was instrumental in bringing a broken family together again. He went on for another twenty minutes and not once said anything derogatory about Jim other than It was his opinion that it was nothing short of greed and he was not going to waste the court's time with any name calling or head bashing when the exhibits provided clearly substantiated that I was indisputably a major contributor and was not seeking anything other for which I was not entitled.

We won the court order to sell our home and divide the proceeds equally. Failure to comply with showings would be deemed a violation and subject to immediate prosecution. But the battle had just begun.

I waited for Mr. Jeffery in the park outside the courthouse under a shady tree. From here I could see Jim as he exited the courthouse to meet with Mr. Henry. He had the stance of a defeated man as he laid his head on his lawyer's shoulder and cried. Was he crying because he was only getting his due – half; or was he afraid to break the news to Sheila?

Chapter Nineteen
Seron

Life was good back in Calibishie. It would be better some day but for now I had all that I needed and Sam. I got together with Carol and Teddy often, read books galore, slept and ate well and tried not to think about Jim and Sheila.

Lionel Sturgess was now a good friend and added to my weekly list of calls from Selina, Bea, Luke, Linda and Jacob. It was now a waiting game until my house sold. Selina was receiving some interest in the house and had a few showings, but no offers were forthcoming.

Jim was never present during these times and she believed he was once again in Canada. Sheila however, was present and refused to leave when the house was being inspected. Often she interfered to the point of foiling the showing.

Often she was drunk and on one occasion, much to Selina's horror, she had not yet dressed for the day and wore a sheer short robe with nothing underneath. She embarrassed the couple to the point where they left without seeing the entire house. I asked Selina, who always carried her camera, to take pictures of Sheila if it happened again.

Eager to have a place of my own, Sam and I drove to areas where land was for sale and I went to see built homes that were on the market. People gave me advice on where and where not to look and all suggested I build my own place. I had enough construction behind me to last a lifetime. Building had no appeal.

My income was sufficient for me and Sam but there was nothing left over for extras. I had to be careful and when I could, I put a little away for a rainy day. I longed for the day when I didn't have to worry about rain.

I bought a second hand sewing machine and resumed a hobby I started when I was in Canada – sewing small lady's handbags. I found fabric with monkey's on it and made that my primary focus. Different straps, lining and clasps made each bag unique and one of a kind. When Selina learned of my project she asked for a few samples. With monkeys rampant in St. Horatio, she believed she could sell the bags. They were selling faster than I could make them in Dominica and the money was a big help for that lemon of a jeep that was now starting to cost me.

There were no eligible men in Calibishie that caught my interest although I would have liked to have someone to go out with. All my friends were teamed up with someone but some of those relationships were not what I would have considered healthy. After Gavin, I had reservations about any man of a different culture but there wasn't much else to choose from.

There was one man who I noticed a few times but mostly because he was so different from most. I had no idea who he was and thought he was from another village and only passing through on the few occasions I did see him. He was never close enough for us to speak but he always had a warm smile and a big wave of the hand for me. He was handsome in a rugged way, with eyes that sparkled in a happy face. His most amazing feature was his hair that fell to his waist.

Needing repairs to my windows, I was told to see the man on top of the hill. I drove by this welding shop daily and never once saw any signs of life and thought the shop was abandoned. It was a pleasant surprise when I discovered the shop was functioning and the owner was my mystery man who, close up, made my heart beat.

Seron was physically beautiful and very unique. He never stopped smiling - his eyes sparkled and he was charming and sincere. He came to my home that same day to repair my window. I learned as we chatted while he worked, he was Rastafarian. I knew nothing about this belief or cult but planned to find out more about it the next time I could access a computer.

After his work was completed, I invited him to have a glass of wine which he downed in one gulp and fled out the door. He was deathly afraid of Sam, insisting I lock him in the bedroom while he worked. As I watched him walk away from my house through the kitchen window, he appeared to glide - his feet barely touching the ground. This was a happy man without a care in the world--a heart and soul made of gold. This strange man loved life.

A week later I found myself locked out of my home. My windows were no longer penetrable thanks to Seron so having no choice, I went to find him. He came happily with me to solve the problem and once again accepted a glass of wine. As before, it went down in one gulp and out the door he fled. I watched him again from my kitchen window. He floated on air.

I was interested in Seron but he didn't appear to share the feeling. He either had a girlfriend or was married. I put him out of my mind and went about my business as usual. I was making new friends and expanding my social life and adjusting to life as a single woman. My favorite hang out was Kokonutz where something was always going on to amuse patrons – usually Carol Ann and Nicky fighting.

Carol Ann was having a birthday party for Nicky at her home on the beach. This was one party I didn't want to miss even without a date. I stopped at the local grocery to pick up my rum contribution and found the shop filled to capacity with shoppers. As I stood chatting with other shoppers waiting my turn to pay for my purchases, a voice rang out loudly enough to stop chatting as heads turned to find the source.

"Hey sweetness, are you going to drink all that rum yourself?"

Seron was standing at the cash wearing his happy face and looking at me. I blushed from the attention of others in the store as their eyes flipped back and forth between me and Seron and the huge bottle of rum I was holding.

I decided there and then I wasn't going to let this opportunity get past me and if the shoppers wanted a show, I would give them one when I yelled to where he was standing.

…."Hi Seron – wanna be my date – I'm going to a birthday party."

Shoppers started to laugh while some men slapped Seron on the back - as in the brotherhood.

"Yes, let me carry that big bottle for you."

Now this was community involvement at its best. The older women gave me an approving smile while the younger ones giggled. What would be called from that day on - The Village Romance, began that evening in the A & A supermarket.

Off we went to the party with Seron carrying my purchases while shoppers, in a festive mood, applauded us and gave their good wishes.

The party was wonderfully romantic on the beach behind Carol Ann's house. This woman could entertain and she left nothing to chance including the food which she prepared herself with the help of a visiting chef from New York. I was so smitten with Seron and the atmosphere, I didn't eat a thing.

Men, mostly local, congregated under a tree in a group. Here they smoked their ganja, talked nonsense and watched the party from a distance, while the women sat on the lounge chairs having a party of our own.

Seron never took his eyes off me and broke custom by joining me with the other ladies shortly after the party was in full swing. When Bonnie Good from Canada started taking pictures at Carol Ann's request, she focused many shots on us. Like a ham, Seron got into the swing by changing poses for each new shot until I encouraged Bonnie to shoot other guests before she ran out of film.

He remained seated beside me holding my hand and then suddenly got down on the sand, my hand still in his and said:

"Could you ever love a man like me?"

"Let's see where this goes." I replied.

Bonnie witnessed the exchange and later came to say:

"You and Seron make a handsome couple. I hope it works out for you."

We saw each other every night following the party and soon became inseparable. Our relationship was everything I claimed I didn't want and yet it was exactly what I wanted once I got to know this man.

By the time we graduated into a full relationship and began living together, we were totally committed to one another. We both wanted the same thing – a loving and long lasting relationship.

Seron's welding shop is adjacent to the home where he grew up and where his sister Ruth now lived with her three children. His humble bedroom located at the back of the shop was his only private space. A pit toilet served his sister and her family as well as Seron. When he moved in with me he had his first hot shower.

The world around us ceased to exist as we frequented the village pubs in the evenings where we danced and hugged. Daily, in late afternoon, we took Sam to the sea or one of the many beautiful rivers where he got his daily exercise and we had a bath. The local residents openly expressed happiness for us and continued to address us as the village lovers. We glowed and people felt our happiness and wanted to offer us repeated good wishes and give us their blessings.

Sam grew to love Seron and waited at the door for him to come home. He took him into the bush for wild adventures or often to his land where he tended his crops. During these times I stayed home to prepare our evening meal or read a book. They always returned hungry and tired. Sam always slept on the floor on my side of the bed but now he had a doggie dilemma - whose side should he sleep on so he alternated between both.

I never lost my love for cooking and went overboard preparing meals for Seron. My budget suffered and before long I couldn't make ends meet. In addition, my jeep was costing me a small fortune every month. If it wasn't one thing it was another and the money was flying out faster than it was coming in. I spared no expense on Sam. If he needed to see the vet which was frequently necessary – he saw the vet.

Seron did not contribute to the rising cost of my expenses. He drove my jeep often and soon began using it for his work which enhanced his customer base but was hard on the vehicle. He brought me fresh produce from his gardens often and helped me plant my own at the back of my house but that was not a financial contribution. Fish was very inexpensive and the only protein he would eat and Sam loved it as long as bones were removed. I made it our main source of protein but I was paying for it.

Lionel continued to call me regularly. We needed each other for support and he was the only person who really understood what I was up against. He was currently involved in yet another court battle with Sheila who, two years after their divorce, was still hacking away at anything she could get out of him and the man didn't have much left.

Jim spent the majority of his time in Canada for health reasons. I could not get any information from anyone on his progress. Either people didn't know or were instructed not to pass on information to me.

Jacob made it a point to keep in close contact with Sheila. He often went to the house to see her and she called him several times a day to seek guidance, complain or invite him to come for a visit. I questioned this but it was a way for him to be in the know and he did pass on information – selectively. He could not be a good cop and not be suspicious. Being close to the situation was the best way for him to stay in the know and he selectively pass on information to me. He was also my only source of information about Jim and even that, Sheila kept closely guarded even from Jacob.

Sheila lived a lavish lifestyle but the house remained boarded up. Her excuse was her fear of me and yet I was the one receiving death threats. The real reason for keeping the house boarded was to conceal what went inside when she entertained various men.

Luke and Linda were spending less and less time in St. Horatio and finally closed up their house to return to Scotland for an undetermined length of time. Luke's mother wasn't well and something else was going on.

"Are you and Luke o-k Linda. You're not separating or anything like that are you?"

"Hell no Laura; we are inseparable. There are just some personal issues that can only be dealt with from home. We will be coming back but first we have to find alternative living for Luke's mom or we have to consider brining her back to St. Horatio with us. Either way, it is not going to be pleasant."

"Give some thought to coming for a visit on your way back. I want you to meet Seron."

"We just might do that. We will let you know and give you plenty of advance notice. By the way, you sound happy Laura and Seron sounds very nice. I wish you all the best."

As much as I welcomed their visit, I had no place to accommodate them and didn't relish them seeing how I was living. Well that was just life and they would understand. Teddy agreed to make room for them if she had sufficient notice.

Hearing from my friends kept my spirits up. Luke did not mention Sheila in our last conversation and I chose not to bring the subject up. Luke had other things on his mind but he was still worried for me – that he did mention.

Seron was everything to me. My little world was complete albeit poor but I was happier than I had been in a long time and held onto my hopes for a brighter future. There was nothing this man wouldn't do for me or me for him.

Our shared dream was to one day build a small Caribbean house somewhere in the hills overlooking the village of Calibishie. Luxury was lost to me forever but as long as I had a loving relationship and a roof over my head, I really had nothing to complain about and I was willing to make even more sacrifices to hold onto what we had.

Seron had a small primitive shack on the property he owned and farmed on the Calibishie ridge. The area was remote, serene and exotically lush with wild jungle flowers, sugar cane, crops of avocado, banana, grapefruit and oranges. It was here we planned to one day built our home. When he suggested we could live there in the shack and start building one block at a time, if we had to, with the money we wouldn't be paying out for rent; I nearly pissed my pants. I had reservations about living in a jungle amidst creatures of some threat such as Boa snakes and centipedes that were ten inches long but I agreed to it anyway.

We gave up my rental house and moved into the shack not long after the idea was born. The property had not been tended to for many years and was a mess. Seron's crops were difficult to access even for him because of overgrowth and I never considered trying.

We had no electricity, no water and a pit toilet. Once the place was scrubbed down and our bed moved in, we had a very clean shack with a bed in it but the work had just begun. I was able and willing to do just about anything if it was the beginning of something good but it wasn't easy to see the light at the far end of a very long tunnel. Even if we started a foundation – block by block, we were headed in the right direction.

Sam loved the shack and surrounding wilderness and it was much better for him. My rental house was surrounded with neighbors who owned goats and hens and a dog to them was a threat. Their fear proved accurate when we had to pay $150 for a wounded goat and had to take the animal away from the property. That's the way it is in Dominica – your dog bites it and you pay for and own it. The little animal had what I would call a nip instead of a bite but that didn't matter – once bitten the animal had to be killed and it was our responsibility.

Seron took the goat to a group of local men who slaughtered and cooked it that same day. The local dish, an island favorite is called Goat Water and although I ate it once and found it not too bad; I would never eat it again after carrying the cute little goat in the back of the jeep to be slaughtered.

We then had to worry for Sam' safety as other goat owners feared a repeat and went gunning for him. He was kept indoors or on a leash at all times but even when tied, one of us had to be close by. These people wanted Sam killed.

Our ten by ten foot tin dwelling was about as humble as humble could be. I cringed to think what my father would say if he was alive to know how I was living. I wasn't deterred from the dream and set out to turn the shack into a castle of any making.

The beauty of the location made up for the misery we lived in for a while. When we had enough saved we added a ten by ten foot addition made of block with four shuttered windows. We moved our bed into the new space and put a small sofa where the bed had once been.

Seron made a corner counter top work space with an upper tier to store our few dishes and some dried goods. He left enough room between the counter and the door for a small propane stove. He also built me an outdoor Mexican sink. With no drainage, I kept a large bucket underneath and hauled it into the bush to empty. We used a large barrel to collect rain water which in turn was used to wash dishes and do the laundry in plastic basins. We carried the laundry to river to give it a good rinsing and carried it back home to hang on the lines.

There were days when I thought my back was going to break from the simple chores to keep the shack clean, the laundry and dishes done. Sam continued to sleep on the floor beside me at night but we could not protect him from large insects that often bit him and a few times got in his ears. It was here in what the villagers called Zion – the jungle, that life as I once knew it ended and a new life began. He was Tarzan and I was Jane.

I was dreaming if I thought life was going to be easy. My life was pure hell. The roof leaked and we were bitten several times during the night in our bed before we bought a net. But Sam had to suffer.

We cleared an acre surrounding the shack and planted vegetable gardens. On one side I planted flowers and carried hundreds of rocks from around the property to make borders. The local people taught me how to plant by the moon – when to prune and when not to. I learned how to prepare foods the Caribbean way – food I had never before eaten and had difficulty swallowing in the beginning.

My pride and joy were my Almond trees. We found 6 to 10 inch saplings along the beach and planted them strategically on the property to achieve shade wherever we could. Within a few months we had beautiful little trees already taking the shape of umbrellas. We learned how to keep them properly maintained and in less than seven months we were sitting under them.

Seron worked his crops when he wasn't busy at the welding shop. The produce was sold to venders who paid small for his hard work and made a bundle when they sold it overseas. It made me want to cry at so much hard work for so little reward. Cooking was done over open fires before we were able to buy the gas stove but we continued to roast on open fires often to save on gas or to cook fish that stunk up the shack.

Each morning I sponged bathed with rain water in a plastic basin that I carried into the shack and placed on the floor. In the evenings we went to the river for a real bath. We used ice in a cooler to keep perishables from spoiling and soon were able to purchase a small fridge that we kept in the shop where there was electricity. We carried only what we needed for a day in the cooler. Candles were used after dark and I learned to use mirrors instead of more candles to give a better glow and enable me to read a book.

My bare hands were my only tools. At night they ached from abuse and soon looked like they belonged to a ninety year old. I was constantly tired but kept going because I had no choice. Local women taught me to take my time and walk away from my chores to rest when I felt exhaustion coming on. The work was difficult beyond anything I could have ever imagined.

I loved my gardens and spent hours tending to them with Sam at my side but many times I sat in the dirt and cried over never ending weeds and beans that refused to grow. My skin became bronzed and weathered from long days in the hot sun. My weight dropped even more but I grew muscles from carrying heavy loads of laundry or basins of water and rocks for my gardens or just rocks to get rid of so many. My hair grew to a length I never would have allowed had I been able to afford the luxury of a beauty salon. The benefit was being able to tie it back.

My prayers became pleas for some resolution. Seron and I were happy as a couple but I knew I couldn't go on living this way much longer. I had shivers from over exposure and shakes from fatigue. I ate little because I was either too tired or didn't care for what I prepared. Nothing was happening in St. Horatio and I was tired of waiting. My anger turned into rage and then the headaches started. That dam Sheila was living my life and Jim was a no good weakling of a jerk. It was then that Seron began to worry about my well being.

He pulled me from the river water; I was barely conscious.

"What happened to you Laura?"

"I don't know. I think I passed out."

"You don't eat enough – you are weak and too small."

"I can't eat, I don't want to eat. All I want to do is sleep. Maybe I just fell asleep in the water."

We changed rivers to one with more shade and less depth. Again I was being swept down stream and screamed for Seron who had walked up the path to the main road to get the towels from the jeep. Sam ran along the water's edge barking. Seron didn't hear my screams but he did hear Sam and knew something was terribly wrong.

I tried to grab onto anything – the riverbed was filled with large boulders. I felt them on my body as the current rolled me over and over. I was being swept out to sea and would never be found in time if Seron didn't get to me before I went under the bridge. I had no strength other than do my best to keep my head above water but even that battle I was now losing.

My body rolled twice and caught between two rocks; I was face down. All I could do was hold onto one rock with enough ridges to get a grip. I prayed I could catch enough air to breath. If my body broke free I would be rushed into the swiftest current and carried under the bridge and out to sea. When I lifted my face to catch a breath, a rush of water was all I got.

I held onto the slippery rock and felt the lower half of my body coming free from the trap that held me when suddenly I felt two magnificent arms lift me clear out of the water and carry me to shore.

"Water calls you Laura – you must never go in the water again without me. I don't want to lose you."

"It happened several times again with Seron always there beside me. To this day, several years later, I never go in water without him. We don't know why it happens but it does and that is enough and all we need to know.

Regardless of our efforts, by mid-month our money was scarce. Many times we ate only from our garden. Dominica was a hard place to live. No man could earn a decent living and the terrain was too rugged for me. We had to look for an alternative.

Sam was my guardian when Seron wasn't around. He never was more than five feet away from me and no goat or hen could distract him from his duty to look after me. When we went to the river he blocked me from entering the water until Seron was with me. Seron taught him to swim under me and re-surface with me on his back. On weekends when locals picnicked by the river, they watched the show we put on – even though I wasn't in trouble. Never before had anyone ever seen a woman ride a dog in the water.

I didn't know what crayfish were until Seron talked about a river deep in the valley on another property his family owned and it was here Crayfish thrived. They were difficult for locals to harvest which resulted in them being extremely expensive, and there were also government restrictions as to when you could. Seron was eager to feed me things he believed I would enjoy. I loved lobster but it also was expensive and beyond our budget.

I was eager to try Crayfish but hadn't planned on accompanying Seron to get them. He was so enthusiastic about taking me to this special place and feeding me until I burst that I went along for an outing – as he called it. We loaded the back pack and set out with Sam for an adventure. He insisted I wear long pants, socks, sneakers and a sun hat. I was sweating before we got out of the jeep.

If I thought I was living in a jungle before, I had a rude awakening when we began the trek down to the crevice in the earth that housed the crayfish I so desired. I was terrified before we travelled a hundred yards. The journey was treacherous beyond belief with overgrown brush, slippery ground and insects. My heart thundered in my chest while sweat poured profusely from every pore. Seron was incredible with his blade as he cut the path before me. He was a true bush man who carried a back pack weighing at least thirty pounds with supplies for the day. He was in the place and space he grew up in and learned from the father he still adored on how to survive in the jungle. Nothing was too difficult for Seron.

When he got too far ahead of me I called him back - he didn't realize how difficult it was for me but Sam did and never left my side.

Several times I lost my footing on the slippery undergrowth and fell. Sam panted and watched me at all times. When I went down he barked to bring Seron back but never left my side until Seron put me upright again. Sam walked in front of me in an effort to protect when in fact, I only tripped over him. If we walked close to the edge of a cliff's, Sam put himself between me and the drop.

Steep cliffs were on either side of our trail and before we began our journey, Seron gave me a lecture on what not to do.

"Laura don't grab onto anything if you can avoid it. The shrubs are small trees rooted in years of rotted vegetation. They will give way if you try to use them. A tree top could appear to be a shrub but if you grab it you will be sixty feet in the air and out of my reach. Don't gab onto anything. If you are sliding on slippery undergrowth let yourself slide, you will eventually bump into something solid that will stop you. The most dangerous is a tree top – you are as good as dead if you try to hold onto one. Don't react to your instincts."

The struggle to reach the bottom was worth the effort. A narrow river of pure mountain water greeted our arrival. For the first time in my life I realized that quiet is actually noisy – I swear I could hear the birds and fish burping. We stripped off our sweaty clothes and hung them to dry in the sun before we stepped into the refreshing cool water. While I played with Sam, Seron set traps of coconut shells to catch my treat.

Within a few hours he had the succulent crayfish cooking on an open fire with a pot he brought with him. The rest were coming home with us. They were incredibly delicious and worth the effort. Sam and I devoured every last morsel while Seron watched and ate fruit. Surprised he didn't take for himself, he informed me Rastafarians don't eat shell fist. All I wanted to do after such an incredible feast and a trip from hell was lie down and sleep but Seron had different plans.

"We have to move now Laura. It will be dark soon and we can't spend the night here – it's too dangerous."

That was all I needed to hear as I put my clothes back on and started moving.

The journey back up was much more difficult than our trip down. Seron's pack was heavier with the surplus crayfish and wet towels. I wanted to leave them behind but he assured me he could handle it.

We had only gone a few hundred yards when I fell. Seron and Sam were at my side in a heart beat to hoist me back up. It was mid afternoon but the sun was disappearing fast behind a mountain. The jungle floor became even more slippery than it had been coming down and I found myself grabbing at anything as we climbed.

Seron repeatedly called back for me to hurry. He moved faster as the day rapidly turned darker. I knew he was worried and carrying too much weight from the sweat on his shirtless body but I couldn't go any faster. The air chilled but my sweating continued and my heart pounded. My arms and legs shook from exhaustion but I dare not stop or look around me. I used his tracks to guide me.

Fear overtook any common sense I may have had as I attempted to move faster than I was capable of or safe. I kept falling and grabbing things and pulled myself up quickly to keep up with Seron. He was getting too far ahead of me and could not hear me when I called out his name. The more I slipped, the more careless I became as panic set in. Branches and shrubs came away from the earth while I was holding them as though they were never attached to anything or they snapped and made my fall worse.

Seron and Sam were out of my sight. Sweat was dripping down my face and stinging my eyes. My hands shook as I tried to wipe my face with my shirt tail and then my feet came out from under me. I grabbed for anything – I was in mid air when I felt a branch and grabbed it.

The branch was brittle – I knew it couldn't hold my weight for long. The lower half of my body was hanging over a cliff and I froze with fear – unable to even call for help. He would never find me if I went over and he couldn't hear me if I screamed. I swear I grabbed the tallest tree top. I couldn't see the bottom, it had to be at least a hundred feet down and it was already dark down there.

I swung my feet a few times in hopes of feeling something solid but there was nothing and I could hear the branch I was holding giving way. Even if I had the strength to pull myself up, I was sure the branch would snap.

Raw fear kept me from moving another muscle. Surely Seron would realize I was in trouble and come back for me soon but he was so intense on getting to the top I couldn't be sure he would even miss me until it was too late. He would never find my body and soon wouldn't be able to even look for me until morning light and he would need help. If the fall didn't kill me I would surely be injured and forced to spend the night alone amidst a world of Boa snakes and vicious insects.

Seron plowed his way up – swinging his cutlass to make a better trail.

His thoughts ran rampant and he kicked himself for brining Laura here. She was no bush woman and probably wouldn't speak to him for a week once they got home.

Next time I will just get the fish myself and leave her at home with a book. I love that woman so much and don't know what I would do without her. He stopped himself short and listened. Holy shit, I am making a new trail for her but she doesn't know it. What if she's following the one we took down? He couldn't hear her or Sam.

She wasn't on the new trail. She was on the old one that was too close to the ridge. Shit! He stood in the silence for a few minutes to get his bearings and let the sounds of nature guide him when Sam began to bark. He headed back down the trail to Sam. He would find Laura before he did.

Sam was the smartest dog Seron had ever known and he loved Laura.

The branch was making noises – dam it's not going to hold much longer. I could hear Sam panting and getting closer as he blazed his way to me. Don't come to close Sam, go get daddy I whispered. He stood above me on the cliff whimpering.

"Sam go get daddy, go go."

Seron appeared behind Sam and flattened himself to the ground.

"Laura don't move."

"Help me Seron."

"Don't talk Laura – just listen to me and do as I say but don't say a word."

He shimmied out of the back pack and sliced his cutlass into the ground. With one arm he held onto it while the other reached out to grab mine with such force I screamed. Just then the branch broke.

"Don't let go of me Seron please."

"I've got you baby….don't move and don't talk."

With one hand he pulled me up and then paused to re-locate the cutlass to another sport. He pulled again and rolled over to dig his heels into the ground. He pushed himself back with his heels as I came slowly up. The dirt he was kicking up with his heels was in my mouth and eyes. Sam stood perfectly still while Seron worked.

"Laura, I'm going to let go of the cutlass and grab you with both hands. Reach out for my other arm and hold on but don't try to help me. Let your body be free and no matter what, don't let your feet touch the side of the ridge. Let me do the work. I have to pull you up fast, the ground is giving way."

Seron moved so fast I didn't have time to contemplate my feet or any other part of my body. He had both my arms with a grip of steel and hoisted me up and on top of him in a flash. Still holding me, his arms now around my back, he once again used his heels to push us further away from the ridge.

Still on top of him, I was smothered with kisses from both my guys.

We lay there panting without saying a word. My arms felt like they would need to be sewn back on but I was alive and never happier than I was at that moment.

"Oh Laura, I'm so sorry. I never should have brought you here."

"You won't ever gain. I can't do this Seron – I can't go on."

"You don't have to Baby. Climb on my back".

*D*eath threats continued even though there was never an actual attempt to harm me, at least that I was aware of. The voice of the caller was always the same – a man with a Caribbean accent that was difficult to understand. His words varied from call to call but the message was always short, no more than a few words and the intent was clear. I was going to die. I

Sheila had to be behind it but the calls could never be traced. The number showed on my cell but police, including Jacob, said they couldn't track it. I believed it was the lack of technology in the islands or inadequate training of police officers or both. There was also the possibility they didn't try to trace the calls at all and that would not have surprised me.

We had four immigration officers come to our shack for a second time to check my papers. They left when they found everything was in order but not before answering my question – why were they checking on me and why four officers? Reluctant at first to give us an explanation; we insisted they give some reason for the invasion at six o'clock in the morning. We told them of the death threats and gave the names of other officers who were aware and that included Jacob. With this knowledge they now informed us they got an anonymous tip which warranted four police, carrying weapons and their early arrival. The tipper claimed I was illegally in the country and wanted for crimes on other islands.

Nothing was happening with my house because of the failing economy now world wide. Selina was doing her best and that was all I could ask of her. It was probably in my best interest to wait until the economy picked up. I was definitely feeling the pinch with the exchange rate between my Canadian income and the Caribbean dollar.

Seron did his best to keep me happy and understood the torment I was going through. He did bring happiness into my life with his constant love and affection. We went to the village almost every night to have a break from our hard day. We were often the only people in the bar aside from a few locals but we were oblivious to them as we danced without music and hugged on the dance floor. Loving him made everything else seem minor.

Life was an adventure whether I liked it or not. Our days ended always with prayer and love.

Chapter Twenty

Hurricane Dean

*I*n was July 2007 when Hurricane Dean ravaged the island. Sam was not welcome in any of the shelters and we were not prepared to leave him alone in the shack. We knew the risks but he meant that much to me and Seron had grown to love him almost as much as I did. There was never a question of whether we should or shouldn't – it was a mutual understanding not requiring any dialogue.

The storm was due to hit us in the late evening. It was hard to conceive we were getting one when the day was so sunny and nice. Kokonutz now belonged to new owners from the U.K., Mike and Chris Connely who we had spent a great deal of time with in the few short weeks since their arrival on the island. They were in a state of panic about the pending storm and very aware their new business didn't stand a chance in a hurricane. They had never been through a hurricane and neither had I but my guy had been through many.

Seron took charge with help from a small crew of volunteers and tied down the flimsy beach hut that served as the bar. He drove spikes into the ground; wrapped the entire structure with heavy duty rope and secured all to the stakes. We emptied all the shelves and placed the contents in containers and stored them in the bathroom. We worked the entire day and then went to check on Seron's sister Ruth and the kids. They were preparing to leave for one of the shelters when we arrived. Winds had picked up as the sky darkened – we rushed to do we what we could to the house but it was in sad shape and vulnerable in its location. We had to think of ourselves now and rushed to the supermarket to get provisions. Sam was with us the entire day and as all animals know long before humans do, his panting told us we didn't have much time left.

We went to the supermarket to get what we would need only to find the shelves almost empty. Everyone in the village with means had been there before us, but we did manage to get the last few bottles of water.

There was nothing we could do to secure the shack. We had no rope and there wasn't time as the storm had begun. Seron removed the back seat from our jeep to make room for a long night. We spread blankets and pillows to soften the hardness of the old jeep. From our own supplies we loaded the jeep with rum, cigarettes, crackers, cheese, fruit, dog food and a potty.

I was about to climb into the jeep when Seron stopped me.

"Not yet Laura, we still have a few hours before it hits."

"What? What do you call what's going on now?"

"The hurricane won't hit for a while. This is just the storm before it. Let's go to bed; I will let you know when it's time to leave the shack."

We did just that with winds roaring outside our thin tin walls which vibrated with the intensity. The only radio we had was the one in the jeep but Seron didn't want to wear the battery down and said he didn't need some weatherman sitting in an office a hundred miles away to tell him when to duck.

Seron and Sam fell asleep almost instantly while I lay awake praying. It was after midnight when the pinging started. I couldn't identify what it was but I had never heard it before. Attributing it to something falling from trees onto the roof, I tried to put it out of my mind but the pinging continued and was getting more frequent.

At 3 a.m. Seron and Sam stopped snoring in the same breath. Still wearing his jeans, something I had not noticed, Seron picked me up and carried me to the jeep without uttering a word. Once inside the jeep, he closed the door and went back for Sam - then he disappeared.

As I sat looking out through the windshield, the horror of the hurricane passed before my eyes. Sam and I were alone and I had no idea where Seron went but the steady rhythm of pounding told me he wasn't far away and up to something. I didn't dare open the car door.

Soaked through, Seron could barely open the door with the force of the wind. Wearing a big smile —he hugged me and Sam and said:

"Pour me a rum."

"Where the hell were you?" I've been sitting here worried about you and scared to death."

"I was on the roof."

"Seron why in the name of roaring thunder were you on the roof in a hurricane?"

"I was pounding the nails back in before the roof came off." PING

He reached behind for dry clothing – something else he thought of which I never would have. I helped him towel dry and change. He was shivering from the cold and exertion and poured us both another rum.

As dawn was breaking so did the storm. For the first time we exited the jeep to have a look around. I was totally flabbergasted to see we had no damage other than the pit toilet was now in a different location.. Our little tin shack was still standing exactly where and how we left it.

We fired up the jeep and set out for the village to help others who weren't as fortunate as we were.. Several fallen trees blocked our way but for Seron it was nothing to heave them out of our way. Ruth and the children were our first stop. We found them sweeping debris and mopping up water from their house. The roof was still in place but would need repair soon. Seron's shop took on water but nothing else was damaged.

We checked on elderly people who already had teams of volunteers working to help them and then headed to check out Kokonutz. It was still standing thanks to Seron and the crew who worked so hard to secure the place. There was plenty of damage but nothing that couldn't be repaired in a day or two. It was the clean up that would require major effort before the bistro cold re-open. What the high seas washed up – years of garbage, all landed in and around the bar. An old tired – a very large one, still leans against a tree not far from where it washed up. Chris painted in bright blue to match the building and wrote Hurricane Dean and the date on it. It's a great conversation starter for new customers.

From there we went to the inn where the owners were staying. The night had been rough on them. We found them drinking rum while mopping water from their suite.

Hundreds of able-bodied men, women and children were fast at work helping each other. When we could do no more, we tackled Kokonutz. Appliances were lost, huge tree trunks were imbedded inside the kitchen and bar area. Sand was two to three feet high throughout the entire structure – making it difficult to maneuver. What was left of the beach was a mess but those magnificent Almond Trees were seemingly untouched by the storm.

Electricity was out all over the island for the next several days. There were no candled to buy anywhere and those lucky enough to own lanterns could not get kerosene and rationed what supply they had.

Chris and Mike donated the food in their freezers to the needy which Seron and I delivered. Aromas of fried chicken and burgers cooking on open fires drifted along streets and alleys for days. We lost all our crops as did everyone else; a small price to pay for the gift of life. Fishermen lost their boats and those that were spared could not get gas anywhere on the island.

Two weeks later on a bright and promising day, we were hit with an earthquake. Seron was working in his shop while Sam and I spent a lazy day in the shack. Everyone was tired from the long hours spent cleaning up after the Hurricane. I was horizontal on the sofa reading a novel with Sam at my feet when the shack started to shake.

Sam was first to react. He ran outside and stood there barking at me. I thought nothing of the shaking as a tin shack will do that in a strong breeze but when Sam persisted I knew it was more than wind. He wanted me to come out with him but if it was a boa there was no way I was going to accommodate him. I tried to beckon him to come back in with no success. I was getting a little irritated with his barking and rose to check out the problem from the doorway when my dishes started falling from the shelf.

The roar brought me to full alert. What the heck was that? Sam and I stood side by side on the lawn without moving a muscle – beneath my feet I felt the earth moving. Frozen with fear, I stood perfectly still as Sam did also so close to me our bodies were touching.

Seron came flying down the road in the jeep.

"Seron what's happening?"

"It's an earthquake Laura. It's passed now but there is a lot of damage south of here."

For the second time in two weeks we were lucky but those to the south and on neighboring islands were not. Within days the quake was forgotten as life in the village returned to normal.

Christmas was fast approaching and with it a visit from Linda and Luke. They were non-committal over their arrival date and could only confirm they would see us during Christmas week. Teddy was willing to put them up at her place but without a firm arrival date she wasn't going to turn down other business and this was a busy time of year for her.

Teddy had a buyer for her inn – a lovely Dutch woman named Hermien, who was staying at the inn and planned to take over the first of the year. I was sorry to see Teddy leave what she worked so hard at it for many years but she was tired of the nonsense that comes with being in the hospitality business and decided to retire.

Luke and Linda did not arrive over the holidays nor did they call. I had no way to reach them and left the ball in their court. By late January with still no word, I called a neighbor of theirs in St. Horatio - a woman I met several times when Jim and I visited the Diamonds at their home.

"Hello Lucille – It's Laura Cassidy from Dominica. Happy New Year."

"Laura how nice to hear from you, and all the best for the coming year to you as well."

"Lucille, I was expecting a visit from Luke and Linda over Christmas week and they never showed up and I haven't heard from them. Do you have a number where I can reach them?"

"Oh my Good Lord – you were not informed. Oh Laura I am so sorry be the bearer of bad news. Luke and Linda had a terrible motor vehicle accident just a few days before Christmas. They were on their way to the airport. Linda died instantly and Luke two days later..

"I didn't know – oh My God – oh Lucille how did it happen, what happened – what about Luke's mother?"

"A drunk driver crossed over the dividing line and into their lane. He hit them head on – they didn't have a chance. The driver was killed instantly and Luke never regained consciousness. Luke's mother died two weeks later but she was never told of the accident. It was Luke's brother John's decision. You know she wasn't well and they had just settled her into a nursing home a few weeks before the accident. John is coming here in March to close up and sell the house.

I cried for days over the loss of my friends.

Seron and I were not making much headway saving money. My jeep was about to die any day soon and still no word on the sale of my house. After a hurricane and an earthquake I needed something positive in my life. I dipped into what little savings I had in Canada to put a bathroom in at the back of the shop. We couldn't afford another vehicle and we couldn't continue to live in the shack on the ridge without one. With no other options, we moved into the shop just days before the jeep took its last chug a lug.

Without my gardens to occupy my days, I was going out of my mind. The shop was dirty and busy with people coming and going all day long. There were hens crowing at 3 a.m. and dogs barking non-stop. Neighbors were out of the homes before sunset chatting with each other in loud voices and then the bread truck arrived at dawn – horn honking to announce his arrival.

I started to sew quilts for Ruth and the children as well as for myself. We gave up our dream for a Caribbean cottage – it seemed useless to have a dream at all. If anything we were going backwards instead of forward and hard as I tried, I could do nothing about anything. Even Sam was miserable.

Seron's business fell off dramatically with the loss of our jeep and before long the shop became a hang out for local guys with nothing better to do than drink rum and smoke marijuana which Seron was also doing at an increasingly alarming and expensive rate.

Without a vehicle Sam didn't get his daily beach exercise and a bath. Seron walked him to the sea a few times but it was never the same again. It was hotter in the shop but at least we had the shower now. When I took Sam into the shower with me to cool him off one day; I came out to find one of the fellows who I didn't care for, with a stupid grin on his face. He questioned me to the point of irritation as to why I would take a shower with a dog. His innuendo and manner was offensive and I was antry with Seron for not putting the man in his place or throwing him out for his rudeness.

My head was sore from thinking of ways to make money. Adding an upper level for two or three rental rooms had appeal but to get anything done would take years. Everything hinged on money and the only money on the horizon was from the sale of my house and I no longer wanted to make a life in Dominica.

I gave up dreaming and lived one day at a time and hated every minute of it. Seron was becoming too comfortable with me as the provider and did less and less to earn his own way. My daughters wanted me to return home to Canada but I wouldn't leave Sam behind and I wasn't giving up on St. Horatio. I also loved Seron very much but we would not have made it together as a couple in Canada.

Chapter Twenty One
Jim / 2008

If I thought about Jim at all I couldn't think after five minutes. I harbored so much anger toward him it wasn't healthy for me. He had a saying that always annoyed me but it was so full of truth that now I played it over in my mind when ever I felt the anger rise to the surface.

"Anger spoils the vessel in which it's contained."

I did have some good memories of him but they were foggy now and I didn't want that to happen. I didn't deserve a lot of what was happening now and certainly not pu t up with a lot of unnecessary nonsense in the years we spent together. He didn't deserve the way I left him and for that I had to take some responsibility.

Jim was very ill and probably not destined for many more years on this earth. I hoped they would be happy for him but doubted they were with Sheila. I had seen and knew enough about her to worry for Jim but if he found comfort by having her around, then that was all that mattered.

Jim was very good at putting square pegs into round holes. He often convinced himself that things were one way when in fact they were not. That was how he justified situations he could not control.

I never regretted ending my marriage – only the way I went about it. My life was of my choosing. I could have returned to Canada at any time and live better but I chose to do what I was doing and to be where I was destined to be. Sheila was not my problem nor would I let her be. She had to answer to God for her own behavior and I had every faith that she would get her due.

Jacob called me in February 2008 to tell me Sheila and Jim were married. The news came as no surprise and other than a brief concern over my house; I put their life out of my mind. The feeling of pending doom hung over me like a cloud but I didn't know why.

Seron didn't fully comprehend the situation in St. Horatio and I hoped he would never have to. My headaches and nightmares increased and with it his worry for me. I knew he would protect me but we were living in his world. What if we had to live in mine?

In the third week of February we walked to the closest river to give Sam a long overdue bath and some quality time with us. By the time we reached the path leading to the river, we were all in need of cool water and a bar of soap after a three mile walk. It was late afternoon – the return trip would be cooler and was down hill.

It troubled me to see Sam unhappy and I was sure it was because he worried about me too. He was more protective me than ever before and stayed so close to me at all times, I was always tripping over him.

Every day presented a new set of troubles to deal with. Seron couldn't make payment of the electricity so I paid and the refrigerator he bought for his sister a year before I met him was being repossessed for non payment. I couldn't let Ruth lose her fridge so I paid for it. Then the washing machine went on the fritz and because she did my laundry for me, I paid for the repairs and then it was the stove and something else again after that. I wanted to float in the river and prayed I would be washed out to sea this time.

We were just about to jump into the cool refreshing water when I heard my cell phone ringing. It was at the bottom of the back pack Seron carried and by the time I fished it out, the ringing stopped. The call identifier showed Commissioner of Police. It was Jacob but I had no time left on my phone to call him back. It was his routine weekly call to check up on me. He would call back another time. I dropped the phone back into the pack and stepped into the cool water where Sam was already having a good time.

I looked forward to those weekly calls from Jacob and Lionel and hated it if I missed one. I never had enough money to keep my phone topped up and had to rely on them to call me, although they didn't seem to mind. We were all swimming when the phone rang again. Seron and I both dove for the back pack.

"Jacob – hi – glad you phoned back. I couldn't get to it fast enough the first time. We are having a swim at the river. How are you?

I could not hear what he was saying over the roar of the river.

"Jacob I can't hear what you're saying. I'm walking up to the road. Hold on."

"Keep talking to me Jacob, I'm hearing you better now and I'm almost at the top."

"Laura, how are you?"

"I'm fine Jacob; it's good to hear from you."

Seron and Sam had followed me back to the road. I should have known my guys would not let me wander the path alone – always my protectors.

"Laura you're not alone at the river are you?"

"No of course not, Seron is right here with me."

"Good, I was hoping you were together. I'm afraid I have some disturbing news for you."

"What, what is it Jacob?

I was out of breath from the climb back up to the road and now the hair on the back of my neck stood up – a frequent feeling I had come to loathe.

I'm sorry to tell you Laura - Jim is dead.

We left the river and walked to the nearest shop to top up the phone. Seron would be eating macaroni for supper instead of fish but this was more important. Lionel told me his guest room was vacant and I was welcome to stay with him. My second call was to my sister Mary. She purchased an e-ticket for my flight on line and called me back with the information. I flew to St. Horatio the next morning.

*T*wo days following their marriage, Jim returned to Canada to resume medical treatment that he had begun the previous December. Sheila did not go with him on either trip. In fact Sheila had never been to Canada with him; had not met his children nor had they visited their father in St. Horatio.

While in Canada he stayed with his daughter Sarah and her husband Tony, who lived in a remote rural area a hundred miles north west of Toronto. Sheila called their house several times a day to speak to Jim. Sarah and Tony owned a farm with many animals. They had few conveniences, one phone in the kitchen being one. They had to stop what they were doing and run from one of the barns to the house to answer calls. They soon became worn out from Sheila's persistent and irritating calls.

Jim was asleep in the upstairs bedroom for many of the calls. It wasn't easy for him to traverse the stairs to get to the phone – he needed assistance every time. The calls became a nuisance and were upsetting Jim. After the second or third day he asked his son-in-law to tape all future calls from Sheila.

The calls kept coming and were increasing in frequency. Jim started refusing to come to the phone. Sheila yelled, screamed and threatened whoever answered the phone – demanding Jim be awakened to take her call. Jim's daughter was getting upset with the calls and in particular the tone used by Sheila who she believed was drunk.

When Jim did take a call, they fought. Sheila was packed and leaving him. She called him horrible names and accused him of being a horrible father to have raised such a rude and nasty daughter. How dare this girl speak to Sheila in that way? Did he not teach his children respect and good manners? Her two sons were well mannered and nice young men – how did he fuck up so badly with his kids?

The situation went from bad to worse, leaving Jim shaking and in tears. His health wasn't good and this was the last thing he needed to deal with. Tony took all calls to spare Sarah further grief. He went head to head with Sheila who was so vulgar he hung up on her and wouldn't answer the phone for the remainder of the day. This hurt their business but the constant interruptions and disruption in their home didn't help business either. These calls were also taped.

Jim slid into a deep depression and openly cried in the presence of his children. They were not happy when he announced upon his arrival his marriage and now they understood the reason why. None of his children had met Sheila but after three years of her meddling in family affairs via e-mail and phone calls, they were all of the opinion their father was making a mistake to be in the relationship. The woman was a gold digger and now with a marriage license to her credit, she had no further use for Jim. She was living in his house and he was too sick to do anything about it.

....Sheila resorted to e-mail messages to Jim and other family members. They were horribly venomous and offensive. In her mind and so stated in many of her messages; she was the victim and not prepared to suffer any more abuse from the family.

She demanded Jim to put his daughter and her husband in their place and defend his wife's honor. How dare they treat her the way they did.

She reiterated in her messages to all Jim's failure as a father and a husband. She wanted out of the marriage and was leaving unless he took her side.

Jim did as Sheila demanded and had a horrible falling out with Sarah and Tony before leaving for St. Horatio. He sent e-mail messages and made phone calls to his other children and called them horrible names and delivered much the same message given to Sarah. He had worn out the welcome mat with all his children and the many friends he bunked in with during his many stays in Canada. He now had no place to stay, abandoned further treatment and returned home. Sarah was so crushed by her father's actions she became ill and was bed ridden for some time after he left.

It wasn't until after Jim left on the 20th of February 2008 that his kids listened to the tapes that Jim himself requested. He left a note on the tape machine, later found, asking the tapes to be kept in a safe place as possible evidence.

After listening to the tapes and discussing the content with James and Kathy, they all worried. Three days later their father was dead.

No longer legally married to Jim, I had no legal rights in any matter concerning him other than our shared property which Sheila now claimed to be totally hers. I wanted to attend his funeral but also had my own affairs to take care of. I wanted to know how he died – as did Jim's children. For the first time in almost four years, his kids were reaching out to me for help. I was the only one who could make enough noise to have his death investigated.

Jim's body remained in the cooler the ten days I was on the island and Sheila never left the house. She called the police several times a day to report I was trying to kill her – she was afraid to leave her own home she claimed.

I discussed my suspicions with Jacob and reported, at his children's request, the events of his final days in Canada and their request for an autopsy. Jacob requested copies of the tapes.

I met with the medical examiner who confirmed Jim died of a stroke but at the time of admission to the hospital, he had no prescribed medication in his body and hadn't been taking his medications for at least 48 hours before his death. His death certificate cited death due to natural causes which I officially disputed on the grounds that without his medicine, he would have had a stroke. This was the sole purpose of the pills he took.

Sheila refused to allow an autopsy and she refused his children's request to ship his remains to Canada. I couldn't convince authorities to override her and requested an autopsy be ordered to rule out the possibility of foul play. On the grounds of expense to the local government, my request was denied. I offered to pay for it but nothing every came of it.

Less than a week after Jim's death, Sheila faxed a copy of his new will, dated January 30, 2008 to his children. Again they made contact with me. He left them nothing - everything went to Sheila including my house. She was named also as the executor and administrator. My Jeffery asked Sheila's lawyer for a copy of the will and was refused.

Mr. Jeffery assured me Jim could not bequeath what he did not own and I had nothing to worry about. As much as I wanted to believe him, how could I when I was sure beyond a doubt she had a hand in his demise. What else was she capable of?

Sheila went temporarily off the deep end when she learned I was the irrevocable benefactor of Jim's pensions. I was certain she knew this already but I was wrong. She talked to Jacob about it and asked him to ask me if there was any pension she was entitled to.

"I don't believe the nerve of that woman Jacob. After all she has done to me she now wants me to help her pick at Jim's bones."

There was one pension that she would have been entitled to but I was not about to help her in any way. She had twelve months to apply or lose it. For the first time in thirty years I prayed for my next birthday. I did not tell Jacob.

"Jacob, I am the sole benefactor of all Jim's pensions. I have already notified them and it has been confirmed. I will begin receiving them at the end of the month. Tell Sheila to get a job."

News of Jim's death spread around the island like wildfire. Along with it came anger from residents. Many times I was stopped on the street by people and questioned. Everyone wanted to know what happened and to give their opinion or voice their suspicions. Many said they saw it coming but not so soon. They wanted to know what funeral arrangements were made. I knew nothing and had no say.

Among the rumors were tales of Sheila escapades to replace Jim only weeks before their marriage. Two recently widowed men were approached by her with an offer to become their companion and care giver. Both men, aware of her reputation and her current status with Jim, sent her away.

Out of money, no service for Jim on the horizon and what business I had to take care of now done, I went home to Dominica after ten days. Jim was buried in a pauper's grave shortly after I left the island. There was no service for him. His children were not given the opportunity to pay their final respects and only a handful of people attended his grave site.

Within days of returning home, a source from St. Horatio who shall remain nameless, advised me Sheila was bragging about two insurance policies in Canada. Jim and I cancelled all our business before moving to the Caribbean. If there were policies – we overlooked them. I booked a flight to Canada.

There were two policies that Jim and I overlooked. Both were paid up for years which explained how we missed them but once I learned that Sheila was making a claim for them, I remembered I was the beneficiary. Of one thing I was certain; if Jim was fool enough to change the beneficiary designations then I was mean enough to make claiming it difficult for Sheila.

The beneficiary designation on both policies was changed only weeks before Jim's death. Even Jim's children who were named contingent beneficiaries were removed.

For over thirty years I worked in Life and Health insurance and knew what to do. I contested both policies which forced the insurance companies to place the proceeds with the Canadian courts. In order for her to get the money she had to hire a Canadian lawyer, pay court costs and be present for hearings. In other words she had to sue me.

I didn't want the money and couldn't afford to take on another legal battle. Let her wallow in this one for several years and I doubted there would be anything left after lawyers and courts got through with it.

After four weeks in Canada, I returned home to Seron and Sam. It was now the first of June. I was receiving Jim's pensions and for the first time in years had a rainbow over my head to replace the cloud.

I could have moved back into my house in St. Horatio but as Jim's wife, Sheila was entitled to live there now too. It would not be a healthy situation for us to share the house and I was not willing to pay for even half the up-keep. The court order still stood and soon it would be sold. All I wanted was what I was entitled to and to make a life in Dominica.

Sheila's lawyer, Mr. Henry, finally provided Mr. Jeffery with a copy of the will in late June. He was anxious to get my house sold so he could get paid. Jim had never given him a retainer or paid any sum of money toward the cost of the divorce and everything else Mr. Henry did on his behalf. Sheila also refused to pick up the tab.

Mr. Jeffery faxed me a copy of the will. The first thing I noticed was the amounts that would be deducted from my share. The American Express tab and a loan Jim supposedly gave me while we were still married.

My lawyer assured me that Jim could not rule from the grave. He didn't cancel the credit card and the court had to assume he intended for me to keep it. I borrowed no money from him but my brother did but that was not my debt to re-pay.

For three days I didn't look at the will again but I did speak to Sarah, Jim's daughter. They noted inconsistencies in the will and drew my attention to them. With a magnifying glass I took a deeper look at the will. How did I miss it?

I dare not get my hopes up and took my time to think it through before taking action. From the internet I found Mr. Curt Baggett - world renowned forensic handwriting analyst. I read many articles on the man and watched an old video of him as a guest on one of the popular late night talk shows.

After several telephone conversations with Mr. Baggett, I couriered the will to him along with several samples of Jim's signature. Three days later Mr. Baggett confirmed the will was a forgery.

During the time I waited to hear from him, I received an e-mail from a Toronto lawyer who had been retained by Sheila. She was offering to split the insurance benefits with me 50/50 if I would sign to have the courts release the funds.

Lionel told me of an insurance policy of his that Sheila forged several years into their marriage. He didn't find out about it until they sold their first home and was furious. It cost him money to undo the damage she did and keep her out of jail.

"Laura you need to get a Canadian lawyer. I'll call my sister who has a friend who is a lawyer in Toronto. I think she specializes in insurance. I'm also going to mail you copies of Sheila's handwriting. Have this guy in Texas take a look."

My Canadian lawyer obtained copies of the beneficiary designation certificates from the two insurance companies and couriered them back to me. Mr. Baggett was well informed and waited to receive my package. One week later he phoned me to give me his findings. Not only was the will a forgery but so were the insurance forms. Sheila was the forger.

Now a police matter, I asked Mr. Baggett to courier his reports directly to Jacob Sylvester with a copy to me.

This discovery changed everything for me, including my life. She wasn't going to get away with it. On the advice of my lawyer in Canada, I agreed to split the insurance benefits with Sheila. I contacted Federal and Provincial police. The insurance fraud was considered a civil matter – they would do nothing about it. The truth was the proceeds were too small to catch their interests and we were two insignificant to waste their time on.

Much the same attitude was taken in St. Horatio. Who was this Curt Baggett? Well some excuse. I was told the FBI would have to do their own forensic analysis and that could take several months. It was all a dam hog wash and the FBI never received the information.

With help and advice from several sources, my plan began to formulate. Down and dirty – that's how it was going to be from now on. I would beat her at her own game and be the victor. I waited for the signal from St. Horatio.

Chapter Twenty Two
Home

*I*t came on November 10ᵗʰ 2008 with a telephone call from St. Horatio.

"Now, come home now Laura. Get on the first plane. Sheila is not in the house – she's in the states. Someone is staying there but it's your house. Take it back NOW. And one more thing, bring Seron with you. I can't protect you round the clock.

Seron and I didn't sleep that night. We packed everything we owned except our clothes and put the rest in storage. I flew to St. Horatio the following day with one small suitcase and my laptop computer. That was all I owned in the world.

Before flying out we booked Seron and Sam on the cargo boat for the following week. It was all we could afford and promised to be a rough voyage.

Many thoughts went through my mind as I watched the beautiful island of Dominica fade from my view out the window of the plane. Would I ever return? I knew the answer but wasn't ready to face it. I was going home and would fight to the death if I had to. I recalled the threat I made to Sheila if anything happened to Jim and now I planned to make good on that. I'm coming to get you Sheila.

I arrived by taxi at my house shortly before sunset. No one was there and her car was not in the garage. The house that was under construction the last time I had been there was now occupied. I asked my new neighbors to look after my things for a few hours and waited in their house until I saw Sheila's car coming down the road. Hurriedly, I got to the gate and inside before Christina, the house sitter was out of the car.

She was startled when she saw me standing there, now in the dark.

I am Laura Cassidy and this is my house. I have to ask you to leave."

"In refuse to leave. I am caring for dogs and house while Sheila is away" said the woman in a heavy German accent.

Just like Sheila she had her cell phone in hand and soon thereafter the police arrived as did George – a so called friend of Sheila's who Christina had never met before. She was given his number to call in the even of trouble.

She refused to leave and so did I. We stood in the middle of the road with the police and George while cell phones were ringing and everyone chatting to who ever on the other end. No one was willing to leave – the police didn't know what to do.

I borrowed one of the officer's cell phones and called Jacob. He told me not to leave, stay put – get into the house and stay there. He called me back ten minutes later and said he had been speaking with police legal counsel. I was to enter the house and stay. He spoke to the officers. Shortly thereafter, Mr. Jeffery called. He had been speaking with Jacob and gave me the same instructions.

"Get inside the house. Don't be frightened – the police are there to protect. Get inside now. Don't stand in the road."

The police were visibly confused but what ever it was Jacob said to them, it was clear they were protecting me. It was either stand in the road until dawn or come to a compromise even if temporary. I didn't fear Christina and had no problem if she remained. It was George I was unsure of. He was authoritative and pushy and I could see no logical reason why he was involved.

We finally agreed for the sitter and me to stay in the house. She was caught in a problem not of her own making and was far away from her homeland doing a favor for a friend. The police insisted George also stay in the house to keep the peace. I didn't like the odds but didn't feel threatened by him and he wasn't willing to leave. I was tired and wanted to get on with it before I lost my nerve. I reminded myself to look at the bigger picture. Get in and take over. The rest will fall into place.

Christina, with the cell phone still glued to her ear, was now talking to Sheila who was giving her instructions to remove her jewelry from the small wooden box on the dressing table in the master suite. I had no problem with that but kept my eyes on her as she moved around the room By this time tomorrow there would be nothing of Sheila's in the room. When Christina was finished I locked the door behind her and changed the bed linen.

I was frightened in many ways but not in the way I anticipated. From somewhere deep within I found the strength and courage to do what I had to do. I only prayed Seron arrived before Sheila returned. I had a week to live through on my own with George and Christina.

....Lionel assured me Sheila would not bump up her return date. She didn't like to spend money unless it was someone else's and it was costly to change an existing confirmed flight. I was counting on this. If anyone knew her it was him but I didn't rule out the possibility he could be wrong. I was prepared either way.

It was rough the first few days but eventually everyone came to an understanding. Christina was scheduled to return to her home in Germany the day after Sheila's return. She wasn't happy with the situation and I couldn't blame her. She was promised exclusive use of the house, pool, vehicle and two weeks in the tropics in exchange for house and dog sitting.

Now she was faced with me living in the house and George who she didn't know and who now took Sheila's car early every morning to go to work and not returning until sunset. I overheard her arguing with him about it but he was of the opinion that he was in charge and could do as he pleased.

George carried himself as if he owned the property and when I told him:

"You behave as if you own this property." His response was:

"I do own this house."

George claimed he was a good friend to Jim and was carrying out his wishes to take care of Sheila. This I found odd given that George had not seen Jim for a few months before his death because of a falling out he had with Sheila and what I knew were miserable last days for Jim. What his relationship was with Sheila following Jim's death was unclear.

I scrubbed my room and veranda where I spent most of my time. Following Mr. Jeffery's instructions I packed everything of Sheila's into several suitcases and large storage bags and placed it all in the center of the great room. Jim's leather jacket, the first gift I ever bought him, was hanging in the closet. I kept it for sentimental reasons.

Under the bed I found a magnificent diamond ring that I suspected was Sheila's wedding ring. After taking several photos of it, I took it to Christina who confirmed it was the wedding ring. She was stunned when I told her where I found it but thanked me and put it in her room – presumably with the rest of Sheila's jewelry she removed from my room the first night.

I sent the photos, using my computer to Jacob and Mr. Jeffery along with an explanation. I wasn't taking any chances.

The only thing I didn't tackle was the bottom drawer of the large credenza that housed our large television. The drawer was heavy to open and contained over fifty old VHS movies. Some were mine and Jim's but others I wasn't sure of and it was not important.

George had a fit when he returned home later that day to find Sheila's belongings where I put them. Christina didn't so much as look at the stack of suitcases in the middle of the floor but I had no doubt she reported everything to Sheila daily.

Several times I overheard George speaking to Sheila on the phone. He ended their conversations by saying "I love you too." When Christina talked to her, they spoke German.

The gates were kept locked day and night. I couldn't get out and no one could get in without the keys. Lionel brought me groceries daily and handed them to me over the fence. I had no way to get into town and had no cell phone. When Seron called me on the house line after not hearing from me for a few days, George told him I was not allowed to use the phone.

He never denied me use of the phone when it was Jacob or Mr. Jeffery and he didn't dare. That was the first serious roar I had with George. He was smug about it but when I told him I planned to have Jacob speak to him, he handed me his own cell phone and told me I could use it for one call a day. I threw it back at him, unplugged the house phone and re-installed it in my room.

After calling Seron back, I then called Jacob who brought me a cell phone later that day. He either knew or anticipated that Sheila would put a secret code on the phone to prevent me from calling out and that's exactly what happened the following day.

My house was set up for wireless computer access but I was being blocked which I assumed George had something to do with. Christina locked the office the first night of my arrival and kept the keys on her person much like Sheila always did. I didn't want any trouble but my computer was my link to the world.

George agreed to connect me and had to go into the office to connect whatever it was that either he or Christina had disconnected to prevent me from internet access. Whoever the culprit was, they were following Sheila's orders.

I stayed clear of the west wing of the house where Christina's room was and made no attempt to access the office. I had plenty of time to do that later and did not want to disrupt what little harmony we had. It wasn't beyond me to kick in any door that blocked me but I had all that was needed for the time being.

Jacob and Mr. Jeffery worried there would be a show down when Sheila returned. I didn't know what was going to happen but I knew I was home to stay and would hold my ground. I set up a journal to record daily activity within the house. If nothing else, I was sure Sheila was going to come out of the gate with accusations and lies to make me look bad. This was her pattern for many years, and Lionel repeatedly reminded me to anticipate her and watch my back.

Legally, neither of us could put the other out of the house but I was going to challenge that and many other things. It bothered me immensely that the police did nothing at the time when something should have been done. It was too late for an autopsy and I doubted I would have any more success if it wasn't.

As little as I knew George, I somehow felt he would become an ally. He believed he was doing the right thing but in time would come to see things for what they were and that included Jim. Christina was scheduled to return to Germany the day after Sheila's return but I still didn't trust or put anything past her. Jacob did get contact information for her just in case he needed to reach her after she left.

Sheila was a pathological liar and there were few people on the island who didn't know it; but Mr. Jeffery just happened to be one of them. I grew increasingly annoyed with him when he questioned me on everything – most of which he was getting from Mr. Henry who had yet to see the whole picture. He had not received any of his fees from Jim when he was still alive and Sheila refused to pay him herself. Jim's funeral was unpaid, again Sheila's doing, and many other outstanding debts were coming to light.

*L*ionel took me to catch the first ferry on the day of Seron's arrival. George left the gate open for me at my request. Lionel was no more than a hundred yards up the road when he slammed on brakes and backed up. He jumped out and ran to the gate and was back in the car and moving again within a matter of seconds.

"What was that all about Lionel?"

"Anticipate Laura – always anticipate." He dropped the lock in my lap.

I waited in the hot sun on the pier for Seron. In my excitement to see my man and my dog, I neglected to bring a hat with me. By noon I was sunburned to a crisp.

The vending machine ran out of everything by noon. I hadn't eaten and the one bottle of water I carried with me was long gone. I walked three miles to a supermarket to get food and water and walked back to the pier.

Needing to hire a truck to carry Sam and his kennel, I walked again to a work shop at the far end of the compound. Here I found a man willing to take us to the ferry for a fee. When the boat had not yet arrived at 3:30, the man gave me back my deposit and left. By this time, most of the workers had left. There wasn't much chance of getting another truck and I didn't know what we would do but was confident Seron would find a way.

Customs officials were now worried when at 4 o'clock the boat had still not arrived and were not responding to the phone or radio.

The agent for the boat advised me to return to St. Horatio on the last ferry at 5 p.m. She was sure the boat would not arrive before then and was encountering mechanical difficulties on the open sea. I had no money for a room and didn't want to be away from my house overnight. Sheila was due back the following day and I couldn't risk her arriving with me absent. The agent drove me back to the supermarket to get water, bread, fried chicken and cigarettes that she promised to give to Seron when the boat came in. My boys would be hungry and were now on their own.

I was half way between islands when I saw the missing boat in the distance but I couldn't turn back. Seron was resourceful and would somehow manage to get to me. I just prayed he got their before Sheila.

I watched the boat come into the St. Horatio pier from my veranda shortly after dawn the next morning. Like a race horse I half ran down the mountain. Seron did not know where my house was and might need help with immigration.

The first pick up truck I saw stopped when I hailed the driver who was willing to help. When I arrived minutes later, Seron was sitting on a railing eating bread while Sam was beside him in his kennel – both were exhausted and happy to see me. We loaded the truck and headed home.

George was standing on the upper deck overlooking the driveway with his arms crossed over his chest and his feet apart when we pulled in. If ever there was a warrior stance, it was George. I hadn't had much chance to fill Seron in on the past several days and there was no time now.

When he saw George standing there, he hesitated and was reluctant to leave the spot he was standing.

"It's alright Seron. Don't worry about him. Please be brave and just do as I ask you."

"I can go stay someplace else Laura. This doesn't look good."

"No Seron, this is my home and now yours. Let's go."

I took Sam out of his kennel and started up the stairs.

"You're not bringing that thing in here."George roared.

"And you are not telling me what can or cannot do in my own home. Get out of my way George."

"He backed away to let us pass and never took his eyes off big Sam. He was visibly shaken at his size and unsure of his temperament.

"Meet Sam George and the man is my husband Seron."

We unloaded the one suitcase Seron brought with him; got Sam settled with food and water and had a quick tour of the house before settling on the veranda off the bedroom for privacy. I filled Seron in on the events since I last saw him. Sheila arrived three hours later.

There was no confrontation or fanfare upon her arrival. George did not go to work that day or the next. Sheila slept on the couch in the living room that first night while George continued to sleep on the front veranda sofa. I didn't set eyes on Sheila until the following morning. We stayed in our space to avoid trouble but it wouldn't last long.

Christina was packed and ready to leave by ten in the morning. – Sheila drove her to the airport leaving George behind – that was the first I saw of her. Upon her return - she wasted no time setting the stage for what was to come. As she slowly climbed the stairs to the upper deck where George waited for her, she went into her act and she was a very good actress.

"Oh George (she hugged him), I feel so sorry for Christina and am so glad I was able to help her."

"Why, what happened?" (looking concerned).

"All her euro was gone from her purse when we got to the airport. Someone stole all her money. Poor girl was so upset. I had to loan her enough to get home."

I was sitting on the veranda and George knew it but Sheila could not see me from where she performed the first act. George said nothing to her about my presence.

George continued to stay in the house. He was gone early every morning with Sheila's jeep and didn't return until the evening. He carried in bags for her each night and carried out the empty bottles the next morning. If he arrived home without bags, she jumped in the jeep and went to get her supply.

Mr. Jeffery called me two days after Christina left and asked me if I took her money. I was outraged but quickly got control of myself. My lawyer had a lot to learn and that would happen quickly. The best I could do for myself was stay calm and lead him to the truth.

"Laura I just got off the phone with Mr. Henry. Sheila wants him to have charges brought against you for the theft of her jewelry and the house sitter's money."

"Do you believe I would do such a thing? I am not surprised at the accusation and you shouldn't be either. I sent you an e-mail to report the little show she put on for George about Christina's money being stolen and you knew Christina removed Sheila's jewelry from my room the first night. I also sent you photos of the ring I found and gave to Christina. This is just the beginning."

"No Laura I don't believe it and I'm not sure either if Mr. Henry does but he did call me and asked me to talk to you. I hope you understand."

"Yes I understand exactly what is happening. I just hope you and Mr. Henry get with the tour soon. Tell Mr. Henry to press charges."

Mr. Jeffery's call did upset me but only because he thought it was necessary to question me. When George came back later that day I asked him if I could speak to him in private.

"George what did you think when Sheila told you about Christina's money being stolen?"

"I didn't believe her. I know Christina had her money when she left the house. She was counting it on the kitchen counter."

"Sheila is accusing me of stealing the money and her jewelry. If you knew she was lying, why didn't you confront her?"

"If Sheila knows I'm onto her, she will clam up and probably kick me out. I need her to believe I am on her side if I am going to help you.."

"Why would you help me George? We haven't exactly been good buddies."

"I'm not as stupid as you may think and I am now seeing for myself that you are not what I was told you were."

"George, you know she's setting you up don't you?"

"Laura, she's setting herself up and she will fall flat on her face. Let it happen."

"Are you willing to make a statement about seeing Christina count her money before she left?

"I already have with Jacob but for now he wants to keep that between us. Mr. Henry, if he knew, would tell Sheila and that's what we don't want.

It is best Laura if Mr. Jeffery doesn't know for a while as well. Lawyers stick together and it's too much of a risk."

For the first time I was glad that George was staying in the house. I confirmed his story with Jacob and felt better that he had told me the truth. His agenda wasn't clear and he didn't know me long enough to switch camps. There was more to George than I gave him credit for but I was sure over time, many things would come to light.

Getting supplies was difficult for us. We walked up and down that mountain many times and took a bus when we reached the main road. We could only carry so much which meant many trips and there were other things in town that demanded my presence; visits with Mr. Jeffery and banking. I also began the process of putting all utilities in my name and met with resistance when I learned Sheila was always one or two days ahead of me to do the same, but as the house was in my name, I was able to achieve my goals.

We were preparing to leave early one morning when George offered to drive us. Sheila went into a fit of rage when she overheard his offer and refused to allow him to drive us.

"No George, you cannot take them in my car. I won't allow it."

"Don't be so stupid Sheila. There's no reason why they should have to walk down the mountain when I'm going down now myself."

"I said no George. They won't be covered by my insurance if there's an accident."

Angry and defeated, George left without us but when we reached the top of the road – he was waiting for us.

"That woman is crazy. She just doesn't want to make it easy for your Laura but from now on just let me know if you need a ride and I will meet you wherever you are."

We took many rides from George and Sheila never knew about it. He reminisced about Jim and told me things I didn't know. They were close friends and it was George who was Jim's care-giver. He chauffeured him everywhere and ran his errands for him. They played chess almost every night together or sat talking for hours. George was very intelligent and well read – Jim would have appreciate and enjoyed his company.

Jim invited his new best friend to move into the guest room. Sheila was drinking heavily and was foul mouthed and combative with Jim. He needed a buffer and George would have been perfect. But one day he found his bags packed when he came home from work and Jim could only say it was Sheila who insisted he move out.

George told me that he stood by Jim's side when he was on the treadmill for his daily exercise. It was he who changed his dressings, help him bathe and get dressed. When Jim was hungry, George prepared food for him.

"Sheila did nothing for Jim Laura. She spent his money and kept the house tidy by having a housekeeper come in almost daily. Jim was paying for it and didn't like what it was costing him. She also had the supermarkets order in specialty foods that only she ate. Just take a look in the freezer on the front veranda. I paid the bills for Jim or when I took him to town, he did himself if he was able. When he was in Canada, I don't know how these things got paid but I know that Jim was always upset when he returned to find overdue bills and warning letters in his mail."

"Did you continue to see him after you moved out?"

"Oh yes, I never gave up on Jim. He needed me and knew it but it was hard because I had no car to get up the mountain and sometimes slept on the sofa when Sheila passed out drunk. A few times Jim loaned me his car."

"What were they like as a couple?"

"Jim ignored her most of the time but he didn't want to be alone. I thought of telling him I would stay with him if she was gone but I was afraid he would misinterpret my intentions and I didn't want to lose him as a friend."

"They must have had something between them George."

"Sheila was always nasty and condescending to Jim. It bothered me when she said things to him in front of me and once I took her on and put her in her place. It was shortly after that I was told to move out."

"What did Jim do when you argued with Sheila?"

"He stayed neutral when I told him he was being foolish to put up with her. He said it was the booze that made her that way and I told him to stop buying it for her. His response was she would go out and get it herself and he didn't want her driving when she was drinking. I gave up after that. It was no use talking to Jim about her. In his mind he needed the companionship I guess."

George and I were becoming friends but we never showed it in Sheila's presence. Her antics continued with George but now we compared notes and I kept making entries in my journal.

Because he was able to maintain a close relationship with her, and she believed he was her strongest ally, George now gave me the heads up when he saw what her next move toward or against me was going to be.

Her drinking was escalating and with it came insanity. We often head them talking late at night on the front veranda. George scolded her for the excessive drinking and often sent her to bed when she was so drunk she wasn't coherent. She accepted this from George and became child like. For what ever reasons, Sheila needed George's approval and he used this to his advantage.

When she started greeting him at the end of his work day with a hug and a kiss in our presence, George realized how much of a patsy she thought him to be and became more cautious around her. When Jacob asked me if I thought there was something between George and Sheila, I knew right away what her strategy was and warned George.

George cautioned Seron to never leave me alone in the house with Sheila. We didn't take the advice seriously and he didn't elaborate on his reasons for giving it. What he was really doing was giving us a warning but we didn't understand that in the beginning.

George did not know until we were in the house for four weeks about the forgeries and my suspicions over Jim's death. Sheila passed out drunk in her room earlier that night as she was most nights and these were the times that George came over to our space to chat.

The look on George's face was one of disbelief and I regretted telling him. I told him of the many death threats, the stalking of me in Dominica and of a few other things that related directly to me with hopes of defusing the previous information.

"George I should not have told you about the forgeries or my other suspicions."

"That's o-k Laura but I am really shocked. What makes you think she had anything to do with Jim's death? He had a stroke – I know that to be a fact."

"He had no prescribed medications in his body when he was admitted to the hospital and he hadn't taken any for several days. The medications were to prevent a stroke. Do you see where I'm going with this George?"

"Jim never missed taking his pills. I sat with him so many nights at the kitchen table while he meticulously filled his monthly container and cut some with a special cutter. It always took him two hours and he wouldn't let anyone help him or come near the many bottles of pills he had."

I gave George the web site for Curt Baggett and suggested he check out the man's credentials. I did not offer to show him the reports but I did tell him it was confirmed Sheila had forged everything. It was up to George to decided what he wanted to believe, but I knew this new information was going to take him a few days to sort out for himself.

"How well do you know Jacob Sylvester George?"

"I've known him all my life. We went to school together."

"If there is anything you know of or have the slightest doubt about, you should talk to Jacob."

Seron was vulnerable and Sheila took advantage of it. When she turned on the charm – complimenting him on his hair or lean body, he swallowed it and thought she was being nice. I tried to warn him but he thought I was being silly. When she came toward him, I got in her way.

Sheila tried daily to find an excuse to get into my room. There was nothing there that belonged to her but she insisted she was missing something and would just take a look. I never allowed it but Seron did once when I went into town alone to meet with my lawyer.

He was on the bed watching TV when she came in."

"Seron, can I just take a look in the drawers for my favorite CD.?"

I learned of this when I arrived home and was very upset with Seron when I found the remote for the TV and the air conditioner missing. Those were the only two things in the top drawer she looked in. She tried continuously with me claiming some of her favorite things were not in the suitcases I packed which were now all in her room.

The first place I searched on the night of my arrival was the medicine cabinet in my bathroom. There were no pills there of Jims. All his clothes still hung in the closet and in the drawers of the dressers he used, yet he had been dead ten months when I arrived. Where then and why were the pills missing?

Sheila confused herself with the lies she told. First she said she took all the pills to the hospital the night he was admitted and they gave them back to her after his death in a shoe box wrapped in brown paper. Later I found a note from Sheila to the hospital and their note back to her. She didn't take the pills as requested but rather gave them a list.

This information along with other accountings of inconsistencies was given to Jacob and Mr. Jeffery.

She didn't relent on the search and when that wore out, she was now in search of Jim's leather jacket which I openly admitted I was keeping.

"Well you can have the jacket Laura but there are other things missing and I need to check the closet."

"No Sheila, you are not coming into my room and will have to take my word for it. There is nothing of yours or Jims left in the room."

"Why can't we be friends Laura? Jim would have wanted that."

"I am not interested in being your friend and you have no idea what Jim might have wanted. He sure as hell didn't want to die."

"We both own this house and until it's sold we have to get along."

"I own this house Sheila and I don't want to get along with you."

"Jim left me his half and I deserve it. I looked after him."

"You didn't look after him Sheila – you killed him."

Later that day and well greased with whatever she was drinking, she asked for Jim's leather Jacket. When I refused, Seron instructed me to give it to her. I didn't want to but I also didn't think it was worth fighting over and she was drunk. I gave her the jacket and didn't speak to Seron for the rest of the day.

Sheila remained in her room drinking for most of every day. She came out only for an hour when George returned from work. She took the dogs into the yard to do their business and sometimes made something to eat in the microwave.

The dogs were not looking healthy and were stressed with their confinement in the dark vacuumof her room. We tried to convince her to let them be free in the house but she refused. When one went missing, it was me who found him not far from home. He didn't want to go with Sheila and cringed at my side when she forcefully dragged him back to her room.

In our fifth week Jacob asked Seron and I to meet him in Mr. Jeffery's office late one afternoon. We couldn't find a ride and walked down the mountain to catch the bus. Both men were waiting for us when we arrived. Something was in the air.

(Jeffery) - "How often do you leave the house Laura without Seron?"

(Laura) - "Not often at all – maybe just a few times I guess when I came to see you. Otherwise we always go together to buy groceries."

(Jacob) - "Seron, has Sheila ever come into your bedroom when you are home alone?"

(Seron) - "Only once she actually came in to look for a CD and Laura has never let me forget it. The two remotes were gone. She opened the top drawer of the night table where we kept them."

(Laura) - "She's always trying to get into our room with one excuse after another but I have never let her in. There is nothing of hers there and you know that."

(Jacob) - "Seron, have you ever gone into her room at any time?"

I bolted from my chair when I saw where this was going. My anger took both men by surprise. Jacob rose to meet me. He put his hand on my arm and asked me to sit back down.

(Laura) - "How dare you go this route when you know dam well what a witch she is."

(Jacob) - "Laura, I don't believe for a minute what Sheila is about to accuse Seron of. She has been bending Mr. Henry's ear about Seron making advances toward her and he in turn has reported it to me out of concern."

(Laura) - "Well fuck Mr. Henry. That man has to be completely stupid. When is he going to wake up and smell the shit where roses never were?"

(Jeffery) - Calm down Laura and don't swear in my office. I think we went about this the wrong way. Hear Jacob out please."

With steam coming out my nostrils I sat back down to hear what better be a good explanation.

(Jacob) - "From this minute on I do not want you and Seron to be more than five feet apart. If you leave the house – even to take the garbage out, Seron goes with you."

(Laura) - "Jacob this is ludicrous and you know it."

(Jacob) - "Yes it is but let me explain where this is going please. Sheila is laying out her game plan and now she has targeted Seron as her means to an end. If Seron is in the house alone with her and if she calls the police to report a rape – there are no witnesses and whether you believe it or not – your dog can't talk."

"Sheila would not call me – she would call the closest precinct and the officers would have to do their job Laura. They would have to arrest Seron and take him in for questioning. He could be held for days before we got to the bottom of it and you know I would do my best but procedure has to be followed."

(Laura) - "I don't believe this is happening – surely Jacob you can't leave Seron and me at her mercy with such stupidity."

(Jacob – now angry) - "You are missing the point Laura. Seron would get out but first he would have to go in. Our only concern here is that you would be left alone in the house with Sheila."

My good God, this never occurred to me. What a bitch this woman was. How could I be so stupid?

We were never apart after that but it didn't stop her from trying to engage Seron in any way possible. She asked him to open a jar of jelly or could he lift something for her or she just sat down on a chair beside him and filled his ego with compliments on what a great looking guy he was.

She tried the same thing on me but I was wise to her and one step ahead at all times. When she came within ten feet of where we were, I told her to get out of our space. She sat her in her lounge chair reading a book and blocking the door to the kitchen. The minute she was out of it, I folded it up and put it away. She got another and another until I finally had them all finally stored in the garage.

Mr. Henry was eager to get this matter over with and asked that we all meet in Mr. Jeffery's office to discuss it with Jacob as mediator. I was not interested in any meeting because there was nothing to negotiate. I wanted a court hearing and my lawyer and Jacob knew it.

"Go along with it Laura. You will have your day in court but for now let's grant Mr. Henry his request to meet. This will be your chance to show him you are not the witch he thinks you are. He calls me three and four times a day because Sheila is calling him twenty times a day with stories about you that make him cringe. Let him see for himself who you really are."

Seron and I were walking down the mountain on our way to the first meeting when Sheila drove past us. I was wearing a white cotton semi flared skirt with a blue form fitting bra halter top that was very striking and a white blouse over it for modesty. Everyone but Sheila arrived at the appointed hour. She kept us waiting forty minutes.

It was a total waste of time but I went along with it. The only purpose for the meeting was to set a price for the house and get it sold. That would put money in the lawyer's pockets and me out of a home. I said nothing. Mr. Henry then made an offer on behalf of Sheila, who sat beside him, for me to move out of the house until it sold and she would pay me rent. I suggested she move out and I would not pay her rent because she had already been living in my house and owed me a year's rent as it was.

Sheila was on her best behavior but when she opened the large bag she brought with her to the meeting and dumped her underwear on the table – the meeting changed.

"This is the way I found my things when I came back from the states. Everything has to be ironed now because of Laura."

"Put your underwear away Sheila, that is not the purpose of this meeting." Said Laura.

Jacob and Mr. Henry were visibly shocked at her inappropriate display of lingerie. It took several minutes for then to regain their composure and carry on.

When Jacob asked Sheila if she was willing to pay me rent as Mr. Henry had offered – she said no.

Mr. Henry and Sheila had obviously discussed this before the meeting but now she was not cooperating with her own lawyer. The meeting was left with several things up in the air. We were all to consider what was being proposed and return three days later to continue.

Sheila was wearing a white skirt, blue halter top with a white blouse over it for the second meeting and was on time. I complimented her on all the lovely jewelry she was wearing and pointed out the wedding ring I found for her. Her face reddened when she realized her own vanity betrayed her.

She was difficult through the entire meeting. She wanted her cake and the icing too. Whatever she may have discussed with Mr. Henry prior to the meeting, she now contradicted him on everything. When the tears began to flow over her on-going grief of losing her beloved husband and her fear of being homeless when she worked so hard to care from him, both lawyers rolled their eyes and I tried unsuccessfully to stifle a laugh.

"Sheila, cut the crap. You didn't give a dam about Jim. You were packed and leaving him just days after the wedding and you didn't bury his remains, you discarded them and have yet to pay the bill."

"Jim wanted me to have my house. He promised me. I really loved him and miss him so much."

No one paid attention to her final remark. Jacob declared the meetings were of no use and brought the current one to a close."

The four of us carried on as before. Sheila was drinking herself into oblivion. Her body was bloated, she sweated profusely and seldom came out of her room. Christmas was only a week away. Mr. Jeffery petitioned the court for a hearing but it wouldn't be scheduled now until after the holidays. The law and the courts had a responsibility to me and to Jim and it was high time they lived up to it.

Seron and I were in town together when Jacob received a frantic call from Sheila. She was locked in her room and Rasta had a knife and was trying to kill her. As Jacob listened to her, he was watching us sitting on a bench in the park in front of Mr. Jeffery's office drinking a beer. It was ten in the morning.

"Where are they now Sheila?"

"They're right outside my door. They have it blocked – I can't get out. Laura is drunk and swearing and yelling."

"Sheila, I was the one who put the new locks on your door. The door opens in, not out. You can't be blocked in."

Jacob did not tell her he was watching us.

Two days later George received a similar call from Sheila as he drove through town.

"George, Seron has a knife. They're trying to kill me. Help me please – come home."

"Calm down Sheila. No one is trying to kill you and you have to stop drinking, it's making you crazy. I'll be home just as soon as I can."

"No George, come now – I'm so frightened. Laura is going to kill me. She been trying to kill me since I met Jim. She wants my house and will kill me. Please come now."

George pulled over to the side of the road to let us out.

"Call me on my cell when you finish shopping and I will come back for you."

"Thanks George. Is there anything we can get for you?"

My kitchen cupboards were getting bare. Every morning something else was missing and within a few days there wasn't a pot, spoon or glass anywhere to be found. Then the paintings on the walls began to disappear.

When an exasperated Mr. Jeffery called me to inquire if I had everything under my bed; we both began laughing. Mr. Henry was concerned after Sheila reported I was stealing anything that wasn't nailed down.

"I sat in the dark on my veranda in the small hours of the morning. Through the window that had a clear view of the great room, office and Sheila's room, I witnessed her come out of her room and many times go into the office which remained locked at all times. When done with whatever she was doing in there, she then roamed the house and hiding all that she could carry back to her room.

George was a sound sleeper and either didn't wake when she was doing her business or he chose not to interrupt. When after a few days passed and he couldn't find the coffee pot, I knew he was truly a sound sleeper. He never asked me about the missing things and I never volunteered what I knew."

Her calls to Jacob, both lawyers and George were out of control. Mr. Jeffery warned her several times not to call his office – he was my lawyer. When she didn't stop, he had her calls blocked. Jacob was weary as well from continuous disruptions from Sheila. He couldn't believe a word she said but as a police officer, he had to listen.

Jacob arrived one evening after speaking with me and George. He wanted all four of us present and Sheila sober. He was on his way.

Wearing shorts and a muscle shirt, the big cop stood on the veranda leaning up against the wall with his arms folded over his chest. He looked tired and concerned. The four of us had no idea why this sudden meeting and waited patiently for him to begin.

"This cannot continue. Someone is going to be murdered. We are going to take a little tour around the house. Everyone stand up and come with me."

We walked into every room with the exception of Sheila's and the office. Jacob pointed to every piece of furniture, rugs, television sets, radios, kitchen appliances and so on. He then asked who it belonged to as each item was identified.. Everything was mine with the exception of very little. What I wasn't sure of, George was. He lived in my house with Jim and knew it better than I did. He confirmed all was mine.

"Sheila, you don't own anything in this house. You didn't buy the house and you didn't build it with Jim. You have made no contribution whatsoever. This house and everything in it belongs to Laura. You have no right to be here and a twenty day marriage to Jim doesn't give you license to anything. Now you can go to court if you want and you can play your games and turn on the tears, but I have enough proof of your lies and other things that I will testify to in court if I have to."

She sat there crying while Seron and I went to our own space. Jacob wanted to talk to her alone but we could hear. She admitted the house was rightfully mine and admitted she lied about me stealing from Christina and her jewelry.

The missing pots and pans were not discussed that night. We did not go into her room because she had the door to it and the office locked and refused to open them. The dogs were in her room and Jacob wasn't eager to be around them. We did go into my room because I had nothing to hide and insisted we identify the furnishings as mine.

Seron cleaned the yard with a minimum of tools. Sheila sold the lawn mower and pool equipment only a few months before I came back. I cleaned the house and was paying the bills. We had to hire a pool service because we had no equipment to do it ourselves. That too had been sold.

When a man came to take my generator I had to send him off the property. He claimed he was taking it as payment for a large sum of money Sheila owed him and had been instructed by her to come for it. I felt sorry for him but he was only one of many who had been scammed by Sheila. He was not happy when I told him I owned the house and all that was in it. Like everyone else on the island, he knew much of what had transpired and was understanding. He offered me his best wishes and left quietly.

Sheila was keeping busy either selling things out from under me or giving them away. Small end tables disappeared and I had no idea what remained in her room. The freezer that was loaded with delicacies was now emptied and it wasn't being cooked in my house. George began to keep his eye on things and if Seron and I had to be away, we coordinated it with George. Someone had to be home at all times. Someone was helping Sheila cart things away but we never found out who it was or when this happened.

It saddened me to see my house in such a sad state. Nothing had been done since I left but I was sure Jim believed the money he was forking over to Sheila was going to keep the house in good shape. George told me she never had the grass cut until a few days before Jim returned from Canada. She didn't pay for services and could never get the worker to come a second time.

When people came banging at my door looking for wages owed to them, I had no choice but send them away empty handed but I did get their phone numbers and gave them the promise of future work if I needed it. I told them to submit their invoices to Mr. Henry or to small claims court. They were all happy I was home.

Christmas came and went. Seron and I had nothing to cook in and little money to buy anything. It wasn't important to us – we were happy to put up my beautiful Christmas Tree and look at the moon and stars on Christmas night.

Sheila went out on Christmas day for several hours. George spent the day with his mother. We had the house to ourselves and only cried over the two dogs locked in Sheila's room.

Jacob's concern was mounting but he kept in close contact with Sheila and promised me it would be over soon. I didn't ask and he didn't volunteer what was going on but I knew something was about to happen.

Sheila was becoming verbally abusive and began having accidents. I couldn't stand it much longer or the stench coming from her room. I suggested to Jacob he get her some help. Call her family if he had to but the woman was killing herself and out of control. I didn't care if she ended up dead – I just didn't want it to happen in my house.

Cock roaches started shortly after the stench from her room. George was fed up and wearing down and I feared he would leave. We sprayed but the house was over infested and required more than a can of spray. We searched everywhere to find the source of the foul smell and believed there had to be a dead rodent in her room and there was no way we could get in without breaking down the door or a window and Sheila refused to give any of us the key.

I worried for the dogs, now lethargic, thin and glassy eyed. Even George couldn't get her to release them from their prison. For the short periods they were out of the room, they ran to me and buried their heads in my lap when she approached. She was brutal when she pried them away and returned them to her room.

My long time good friend Karen is a psychiatrist. We always kept in touch by e-mail and were like two school girls when we got together in Canada. I wrote to her daily with reports of what was going on in my house. Karen specialized with alcohol and drug addiction patients of the worse kind. She believed Sheila was at the breaking point and diagnosed her as psychotic and dangerous.

I discussed this with Jacob who wanted to communicate directly with Karen. I could see Jacob's concern with every new day and this was an area where he had no training and likely not a great deal of knowledge. Karen gave him her professional evaluation of Sheila with the understanding she had never met the woman but felt comfortable enough to provide him with some basics he should be aware of.

She sent him clinical papers defining sociopath- psychopath along with case studies. I read all this also and although not a health provider, I could clearly see where Karen was going with it. Jacob found the information disturbing as well as informative and realized something had to be done soon before someone did get hurt.

Karen's closing remarks to Jacob were even though Sheila led Jacob to believe she accepted the fact of my ownership of the house, it was just another trick on her part. She did not believe I was owner or entitled to anything and she would never let go of that belief. I was the target and had been long before Jim died when she learned how the house was registered in both our names, irrevocable benefactors each in the event of death.

It was also Karen's belief that Sheila was insanely jealous of me for many reasons. The episode of the white skirt and halter top was one. While my ego was having fun at the thought of someone being that envious to copy my exact outfit, I was way off base and Karen was very quick to point that out to me.

Sheila was obsessed with my hair and asked me what products I used to make it so healthy looking. When she saw me after shampooing and noticed the curls, her reaction was indescribable. She was angry I had curly hair that I chose to straighten. Again my ego dominated and I happily surrendered to my ego and told her what she was doing wrong with her own hair. She wanted to be me.

Sheila asked about my teeth – were they real? She told me how much Jim talked about my intelligence, my successful career, my warrior attitude and relentless will to achieve. Lionel said she never worked a day in her life but bragged of her success at various jobs that were a totally fabricated to impress others.

Her unrelenting advances toward Seron were again misinterpreted and a rude awakening when Karen drew my attention to it. She didn't want Seron so much as she didn't want me to have him. When I looked at it from this angle I saw what I should have been seeing all along.

She didn't want Jim either, only what she believed he had to offer and that was to fill the vacancy I left open. She wasn't liked by many people whereas I was. I had my own business and although it was short lived, it was successful.

What Karen made me see after some head bashing was the way Sheila was seeing things. It was hard for me to put myself in the head of another person. God knows Lionel was trying but how does one think with the mind of a psychotic? Sheila did not see the envy or jealously that motivated her. I was the enemy and that was what I had to keep foremost in my own mind at all times.

Sheila's pattern could not be overlooked. Her cries of fear for her own life, was her way of getting people to take her side. She needed Jacob – the big cop with a great deal of influence and the lawyers and what friends she had, to believe I was a threat to her. Then when I was dead and Sheila had all that I owned, she would be the winner and all these ignorant people would believe I deserved to be.

Her closing comments to Jacob were to see me as the victim and in danger. Sheila's behavior was changing rapidly and being fed by mind altering drugs. Her recommendation was for me to be removed from the danger zone. As long as Sheila was within reaching distance of me, my life was in danger. As long as I lived, Sheila would lose and she knew it. There was only one solution – in her mind.

Lionel's words about playing hard and dirty were easier said than done. I relied on logic and placed great faith and trust in people. To him that was a mistake for the situation I was in.

"Trust no one Laura – not even Seron. You can't expect others to anticipate what you yourself seem unable to do. Treat everyone as though they are blinder than you are. If you don't see it first, you can't expect them to."

He also had a phrase that I will never forget. "The enemy of my enemy is my friend."

Aaron and I took turns sleeping at night. Sheila fell often and a few times cut herself on a broken glass. We feared she might burn down the house if we didn't keep watch. When she began to wake George up while he slept, he also began to stay alert and set up devices close to where he slept to alert him when she approached. She was possessed.

She tried to befriend Sam with cookies but I quickly put a stop to that. She knew how much I loved my dog and when she was around I kept him at my side or scolded him for taking a cookie from her. I let her know I did not want her anywhere near him but she kept trying. I bleached and scoured his food and water dish daily and never left uneaten food out for him.

I kept recalling a workshop I attended a few years before Jim and I left Canada. It was called the Landmark Forum. Our host and leader spoke of knowledge. We all know what we know, we all know what we don't know, but when we don't know what we don't know, that is when we get kicked in the head. There was so much I didn't know and I didn't like not being told what others knew and were not saying. Jacob knew more than he was willing to share and I accepted that as police confidentiality but if my life was in danger, I had a right to know whatever it was I didn't already know if it meant my my safety.

Jacob called me one morning just before the New Year to report Sheila had an accident in her room the night before and would I check on her.

"What happened to her Jacob."

"She said she got up in the night and there was water on the floor from a leaking pipe. Her foot slipped on the wet map and she fell and knocked herself out."

"Jacob, the dogs would have barked or I would have heard her fall. We all take shifts sleeping now for fear she will kill herself or burn down the house."

"Have you seen her yet today?"

"No."

"Well when you do, I want you to report back to me."

It was only a few hours after my chat with Jacob that she came out onto the veranda wearing a thick white towel to cover her neck and upper chest.

"What happened to you Sheila?"

The story she told me was quite different from the one she told Jacob. I listened and said nothing. Later, when she was back in her room, I looked in the hall outside her door for signs of a leaking pipe. When I went into the power room to check the plumbing, I found broken glass on the floor and in the sink which was clearly a wine glass. There was no leaking pipe.

George was home less and less and that troubled me. Things were going to come to a head and I needed and wanted him close by. When he was home, Sheila hauled out bags of garbage from her room for him to take down the road immediately to the dump site.

When I asked him why so many garbage bags, he told me they were empties.

The stench we determined was coming from her room. There was nothing I could do about it for now and Jacob told me to ignore it.

"That's easy for you to say Jacob, you don't have to live with it."

Jacob started showing up unannounced daily to speak with Sheila. They sat together on the front veranda and spoke in hushed volumn. He did tell me he called her son in New York after I told him she needed help and they were trying to get her home and into rehab. That was good news but would she come back to St. Horatio when she thought she was cured?

She looked terrible, was incoherent and had not bathed in some time. When she came onto the veranda and started hugging Seron up, I remembered hard and dirty and went for it.

"Go take a good look at yourself in the mirror Sheila. You're an old bag. Look what you are doing to yourself. You are bloated and smell foul. Can't you stay sober long enough to take a little care of yourself and I will tell you this only once. Keep your hands off Seron."

My words got the desired results. She retreated to her room and I never saw her again.

On December 30th Jacob came to tell me and George that Sheila was gone. He didn't say where other than she was on another island to think things over. I didn't believe it. She wasn't well enough to change her clothes let alone travel to another island for the weekend.

George released the dogs from the room and bolted it shut behind him. It seems he had a key after all. We kept the dogs with us and did our best to nurture them back to better health. They were in bad shape but happy to be free.

George was upset that he had not been in the loop where Sheila's departure was concerned. I couldn't blame the man but I thought he had seen enough to know better. Perhaps that was what upset him.

Jacob was again vague with his information. Was she coming back or not? That's all I wanted to know. I didn't care if she was spending the weekend on the moon. I just didn't want her to return.

Jacob asked me not to attempt going into her room for the time being.

Other than the stench, I had no desire to go into that room and George had the only key.

On January 1st, Jacob and George went into Sheila's room and closed the door behind them. When they emerged a half hour later, one of them was sick in the powder room just outside the bedroom door. I was again asked not to go into the room but I was also told Sheila had returned to the states to be with her sons and that was good news.

Chapter Twenty Three
Closure

On January 3rd we could no longer stand the stench and roaches in the house. Seron went to the garage for an axe to break down the door. Nothing could have prepared us for what we found. Every pot, pan and dish was piled high to the ceiling along with wall hangings, linens and tools.

Several large green garbage bags were the source of the foul odor along with human and animal feces on the bed, floor mats and the mounds of clothing strewn everywhere. All food stuffs, once located in the kitchen pantry filled every available space. It took both of us to push open the bathroom door where more spoiled food and dirty dishes filled the tub and sink. It was totally disgusting and I wondered how much, especially the human waste was deliberate.

It took us three days wearing rubber gloves and face masks to clear out the room. Everything was burned with the exception of one thing – Jim's leather jacket. We hired two local men to scrub and disinfect from top to bottom and I personally took on the bathroom.

I called Jacob when we first entered the room to tell him. He sighed with relief, telling me he had been trying to find someone to do the dirty job. He didn't want me to have to face such a horrid task. No one was willing to come to my house for any price. Sheila's reputation had put the fear into the local people and Jacob, in fairness, forewarned potential cleaners what they would be up against.

We hired someone to spray for roaches but the cost was prohibitive. We bought our own sprayer and did it ourselves. It took eleven weeks with several sprays each week before we were roach free. In the meantime, the rats came causing another major initiative to rid the property of the little beasts that ate through several cushioned chairs and window screens.

Finally we relaxed and settled in to enjoy our home. We kept front and back gates locked at all times and still feared she would return. I thought about her many times but could only feel pity for someone so messed up and tortured. I didn't understand the psychosis she suffered but I also wanted her to get help and live out the rest of her life in peace with her family. If anyone could help her, it was them.

Seron started work with a local welding company while I cleaned house until I thought my hands would drop off. I didn't lack for things to do just the money to do the major things that were long overdue.

Sheila's dogs returned to good health and roamed free with Sam through the house. George moved out a week after Sheila left but came regularly to help with the clean up and to walk the dogs. He was now a good friend who suffered himself from the ordeal. We discussed many things on the evenings when he shared a meal with us. He had been used in the worse way and now looked at Jim in a different way. Only he could come to terms with how he had been treated in the past few years.

George was a good man who only had good intentions, first with Jim and then with Sheila. Jim's weakness in dealing with Sheila was a betrayal of the friendship George believed he had. I gave him the marble chess set he played so many times with Jim and told him the history of the set which Jim never did.

We bought the set on our trip to Greece in 1994. It was very expensive and heavy. Jim so much treasured it, he carried it back home rather than place it in our luggage or ship it. It sat on our coffee table in our all three of our homes in Canada. He taught our grandchildren how to play and was trying to teach me. It was a source of many hours of pleasure for Jim and I was sure he would want George to have it.

There was a time when many people on the island did believe I was a threat to Sheila and had done Jim wrong by leaving him. Sheila was a master at telling lies and did as much to taint the memory of Jim as she did to me.

Lionel and a few other friends spread the words of truth. Sheila wasn't gone a month when she began pressuring Mr. Henry to force the sale of my house so she could get her share and demanded I pay her $2,000 U.S. a month rent until the house sold.

She submitted a sworn affidavit, prepared in the U.S. and had it sent to Mr. Henry and Mr. Jeffery. In it she stated that I was the one drunk all the time. I was filthy and the house was such a pig sty that she could stand it no more and left. She also claimed I stole money from her house guest and had yet to recover the missing jewelry.

The ten page affidavit got more vicious as each page was turned. Clearly the woman was not in her right mind and prepared the paper herself. It is hard to conceive that any decent lawyer would be party to anything so libel and offensive without proof.

The few friends Sheila did have, abandoned her soon after she left. They, too, recognized how she had used them for her own purpose. She left her car behind and told George he could have it. Two weeks later, a couple showed up and demanded the car. They claimed they were friends of Sheila's and were promised the use of her car while they vacationed on the island for a few months.

Jacob intervened and contacted Sheila. She claimed if George wanted the car he had to pay for it. He didn't have funds to purchase it and Jacob in turn, bought it for his son. When he wired the money to Sheila, she refused to sign the car over to him.

Mr. Jeffery did not want to go any further with my case and resigned. The next phase, if it ever came to pass, was to contest the will and go for damages. I wasn't letting Sheila off the hook and I wasn't going to live my life in fear she might return. I wanted closure and justice for Jim. As my case had the potential for criminal charges, Mr. Jeffery admitted this was not his area of expertise and he felt it best for me to find another attorney.

I was saddened that he no longer represented me but was totally grateful for what he had accomplished. He is a man of great integrity and talent and I would miss his friendly smile and sparkling eyes.

My friend Karen's words that Sheila believed the house belonged to her were confirmed when we received the affidavit. Jacob was shaken when he read it because he believed he convinced her to walk away. He now knew she used anyone including him, said whatever the situation demanded and was capable of anything. When George told me the same thing over dinner one evening, I asked how he knew that.

"She always believed the house was hers. She doesn't want half Laura. She wants it all and we are not out of the woods yet with her."

As the months passed with no further sign of Sheila we became more at ease. We purchased a used vehicle, making life so much easier. I hate to think even now how many times we walked up and down that mountain. Seron had to return to Dominica in March for a short trip and the night he left I got my first death threat since arriving home. Someone was watching me and knew I was home alone. George came to stay with me until Seron returned.

Major plumbing problems cost us more than we could afford but we had to do what we had to do. At first inspection by our plumber, he informed us that much of the problems were caused by sabotage. I put nothing past Sheila. It all started in the room she used, spreading throughout the house causing damage to floor tiles and walls. We repaired only what was necessary to prevent further damage and worked out a plan with our plumber to spread out the expenses.

The water tank that supplied water to the house from the cistern was too small to support the house. The original one was somehow damaged as was the pump. Sheila replaced it soon after Jim passed away with a tank too small and a cheap pump. We would soon have to replace both for a significant price. The windows on the east side of the house were rotted out and needed replacing but we had no money to do it. It seemed so never ending and we questioned the wisdom of keeping the house but as long as Sheila as in the picture, even from afar, I wasn't about to leave my roost.

The plumber, Leonard, was due to arrive to do some more work for us. Seron needed to go into town and I couldn't leave until Leonard did. He left the car for me to join him in town and walked down the mountain to catch the bus. Seron was so reliable, loveable and wonderful. I hated being apart from him even for a few hours.

Forever tired I flopped on the sofa with my novel. Sam was at my feet on the floor snoring before I opened the book and I wasn't long before I too was snoring. Sam was my door bell and would let me know when Lennie arrived and my plumber was one of the few locals who wasn't afraid of Sam and always brought him a treat.

Sam' whimpering woke me. I loved my mid day naps and didn't want to wake up. My pillow was already wet from my drooling when I reached down to the floor to pet my big boy and he wasn't there.

"Sam be quiet – mommy's sleeping. Let me sleep."

I was alone, but something came around my neck with such force, my head slammed back onto the arm of the sofa so hard I felt the wood beneath the thick cushioning.

I grabbed at my throat trying to get at whatever was choking me. My fingers felt a cord and I almost had it when my head was slammed back again, half lifting me from the sofa. With my head tilted back painfully, I saw her face. Sheila you are one miserable bitch.

Sam' whimpering had my attention. Where are you dam dog? I could hear him running back and forth on the pool deck. He was panting and growling between whimpers.

Her distorted face hung over mine. With eyes that bulged from their sockets, I saw such evil that brought back so much of what Lionel had tried to warn me of. This woman was crazy out of her mind and I was alone and Sam was locked away from me. Oh dam, what am I going to do?

Her mouth was twisted in a snarl that housed fangs I was sure. Sweat dripped down her face – her hair was stringy and matted to her head. I could see the rope. t It was our orange electrical cord that Seron had just used yesterday and left on the veranda. It was so tight around my neck I could feel my flesh burning from the tension. My head was going numb and I couldn't breath.

She tugged at the cord over and over. When I thought I had a break and could do something, she slammed me down again.

I gasped for my last breath. Oh shit, why didn't we see this coming? This is what she had in mind all along. Why didn't Jacob throw her sorry ass in jail when he had the chance? What is wrong with these people?

On his way down the mountain Seron waved to our friend Samuel – the taxi driver who so often gave us a ride with our groceries and charged us next to nothing. Why was he coming up the mountain road? This wasn't his usual run unless he had a private fare – thought Seron.

Seron stopped at the bus shelter and pulled out his pack of cigarettes. It seems he supplied most of the males in the village when he was around but he didn't mind and neither did I. They were all good guys who were always willing to lend us a hand when we needed it. They chatted and smoked and smoked and chatted and no dam bus came along. Didn't matter, he wasn't in a hurry and he hadn't seen Lennie go up yet to our house so it would be a while before I joined him in town.

Seron had what he later called a brain freeze which he meant was the top of his head went very cold just before his ears started to buzz. His subconscious met his conscious mind while he stood there mute with his buddies looking at him as though he had sprouted a second nose.

Samuel had a passenger. He thought nothing of it when they waved to each other but now his awareness took hold and he realized he recognized the passenger who did her best to keep her face from view as the bus passed. It was Sheila.

He said nothing to his friends and started running. They called after him.

"Hey, where you going?"

Seron ran as fast as his legs would carry him while his friends started to run after him.

"Call 911" – he yelled back and kept running.

Lennie was taking his time driving up the mountain in his old truck when Seron suddenly leapt in front of him. Like a monkey he was in the cab before Lennie could change gears.

"Drive this bucket as fast as you can. She's back. I just saw her and she's going to kill Laura."

Sam was no longer whimpering - he was howling and scratching on the screen. I had no strength or voice. It was all I could do to take the next breath which could be my last. Insane people have amazing strength.

My throat was on fire. I was sure my head was no longer attached to my body when everything went black.

"Dam it Lennie. I don't have the keys to the gate. I left them with Laura. Ram the sucker – I'll pay for any damage to this heap. Just ram that back gate at full speed."

"Hey no charge man. This one's on me."

At full speed Lennie did just that and sent the double gates flying into the air. With Seron in the lead, they two the stairs three at a time – ran past Sam and burst through the locked screen doors.

"You no good mother-fucking bitch--I'll kill you!"

He lunged at Sheila's head and whipped her off her feet as most of her hair came away from her scalp. She fought back crazed with her teeth bared and her face wet with perspiration. He punched her in the face with his fist and she came right back at him trying to sink her teeth into his neck. Seron showed her no mercy. From the corner of his eye he saw me unconscious and slightly blue in color.

Lennie tried to help but got kicked in the nuts hard enough to take him to the floor.

"Get to Laura Lennie. I'll take care of this one. Take care of Laura."

He couldn't believe how strong she was. Man alive he had been in bar room brawls over the years and never met anything like this. He knew he could take her out but he didn't want to kill her – not in the Caribbean. He could see the headlines…Black Rasta man kills innocent while lady in her own home. No way, she wasn't worth spending the rest of his life in prison.

He gave her one final blow that guaranteed a knock out but wouldn't do permanent damage and she was down.

Lennie had the cord off when Seron got to me. He breathed into my mouth and pushed on my chest while Lennie and Sam cried.

"She's dead Seron. She's dead."

"No she's not dead. I won't let her die."

When I gasped and took in much needed air, my eyes opened to see three spooky looking characters dripping tears on me.

"What baby, what happened? " Seron asked.

"She was here, she tried to kill me," I sobbed.

"Hey, there's no one here but me and Sam,"

He held me close while I tried to sort out what happened.

" Look at my neck Seron."

"It's a smooth and beautiful as ever."

"Seron she was here. She tried to kill me."

"No baby. You had a bad dream. I won't let her or anyone else ever hurt you."

I pray that he's right.

Epilogue
Six Months Later

It was just a bad dream I had that day but I will never forgot it for a minute.

My new lawyer assured me I owned the house and was prepared to take my case to the limits. Following Sheila's departure, many pieces of incriminating information were found in the office. What she had stolen from Jim and stashed in an account on another island gave proof of this and other scams she pulled before and after his death. What she managed to steal was far more than she would get if she was awarded half the house.

She did take the hard drive from the computer on Jacob's advice. Jim's computer, kept in the office, was old and clumsy. Sheila did not want to leave the information behind. Jacob helped her remove it.

When I finally got around to that big drawer under the TV in my bedroom with all the old movies in it, I found a Derringer Ladies Purse Protector concealed inside a bible that had Sheila's name written on the inside front cover.

Jacob came soon after I reported my find to him. The gun was loaded with .45 caliber long colt bullets. Also found in the drawer were two full boxes of bullets – one box being .410 gauge shotgun shells and the other the long colt bullets.

Jacob confiscated the gun and ammunition. He traced the serial number back to Sheila and register in the U.S. She had no permit for St. Horatio – an automatic five year prison term.

I asked Jacob for an official receipt when he took the gun and have yet

237

to receive it one year later. When I asked why he didn't press charges, his response was too much time had passed.

Was she looking for her favorite CD, Jim's pills or was she trying to get at the gun? You tell me.

Jacob did send me an e-mail in which he stated he was now convinced she intended to kill me.

It's not over yet!

Thanks for reading my story. Pato - August 21, 2010

Lightning Source UK Ltd.
Milton Keynes UK
30 September 2010

160592UK00001B/46/P

9 781452 078786